In Their Own Words

In Their Own Words
Letters from Norwegian Immigrants

Edited, translated, and introduced by

Solveig Zempel

University of Minnesota Press
Minneapolis   London
in cooperation with
The Norwegian-American Historical Association

Published by the University of Minnesota Press
111 Third Avenue South, Suite 290, Minneapolis, MN 55401-2520
http://www.upress.umn.edu
Printed in the United States of America on acid-free paper

Fourth printing, 2000

Cover photo: (Norwegian-American sisters reading a letter, Kerkhoven,
Minnesota, ca. 1890), by C. L. Merryman, courtesy Minnesota
Historical Society.

Library of Congress Cataloging-in-Publication Data

In their own words : letters from Norwegian immigrants / edited,
    translated and introduced by Solveig Zempel.
        p.   cm.
    Includes bibliographical references and index.
    0-8166-1859-3 (pbk.)
    1. Norwegian Americans—Correspondence.
I. Zempel, Solveig.
E184.S215   1991
305.83'982073'09034—dc20   90-11012

Contents

Preface

In the spring of 1983, the University of Minnesota Press proposed an exciting project: to collect, translate, and edit a volume of Norwegian immigrant letters. This book has grown out of that proposal and complements previous translations of letters from Norwegian immigrants such as *Their Own Saga* (Hale, 1986), *Land of Their Choice* (Blegen, 1955), and *Frontier Mother: The Letters of Gro Svendsen* (Farseth and Blegen, 1950). *Land of Their Choice* contains letters and documents written by many immigrants between the 1820s and the 1870s. Some of these letters had been published in newspapers or otherwise widely circulated at the time they were written. *Frontier Mother* tells the story of one pioneer through the letters she wrote to her family during the 1860s and 1870s. *In Their Own Words* picks up where these two earlier volumes leave off, telling the story of nine individual immigrants with widely differing backgrounds and experiences, through their personal letters to families and friends in Norway between the 1870s and the 1940s.

I began searching for material for this collection by examining the letters available in the archives of the Norwegian-American Historical Association at St. Olaf College in Northfield, Minnesota. Other letters were found at the Minnesota Historical Society. Publicity about the project, both in the United States and in Norway, prompted donations of letters from private family collections. A generous grant from the Royal Norwegian Ministry of Foreign Affairs enabled me to spend the summer of 1984 in Norway, where I collected photocopies of more than a thousand letters. I am indebted to the Regional State Archives in Stavanger, Kristiansand, and Trondheim, to the University of Bergen Library, to the Emigrant Museum at Hamar, and to Nils Kolle of the University of Bergen History Department for allowing me to photocopy letters in their collections. Many individuals at these institutions were generous in giving their time and assistance, and I am grateful to all who helped me with this project. A list of donors and sources follows the Introduction.

I discovered that the archives, libraries, and museums in Norway contained extensive collections of America letters. And, in the course of the collecting phase of this project, I acquired far more letters than I could ever translate and present in published form. All the letters collected in conjunction with this project and the indexes to them are available in the archives of the Norwegian-American Historical Association.

Many American archivists, historians, and librarians have also been generous with their time and assistance. I wish it were possible to thank them all individually. I am grateful for the support of a Bush Foundation Faculty Development Grant, which enabled me to work full-time during the summer of 1985 on the task of reading, evaluating, and indexing the letters. With the aid of a sabbatical leave from St. Olaf College, I was able to finish selecting, translating, and editing the letters during the 1987–88 school year.

In addition to institutional support from many sources, I am greatly indebted to family, friends, and colleagues for their willingness to listen, read drafts, and make comments on my work. I would like to thank my two department chairs: Odd Lovoll, who suggested that I participate in this project, for his constant help and encouragement and for the inspiration of his own work; and Lloyd Hustvedt, who stimulated my interest in Norwegian America many years ago. Many people in Norway offered me advice and assistance, especially Ingeborg Kongslien, Dagfinn Worren, and Orm Øverland. Both Bjørn Jensen and Halldis Moren Vesaas deserve thanks for their help with travel arrangements and housing during my stay in Norway. My mother, Ella Valborg Tweet, my sister, Torild Homstad, and my husband, Elden Zempel, have all provided immeasurable support, and my children, Liv, Synneva, and Torfinn, have patiently endured my preoccupation with this project and my several long absences.

Introduction

Norwegian migration to America began in 1825, when a small group of religious dissenters left Stavanger on the sloop *Restauration*. Immigration from Norway was sporadic until 1836, when it became continuous. During the founding, or pioneer, period (1825–66), immigration was primarily undertaken in family groups, and the numbers in any given year were not large. Even so, by the end of the 1860s, more than seventy-seven thousand Norwegians had settled in the United States, moving from the first colony in New York to the Fox River Valley area of Illinois, then spreading gradually into rural settlements in Wisconsin, Iowa, and Minnesota. These first immigrants, in spite of the rigors of pioneer life and their relatively small numbers, established cultural institutions and created a Norwegian-American society ever eager to welcome new members and fresh blood from Norway.

America acted as a powerful magnet in the period following the Civil War. Emigration offered opportunities never before imagined. The discontented, the financially hard-pressed, and the adventuresome found a new outlet for their frustration or creative energy. The six decades from the mid-1860s to the mid-1920s witnessed mass immigration, when over 770,000 people left Norway to start a new life in a new land.[1] The family groups that had predominated during the pioneer period were largely succeeded in the period of mass immigration by younger, often unmarried men and women. The traffic was not entirely one-way, however, and it is estimated that of all the emigrants who left Norway after 1880, about one quarter returned home again.[2] The flow of immigrants into the United States finally slowed to a trickle in the late 1920s, ending a century of direct linguistic and cultural contact between Norwegian America and the homeland.[3]

During the period of mass immigration, Norwegians settled not only in the traditional, strongly Scandinavian areas of the Midwest, but also spread to the Pacific Northwest, to Texas, Montana, California, and Alaska. They lived not only in rural areas, but also formed urban colonies in the cities of New York, Chicago, Minneapolis, and Seattle. They became not only farmers, but also lumberjacks, laborers, gold miners, professionals, politicians, businessmen, and bums.

Various emotional and personal reasons for emigrating affected individual decisions. However, during the period of mass immigration, the desire to attain better economic conditions was clearly the primary motivating force. Historians of migration sometimes refer to "push" and "pull" factors. The first large-scale migration from Scandinavia came during the years of sporadic famine at the end of the 1860s, which closely followed the Homestead Act of 1862 on this side of the Atlantic. Thus the landless of Norway were able to obtain free land in America—a powerful "pull" factor. Demographic, social, and economic changes in Norway, which led to an increase in the landless class and a surplus of labor, were "push" forces, though changes in American economic conditions generally led to fluctuations in immigration curves, indicating that "pull" factors were a stronger influence than "push" factors. Once emigration from Norway had begun, earlier emigrants, through letters and return journeys, exerted another powerful pull, as did advertising by states, steamship lines, and railroads.[4] Einar Haugen has described the situation of nineteenth-century Norwegian immigrants more poetically, saying that they "were like Adam and Eve after they had tasted the apple of knowledge: they suddenly discovered that they were hungry. The apple they ate was the news of America. . . . They emigrated because they had learned to be dissatisfied, and because a changing world had provided them with a hope of escape from their dissatisfaction."[5]

The full story of Norwegian immigration, much too complex to relate here, is well documented in a number of excellent books and articles by such historians as Odd Lovoll, Ingrid Semmingsen, Theodore C. Blegen, and many others.[6]

For most Norwegians in the nineteenth century, America remained a remote and exotic place until the first immigrants began to write home. Their letters were among the most valuable, accessible, and reliable sources of information about the new world, the journey, the background for and consequences of the decision to emigrate. Thus the spread of information via letters was of great significance in encouraging emigration, particularly from areas where the idea had already been planted and the social and economic conditions were ripe. Reliable knowledge of the new land and the promise of personal success, freedom, and equality that the first immigrants reported in their letters was often a deciding factor for others who were considering emigration. Frequently these early letters were intended as much for public consumption as for private reading, and many were widely circulated and even printed in newspapers. The letters praising America written by Gjert Gregoriussen Hovland between 1831 and the 1860s are good examples of this phenomenon. Some of Hovland's letters are translated in *Land of Their Choice*, Theodore C. Blegen's collection of early Norwegian immigrant letters.

The earliest letters were written for the most part by people who had never before needed to write letters. These immigrants came from a relatively stable rural society, where the same families had lived for generations in the same neighborhoods. There were long-standing traditions, and communication among family, friends, and neighbors was direct. This direct communication was broken abruptly by the decision to leave for a new land.

The "America letters," as they were called, were important in their time, not only because they conveyed what their recipients naturally considered to be reliable information and thereby encouraged further immigration, but also because they kept open the channels of communication between the two worlds. This was, of course, a two-way exchange, with letters flowing in both directions, keeping the immigrants in touch with what was happening in Norway as well as informing Norwegians of what was happening in America.

Letters had great personal significance to the immigrants who wrote them, as well as to the recipients who stayed behind, and helped make the separation less painful. In writing, those who had left were able to share their new experiences, as well as entice others to join them, and to maintain ties with family and friends. One can often detect in the letters a compulsion to defend the decision to emigrate. For a few immigrants, writing letters home was their only, and consequently cherished, opportunity to communicate their thoughts and feelings in their native language.

Colorful individuals, such as Hovland the letter-writer and the enigmatic Cleng Peerson, pathfinder for the very first Norwegian settlers, dominate histories of the early period of immigration. The story of mass immigration, however, has of necessity been told through statistics, generalities, and groupings of immigrants. As Ingrid Semmingsen states, "When thousands make the same decision every year, the individual personality is submerged."[7]

Immigrants during the period of mass migration faced different problems than the pioneers. These later immigrants came to established communities. Instead of struggling to found a kingdom, they endeavored to find a meaningful place within it. Instead of struggling with a harsh nature, they faced political, social, and personal problems—problems that do not as readily capture our imagination as the hardships of the frontier. Because the history of this period is so often told in terms of statistics and generalities, we must seek out other sources to help us find those individual personalities concealed within the mass and understand how individual immigrants perceived and experienced the process of migration, assimilation, and acculturation. Reading the personal letters of immigrants of the period helps us to do this.

The reader of today who expects these letters to illuminate particular historical incidents may be disappointed. Major historical events may be mentioned not at all, or only in tantalizingly brief asides. In the midst of wars, depressions, elections, and other exciting events, the writer may instead choose to tell about fixing supper, the antics of the children, and how much the wheat crop sold for. On the other hand, as documents of social history, as a means of understanding everyday life of a previous era, and in telling the story of an individual immigrant, personal letters can be invaluable.

From letters alone, however, we can never know the whole picture, even on the personal level. We don't know how many "America letters" were tossed into the fire, lost, or otherwise destroyed. Of course there were also many immigrants who never committed their experiences to paper at all, and those who did had a great variety of skills and motives. For example, those who wished to entice family and friends to join them were unlikely to emphasize the negative. The failed immigrant is a story that is not often told in personal letters, unless the writer is describing someone else!

The news value of letters fades rather quickly—except, perhaps, to the genealogist—but the immediacy of personal letters preserves much of their emotional and aesthetic value for the contemporary reader.[8] Today, we read these letters from a double perspective. Our knowledge of the fate of the letter-writer leaves us with a sense of poignancy not felt by the original correspondents. We know as well about wars that end, droughts that are followed by rain, depressions that are followed by prosperity, or prosperity that is followed by hard times.

As Elizabeth Hampsten explains in *Read This Only to Yourself*, we usually read private writings in search of a sense of presence. We also read them in the expectation that they will be true to life. However, we must not expect them always to be factually accurate, or even always interesting. After all, "both inaccuracy and boredom may also be true to life."[9] In letters from Norwegian immigrants, for example, the same person may be referred to by many different names, dates may be inaccurate, religious platitudes may abound, and there are frequently long lists of people to be greeted. The letters in this collection have been carefully edited to remain faithful to the original writer while at the same time holding the interest of the present-day reader.

Although both historians and authors of fiction can use personal narratives as raw material, what makes letters so special in their own right are the ways in which they differ from both works of historical scholarship and of imaginative literature. Personal letters present an individual and subjective view of historical events, or ignore the larger picture completely to focus entirely on the minutiae of daily life. The historian uses letters, together with other sources of information, to interpret events and synthesize individual experiences into a broader collective portrayal of the story of immigration. The writer of fiction explores the psychology of the immigrant, and portrays in literary terms the universal and mythic aspects of immigration. In comparison to fictional and historical accounts, personal letters may seem mundane, repetitious, and formulaic. Letters do, however, reflect the character of the person who wrote them, giving insight into the daily life and feelings of the individual immigrant. We read personal letters precisely because they offer a different perspective from either the historian who interprets and synthesizes, or the novelist who universalizes, thus supplementing the insights offered by both. Writers of personal letters tell their own stories in their own words.

Most immigrant letters are filled with the ordinary details of everyday life: births, deaths, marriages, sickness and health, children, crops, and weather. News of friends and neighbors is frequently exchanged. Religious sentiments are often expressed, and greetings are sent to all and sundry. Many writers emphasize their hopes for the future, their belief that the struggles of their generation will make a better life possible for their children. Some of the common topics and threads running through these letters may be attributed to the conventions of letter writing, and some to the common experiences shared by all who leave one home to build another. However, each letter also reflects the character and personality of the individual writer, and in this way the letters are as varied as the many different people who wrote them. These private letters represent personal responses to unique events and experiences.

One of the distinctive aspects of letters is the degree to which they are colored not only by the writer but also by the person they are addressed to, and by the relationship between the writer and the recipient. The task of interpreting these letters is made doubly difficult because we often know only as much about that recipient as we can infer from the letters themselves. Reading these letters today is a bit like listening to only one end of a telephone conversation, albeit a fascinating one. The contemporary reader lacks the shared body of knowledge, the common memories and experiences of the original correspondents. The letters are full of tantalizingly cryptic references to people, places, and events unknown to us. Even when we have an extensive collection of letters from one individual, we may be puzzled by our incomplete knowledge. When writing to family, friends, and neighbors, these writers had no need to relate facts that we as strangers might like to know. Occasionally a letter from someone else, or some other source of information, or even our own imagination will help to paint a more complete picture. Often, however, the frustration of wanting to know more remains.[10]

The stories told in these letters are characterized by fragmentation. By their very existence, letters indicate a separation in time and space between sender and receiver, though at the same time they represent the effort of the sender to bridge that gulf. Fragmentation is inherent in the letter form as well, with long gaps in time between events and the reporting of them, between the sending of a letter and the receiving of a reply. Letters may grow more and more infrequent as time passes, and the focus of the letters may also change over time. Even the style and the very language in which the letters are written are subject to change, though the same person is writing to the same recipient. Yet another type of fragmentation is caused by missing letters. Writers frequently complain of lost or stolen mail, and many letters or portions of letters that were received by the addressee are absent from collections or illegible for any number of reasons.

Working with personal papers presents many special problems. In addition to the problems of legibility, of missing pages, of gaps in the sequence of letters, and cryptic references, there may be problems with idiosyncratic spelling and punctuation, with deciding where to divide a stream of words into sentences and paragraphs. Also, these "America letters" tell the stories of flesh-and-blood immigrants—or at least as much of those stories as the writer cared to reveal to family and friends—and may sometimes contain passages that are too intimate or sensitive to be shared with strangers.[11]

This collection contains letters from nine writers, for reading many letters from the same person illuminates the story of that individual. In contrast to most other collections of Norwegian immigrant letters, all the letters from each writer have been kept together, and each chapter therefore focuses on the story of one person or family.[12] Only private letters have been chosen, and any that were intended to be widely circulated outside of family and intimate friends, or even published, have been avoided. In choosing which writers to include, those whose letters were interesting by virtue of their content and style have been selected.

The letters in this collection were also chosen to represent a broad sample of Norwegian-American life, balancing geographic areas, urban as well as rural immigrants, and letters from men and women. There are letters from the East Coast, the West Coast, Alaska, and, of course, the Midwest; from prairie farmers and from gold miners, from politicians, businessmen, workers, unmarried mothers, and housewives. There is even a series of letters from what might be called a failed immigrant, that is, one who gave up and returned to Norway. The letters span the period from the 1870s up to World War II, with the chapters arranged so that the stories flow in an overlapping chronological order. From these letters we can put together a mosaic of different voices, different experiences, different times, places, occupations, sexes, and generations to form a complex, intricate, and colorful picture of the immigrant experience.

These are the stories of individuals. Many other interesting stories could also be told, but constraints of time and space have limited what could be included here. In the translation of these letters, it was important to preserve the voices of the individual writers as much as possible. The style and language of each group of letters vary to reflect the differences in the style and language of each writer. One common element in the letters chosen for this volume is a flair for description or communication that continues to hold our interest. I sincerely trust that my translation and editing will communicate that flair to readers of this volume.

NOTES

1. Odd S. Lovoll, *The Promise of America: A History of the Norwegian-American People* (Oslo, 1984), 8.

2. Ingrid Semmingsen, *Norway to America: A History of the Migration*, trans. by Einar Haugen (Minneapolis, 1978), 120.

3. Semmingsen, *Norway to America*, 157.

4. Hans Norman and Harald Runblom, *Transatlantic Connections: Nordic Migration to the New World after 1800* (Oslo, 1988), 61–63, 112–14.

5. Einar Haugen, *The Norwegian Language in America: A Study in Bilingual Behavior* (Philadelphia, 1953), I, 22.

6. See the Bibliography.

7. Semmingsen, *Norway to America*, 99.

8. See Susan S. Kissel's interesting discussion of the appeal of private letters in "Writer Anxiety versus the Need for Community in the Botts Family Letters," in Leonore Hoffmann and Margo Culley (eds.), *Women's Personal Narratives: Essays in Criticism and Pedagogy* (New York, 1985), 48–56.

9. Elizabeth Hampsten, *Read This Only to Yourself: The Private Writings of Midwestern Women, 1880–1910* (Bloomington, Ind., 1982), 14–15.

10. For interesting discussions of the epistolary form, see Janet Gurkin Altman, *Epistolarity: Approaches to a Form* (Columbus, Ohio, 1982), and Ruth Perry, *Women, Letters, and the Novel* (New York, 1980).

11. Hampsten, *Read This Only*, 14.

12. See the Bibliography.

Sources of Letters and Photographs

LETTERS

Andreas A. Hjerpeland — Minnesota Historical Society
Berta Serina Kingestad — Regional State Archives, Stavanger
Gunnar Høst — University of Bergen Library Manuscript Collection
Hans Øverland — Orm Øverland and Berge Øverland
Barbro Ramseth — Rolf H. Erickson
Hans Hansen and Sivert Øien — Regional State Archives, Trondheim
Bergljot Anker Nilssen — Jens T. Anker
Christ Gundersen — Regional State Archives, Kristiansand
      Additional letters have been collected from the Norwegian Emigrant Museum in Hamar as well as from other private donors. Copies of all letters collected in the course of preparing this book are deposited in the Archives of the Norwegian American Historical Association, Saint Olaf College, Northfield, Minnesota.

PHOTOGRAPHS

Cover — Minnesota Historical Society
Berta Serina Kingestad — Margrete Indrehus and Nils Ladstein Vestbø
Gunnar Høst — North Dakota State Historical Society
Hans Øverland — Regional State Archives, Stavanger
Barbro Ramseth — Rolf H. Erickson
Hans Hansen and Sivert Øien — Thos. Ostenson Stine, *Scandinavians on the Pacific, Puget Sound*, and Ragnar Standal, *Mot nye heimland: Utvandringa frå Hjørundfjord, Vartdal og Ørsta.*

Bergljot Anker Nilssen—Jens T. Anker
Christ Gundersen—Mrs. Bernhard M. Christensen

In Their Own Words

1

A Peripatetic Schoolteacher

Andreas Hjerpeland, 1871–1893

*A*ndreas A. Hjerpeland was born on October 28, 1835, in Lardal, Vestfold, Norway. He attended teacher's college, and taught in Vågå, Gudbrandsdal, in the 1860s, where Ivar Kleiven, the man he corresponds with in this collection of letters, was one of his pupils. Kleiven, who lived from 1854 to 1934, became a local historian and writer. In one of his collections of anecdotes about his home community, Kleiven wrote about Hjerpeland coming to the school in Vågå in 1866. As the first trained teacher in the community, Hjerpeland introduced such newfangled teaching aids as wall maps and blackboards. He quickly won the respect and affection of his pupils, and was considered a kind and good teacher.[1]

Hjerpeland (he started spelling his name Jerpeland sometime between 1881 and 1889) came to Fillmore County, Minnesota, in 1870, where he was in great demand as a schoolteacher among the Norwegian-Americans, and taught in Norwegian schools for a number of years. After spending some years in Highland, Minnesota, alternately doing farm work and teaching, he traveled west in 1874, going to Portland, Oregon, and traveling about on the West Coast. By 1876 he had returned to the Midwest, staying first in Worth County, Iowa, and then in Fillmore County, Minnesota. He homesteaded in Barnes County, North Dakota, in 1879. In 1880 he married Oline Erikson, and they lived on their homestead near Kathryn, North Dakota, for thirty years, until moving to Fosston, Minnesota, where Hjerpeland died on May 16, 1916.[2]

Hjerpeland is an interesting correspondent who tells in some detail about the conditions around him, and also comments on political, religious, and philosophical issues. He traveled a great deal in his early years in the United States, and wrote of himself: "The bird of passage instinct is powerful. . . . when I see the railroad train roar away, I always wish I were on board." As we might expect from an educated man, Hjerpeland writes well. He uses complex grammatical structures and many *biblical and literary allusions. Occasionally he adopts a rather unusual style, using direct quotes to write an assumed conversation.*

Transcriptions of Andreas Hjerpeland's letters are available in the archives of the Minnesota Historical Society. Unfortunately, portions of some letters were omitted when the transcriptions were made, and the original letters are no longer available. The earliest letter in this collection is from Highland, Minnesota, in 1871. However, in it Hjerpeland refers to previous letters, so we know that it is not the first one he wrote to Ivar Kleiven. The last letter was written in 1893, giving us a correspondence spanning a period of over twenty years in the life of this peripatetic schoolteacher and immigrant.

In this letter, Hjerpeland refers to Vinje, Bang, and Dunker, who were all prominent Norwegians at the time. Vinje was a poet, Bang an author and journalist, and Dunker a leading lawyer and attorney general.

Highland, Minnesota
June 24, 1871

Dear Friend,

I received your letter dated October 12 of last year in good time and I thank you for it; as it pleases me very much to see that you have not forgotten me, and I am also happy to hear that you and yours are in good health. I also thank you for the news you told; although much of the biggest news I had heard before, such as that Vinje, Ant. Bang, and Dunker are dead; for I read the newspapers, and often there is a piece from Norway, where the most remarkable news is included.

First of all, I must now tell you that I am still, by the grace of God, so fortunate as to have good health and am still doing well. I cannot remember when I last wrote to you; presumably it is almost a year ago. I must tell you, therefore, that last summer I received three dollars a day during harvesting for binding and one and a half dollars a day for stacking as well as a week of threshing. Since then I have gotten one dollar a day until November 3, when I began teaching school. I taught school for three months and got twenty dollars a month. Then I didn't do anything for awhile as I pondered what I should try next; I had decided to travel west and take land; however, nothing came of this, and I am still in the same place. You probably already know that anyone, be he native or immigrant, has the right, according to the Homestead law, to take a quarter section of land, 160 acres (pronounced "aker"). You get this by just paying for the papers, about fifteen dollars. When you have lived there for five years, the land is your legal property.

Now I must answer your questions. As for the first, I must say that I have not seen such natural beauty as in Norway. Here there is rolling prairie with a little woods and some valleys. Still, there is beauty in nature here, too.

None of the animals you mention, other than deer, are found in the woods around here; and even those have just about been destroyed by exploiting hunters. There are many kinds of horses, cattle, and sheep here, some large and some small. Though on the whole I believe that the horses are somewhat larger, but not better, scarcely as good as in Norway. The cows are generally larger and better, the sheep also. Most people don't keep more cows than what is needed for household use, at least around here, it is different in other places. It would be a bit too complicated to try to give you a complete picture of farm work here. I'll just tell a little bit now and a little more another time. They seed with machines, they mow mostly with machines, and they cut and thresh with machines too. During the winter the men don't have so terribly much to do. Their work is to take care of the horses and cattle, to drive and cut wood, as well as to haul wheat to town. The women don't do anything all year around other than take care of the housework.

Now I must close my letter for this time, as this piece of paper is about full. Write to me soon, please. My address is the same as before. Greet your parents and family from me as well as other acquaintances.

Finally, you are heartily greeted from your always faithful,

A. Hjerpeland

Highland, Minnesota
May 20, 1873

Dear Friend,

I have received both your letters . . . for which I give you my heartiest thanks. I am very happy that I still have at least one friend in Vågå who has not forgotten me, and I cannot find words to tell you with what emotion I read your letters. Both should have been answered long ago, and I can scarcely expect that you will forgive me my neglect. . . .

I see from your letter that you hope to become a Norwegian warrior, but you add "I don't believe you would appreciate this very much." Well it would be lots of fun to hear that you had become a warrior in the true meaning of the word; for I believe you have greater talents, and wish that you would become a spiritual warrior, a fighter "against principalities and powers, against this world's rulers, who rule in this time's darkness, against the spiritual army of evil under the heavens." In other words, I wish that you would become a minister. "A minister?" you say. Yes, exactly, a minister. I believe that your spiritual strength is greater than your physical strength, and I am convinced that you are capable of becoming a minister, if you only have the desire. I have now taught several hundred children in school, but I have never yet met anyone who can come close to you in ability and desire to learn. It is not my intention to flatter your youthful vanity and make you proud, God forbid! . . . No, instead of becoming proud, I hope that you will rather thank God because He has given you these abilities, as well as pray to God that He will help you to use these abilities to His glory and for the benefit of yourself and your fellow human beings. In Norway it costs much to become a minister, but here in America it is easier. You certainly understand what I am getting at; think more about it until another time. . . .

My own story is soon told. . . . From the middle of November until two weeks ago, I have been teaching school. The first four and a half months I got eighteen dollars per month, for the last I got twenty dollars. I have been in good health all the time and have been doing well. I will not teach school any more this summer, perhaps I won't teach any more at all. You wish that I would come back to Norway, and write enthusiastically of awakening in me a patriotic love for "old mother Norway." Norway is a pleasant country, that cannot be denied, and you have never heard me speak with contempt about my fatherland. I would very much like to see the country again, as well as friends and family, but I don't believe that will ever happen. For I cannot afford to travel to Norway just for a visit, and it would not be profitable to go there in order to live. Instead of traveling east, I will go farther west, perhaps this summer, as I have now made a firm decision to take land for myself. America is no paradise, but it cannot be denied that it is a good land. The soil bears abundant crops and repays the industrious worker richly for his trouble. The working man gets a large daily wage, so that the diligent and thrifty person can save up money. When he has saved up 400–500 dollars, he can travel farther west, which is now my plan, and take land on a homestead (160 acres) for nothing. At first it is not so easy for the settler, but soon he has, almost without noticing it, become a wealthy man. Wheat this winter has been worth from one dollar to one dollar and twelve cents per bushel. Pork has been selling for three to four cents per pound. Good buys!

Now you have certainly had enough of this nonsense, so I can safely close. Write to me as soon as possible; as I mentioned above, I may leave this summer. Greet your parents and family from me, as well as other friends and acquaintances. And last of all, hearty greetings to you from your always faithful,

A. Hjerpeland

Portland, Oregon
January 12, 1874

Dear Friend,

Now I suppose that you have waited long enough for a letter from me, as it is a long time since I wrote to you. But please excuse me, dear friend! The reason I have not written earlier is that . . . I have taken a long trip to the West, so long that when we two are standing up, our feet point almost straight up and down toward each other, and when you have morning, I have evening and vice versa. "Where in the world have you gone?" you surely wonder. Well, I have traveled to the Pacific Ocean. I left Minnesota on November 5, journeying through Iowa, Nebraska, Wyoming, Utah, Nevada, and California to Oregon, a distance of over 2,000 English miles (seven English equals one Norwegian). I took the train from Minnesota to San Francisco in California. From there I took a steamship on the Pacific Ocean to Portland in Oregon. The journey took exactly three weeks. I paid just 81 dollars for the trip, besides all other expenses, which I believe came to almost as much as the tickets. Portland, a city of nearly 11,000 inhabitants, lies about 100 miles from the Pacific Ocean on the Willamette River. East Portland lies on the east side of the river, a little city by itself, where I now live. The two cities are connected by steam ferries, which go back and forth daily. The river is navigable for larger ships, so that besides the small steamboats going back and forth constantly, there are also large ships that have come all the way up from the ocean. At Christmas time a ship from Stavanger was here loading wheat. On both sides of the river there are railroads. The one from East Portland runs on the east side of the river; it is finished for 200 miles and is supposed to connect with a railroad that comes from Sacramento in California; another has been completed for only 48 miles.

Since I came here, I have made several trips to observe the country. Most of the countryside, which isn't settled in the western part of Oregon, is forested (huge pine forests!). I don't much like the land I have seen so far, and I have decided that I will stay here for a year and see how I like it, before I look for land. The winter weather is excellent here. Soon after we came, we had a short cold spell with a little snow, but the snow disappeared long ago, and we have rain and sunshine alternately—though mostly rain—and the earth is as free of frost as it is at home near midsummer. To give you a little notion of the temperature, I can tell you that I am sitting and writing these lines in an unheated room, totally unaffected by cold. I came here because I knew about the good climate; however, whether I will be happy I cannot yet say. I have only worked for two weeks since I came, and have gotten one and a half dollars per day for eight hours of work. Otherwise, I am in good health and doing well. . . .

Greet . . . friends and acquaintances, and finally, you are heartily greeted from your always faithful,

A. Hjerpeland

When Hjerpeland accuses his friend of writing in the "country language" he is referring to the ongoing language controversy in Norway. Norway was united with Denmark for some four hundred years, until 1814. During that time, the written

Norwegian language had gradually been replaced by written Danish. Many Norwegians resented this, especially after independence, and several solutions were proposed. One of these was the creation by Ivar Aasen of a new language, based on rural dialects. Called Landsmaal *(country language or national language) when it was first introduced in the mid-nineteenth century, it is now known as* Nynorsk *or* New Norwegian. *Many Norwegian authors (including Kristofer Janson, who is mentioned in this letter) began to write in the new language. Ivar Kleiven was a proponent of* Nynorsk, *and used it in his own writing.*

In his discussion of religion, Hjerpeland expresses dismay that his friend and former pupil has become a follower of Grundtvig. Nicolai F. S. Grundtvig was a Danish pastor, author, and historian. He was a national and religious folk revivalist and a proponent of "happy Christianity." The followers of Grundtvig formed a low-church movement that emphasized the sacraments.

The minister referred to as a "fool" in the closing of this letter is probably the eccentric Reverend A. E. Fridrichsen, who came to Portland in 1871 and organized the first Scandinavian Lutheran church in Oregon. In November 1873, Fridrichsen wrote that Andreas Hjerpeland had arrived from San Francisco by steamer, and that he had helped Hjerpeland and his companion in finding a little house near his church for four dollars a month. He reports that they seemed pleased with Portland.[3]

Portland, Oregon
June 23, 1874

Dear Friend,

Many thanks for your most welcome letter, which I received several days ago just as I came back from a trip to Washington Territory. I have done almost nothing since I came to the West Coast other than travel around looking at the country. . . .

I see that you have become an advocate of language reform, as you write for the most part in the "country language." What language do you think you're using then? Are you writing in your true mother tongue, the Gudbrandsdal dialect? Or are you using the language that Kristofer Janson and Ivar Aasen have served up? I suppose it is the latter. You are surely not trying to convince me that this hodgepodge they call the real language is genuine Norwegian? No, it is just a patchwork, pieced together from several country dialects. You also say that if I wish to hear the sound of the language of our dear forefathers, then you will write me a letter in *Landsmaal*. I would like to hear the language of our forefathers, but, my dear friend! Neither you nor I can write, speak, or understand it. If you want to hear the language of our forefathers pronounced purely and cleanly, you must travel to Iceland, for there the Norwegian language is spoken in its authentic form. . . . If I were close enough to speak to you in person, I would talk more about this issue, but from here it isn't possible. I really don't understand how language reform will improve the lives of people in Norway. I think that it is unnecessary, fruitless nonsense.

So, my dear Ivar, you are on the way to becoming a follower of Grundtvig! Doesn't your old childhood Lutheran faith suffice for you any longer? Do you now believe that the word of the Bible is nothing but a dead text? Don't you believe any longer that "the Gospel is God's power of salvation for all who believe"? Don't you believe any longer that the word of the Bible is "powerful and sharper than a two-edged sword"? I see from your letter, as I actually knew already, that this summer you will celebrate your twentieth birthday, so I cannot expect you to sit now, as you did when you were a child, and listen as an attentive pupil to teaching from my mouth. Only one thing I ask of you, think very carefully before you desert your old, authentic Lutheran childhood faith.

I see that you also believe people in Norway today are too preoccupied with politics. Here too, I am of the opposite opinion. Don't you think that the Norwegian people have too long allowed themselves to be tyrannized by the dominion of the aristocracy? The Norwegian constitution gives the people the right, through parliament, to make their own laws and rule themselves, and I think it is none too soon if the people now open their eyes and make use of the rights given to them by law, as well as casting off the tyranny of the aristocracy. You say that you think it would be good for you if I were close enough that you could sometimes talk with me. It doesn't look like this would be the case, for as you see, I would be your opponent in many things. If I were in Norway, I would leave the advocates of language reform and the Grundtvigians to their own fate, while at the same time, I would do what I could with regard to politics in the service of the People's Party.

At the beginning of my letter, I told you that I haven't done much other than travel since I came here. When I came, I had decided that I would travel around and observe, and if I found a place I liked, I would take a piece of land. In any case I have not worked toward any particular goal for a long time; I have been as one who beats the air. I still haven't found any place that suits me. . . . I like the climate here on the West Coast, but then there is much that I do not like, so it is very uncertain whether or not I will settle down here. Wages are good, from forty to fifty dollars a month, if one can only find work; but there are too many people seeking employment, so sometimes it is difficult to find a job. There are lots of Chinese here, which is a great misfortune for the white working man. They work for such low daily wages that the white worker neither can nor will work for so little. The reason that they can work for so much less than the white man is that it costs them so much less to live, for they live like swine.

The land here is mountainous, and as far as I know, there is no land in America that resembles Norway as closely as Oregon and Washington Territory. There are both valleys and mountains here, mountains so high that they are always covered with snow. The lower mountains are closely overgrown with large pine and fir forests. The whole area west of the Cascade Mountains was at one time mostly covered with forest, but now much has been cut down and placed under cultivation. East of the Cascades are huge treeless prairies, fertile, but for the most part too dry unless irrigated, for it seldom rains there.

There are quite a few Scandinavians here, but no Scandinavian settlement, as those who have taken land have done so here and there amongst the Americans. There is an old Norwegian fool in East Portland, who has built himself a church and calls himself a minister, but he has no congregation. He is, as I said, a fool, and no one cares to listen to him.

Dear Friend! If only I were near enough to speak with you in person, then I would find more to discuss. Now that I can only communicate through the pen, I don't have much more to say. I will therefore close for this time. Greet your family . . . and all other friends. You are most heartily greeted from your faithful,

A. Hjerpeland

Fertile, Iowa
July 7, 1876

Dear Friend,

Your letter of October 14 of last year has now come into my hands, and I thank you for it. I must admire your persistence in hunting me down, and I am ashamed by the thought, though in part I am innocent, that you have not received a letter from me in such a long time. I did not receive your last letter, and I have traveled so much lately, and stayed for such a short time in each place, that I thought there was little use in writing. . . . If you have thought that it was due to any personal dislike for you, then you are greatly mistaken. I certainly do not like the idea that you have become a Grundtvigian, but I would love you no less even if you had become a Mohammedan. I know Grundtvig's teachings so thoroughly that it would do you no good to try to convince me of their rightness, and yet I would like to hear what you have to say in their defense.

Well . . . now I will tell you how the "bird of passage" has traveled since last you heard from him. I see that my last letter was dated June 23, 1874. I was in Portland then, and you certainly took your time before you answered it, as I didn't leave there until October, and then I went to Astoria, or rather thirty miles north of Astoria, and took land. I stayed there for awhile, but I didn't like it at all, and so I gave it up and left. Since then I have been several different places, always with the thought of moving on, as I was never happy. Still, this did not become a reality until spring; but then I made a journey of between two and three thousand miles. On the first of April I traveled from Portland, Oregon, to San Francisco, where I stayed for two days to see the wonders of this great city for the last time. From there I traveled over the Rocky Mountains and didn't stop until I got to the place in Iowa where I am now. You can believe that I have seen a lot on my wide-ranging journeys. I have seen almost all the races of the world.

I have taken up my old profession again — teaching school. I started a few days after I arrived here, and now I have taught for two and a half months, and have gotten twenty dollars a month plus board, or one dollar a day. (A school month is considered to be four weeks and a school week five days.) I don't know that the place I have come to is the best in the world, yet I am ten times happier here than I was in Oregon. . . . I am thinking about traveling to Norway again, too, but nothing will come of that for awhile at least. Now I will break off for this time. If you will answer this letter quickly, I will promise to keep up a steady correspondence with you.

Yours faithfully,

A. Hjerpeland

Lanesboro, Minnesota

May 3, 1877

Dear Friend,

Hello, Ivar! Are you home today? Well, listen here! Now you are finally getting a message from the "bird of passage" who has been out traveling again. "Traveling?" you say. "Yes, you travel so much that you travel away both your wits and your reason." But excuse me, now I will get hold of myself and try not to make so much noise.

I thank you for your most welcome letter, which I received some time ago. I know you have been sick and tired of waiting for a reply; and I admit with shame that I should have written to you long ago, and worst of all, I don't have any good excuse, except that due to laziness it has been put off until now, so once again I must beg for forgiveness. As you already could guess from the beginning of my letter, I have now left Iowa, where I was when I last wrote to you. It happened this way. I went to Minnesota for the harvest, as the day wages are generally higher than in other places at this time of the year. When the binding was over I went to Fillmore County to visit my old friends, and when I got there, they absolutely wanted me to be their schoolteacher again. As I liked it last time, I didn't have anything against the idea, so I accepted the offer. I went down to Iowa for my things, came here late in September and began teaching October first. Since then I have taught school the whole time, that is for seven months, and have gotten twenty dollars per month plus board and washing. . . .

According to your wishes, I will tell you a bit about the school system here. There are public schools everywhere, where the ordinary school subjects are taught: reading, writing, arithmetic, geography, and grammar.

School is held in well-equipped schoolhouses, usually for seven or eight months of the year. The cities are full of higher schools and universities, so the youth have good opportunities for learning. Because there is freedom of religion, and no state church, the public schools have no religious instruction, leaving that up to the parents themselves. This is the reason the Norwegians, as well as other nationalities, establish parochial schools, so that the children will receive religious instruction. But the parochial schools have a low status (about like the ambulatory schools in Norway). There are not enough qualified teachers, the school session is too short, and the buildings are poor. It is quite difficult to hold Norwegian school here, and twenty dollars a month is considered poor pay here in America.

Last summer it was rather dry, so the crops in most states were poor. But then the farmers were well paid for what they had to sell. Wheat now fetches $1.75 per bushel (about a quarter of a barrel), mostly on account of the prospect of war in Europe. . . . There is much complaining of unemployment and hard times; and yet I don't believe anyone is suffering. Now it is beginning to look like business will get a little livelier again. For the moment I am doing nothing, and I don't know what I will take up next. I could continue to teach school, but I am tired of that. . . . I believe I would rather go without work for awhile and bide my time.

It looks like we can get a little religious war going, that is to say, a war of the pen. I don't have any great desire for such a war; nevertheless, I want to say just a few words about your defense of Grundtvigianism. The first I would ask is, how would you prove that the creed is from the mouth of God, in other words, that the creed is used at baptism? The proof you give in your letter is insufficient. . . . This is all I have to say about the matter, at least for this time. Even though I waited a long time before I wrote to you, I will ask you not to repay me in the same coin, but write to me soon. . . .

You are heartily greeted from your faithful friend and former (false) teacher,

A. Hjerpeland

Lanesboro, Minnesota
October 27, 1877

Dear Friend,

Once again I have waited too long before answering your most welcome letter, which I received some time ago, and so again I plead guilty and must be placed under indictment for neglecting my duty. Now as previously I beg for forgiveness. . . .

When I wrote to you last spring I had just finished school, and I believe I said that I would not work for awhile but would just take it easy. I did that for about three weeks, but soon I got tired of it, and so I started to work, and since then I have worked steadily until the tenth of September, when I began teaching again. During this time I earned about ninety dollars. Around here and over most of America it has been a good year, except for a few small areas in the western states that have been visited by a grasshopper plague, though less this year than in the previous years. It is our hope that the plague is now over. Times have begun to turn to the better again. . . . Day wages during harvest were three dollars a day, one and a half in stacking and one dollar a day during threshing. I was binding for eleven and a half days, and thus earned 34 and ½ dollars for those few days. Clothes and other supplies are very cheap. Wheat now fetches 93–95 cents per bushel at Lanesboro, our nearest marketplace.

You say in your letter that you would like to hear that I have taken a year-long rest. This I have now done, so your wish has been fulfilled, as this year I have not traveled much and I suppose that will be the case in the coming year as well. Still the bird of passage instinct is powerful, and when it gets too strong, I have to take some short trips. Thus this year I have traveled two or three times to Rushford . . . for when I see the railroad train roar away, I always long to be aboard.

. . . Now I must break off, as the womenfolk want to chase me away from the table. Let's declare a truce in our religious war. . . . My dear Ivar, you are heartily greeted from your always faithful,

A. Hjerpeland

At the end of this letter Hjerpeland writes that he has "served up too many love stories." Unfortunately those love stories were omitted from the transcription.

Lanesboro, Minnesota
April 6, 1878

Dear Friend,

Well, now I probably ought to begin by scolding you for waiting so long to answer my last letter, but when I remember that I have often been even more negligent in answering you, then it is probably best if I keep quiet on that matter, and instead thank you very much for your most welcome letter. . . .

I am living with the same man that I have lived with the whole time I have been in Minnesota. . . . His family is unusually kind. The Norwegians here keep more or less to the old Norwegian ways, though they have had to abandon some traditions due to conditions here. One Norwegian custom that has been abandoned is the damnable one that dictated that the workers and servants in many places had to eat in the kitchen and were scarcely allowed to stick their heads into the owner's parlor. Here in America everyone eats at the same table.

I won't have an opportunity to tell you anything about the Norwegian school this time, because I have served up too many love stories, but I will do it another time. I have, thank God, my health and am doing well, and carry on with the school every day.

Greet your parents and brothers and sisters . . . as well as other acquaintances from me. Now you absolutely must write to me soon.

Live well! Always live well!

Your always faithful,

A. Hjerpeland

The degrees Reaumer used by Hjerpeland in this letter refers to a temperature scale not used anymore. The temperatures he mentions are equivalent to about 35–38 degrees Celsius or 95–100 degrees Fahrenheit.

Lanesboro, Minnesota
July 24, 1878

Dear Friend,

Many, many thanks for your most welcome letter, which I received yesterday. You were really kind this time, and answered my letter immediately, so in return I must answer yours at once, so that you will have no reason to accuse me of being ungrateful.

I received your congratulations on the occasion of my engagement with greatest thankfulness, as I know that it is not merely empty words, but comes from a heart that truly wishes me happiness, joy, and everything good. . . .

This year I can't complain that I haven't been teaching long enough, as I taught for nine and a half months. I closed the school on June 14, and since then have only worked for ten days. But now there won't be any free time for awhile, as the harvest begins in a few days. A month ago, it looked like we would have the best crop in many years. But that hope was crushed for some. Three weeks ago, just when the wheat was well along, we had a terrific rainstorm with oppressive heat (from 28 to over 30 degrees Reaumer in the shade) which had a destructive effect on the wheat. Many heads are completely withered and many from the top to the middle. Much wheat has lodged early, and is perhaps not worth cutting. Nevertheless, it will be a difficult harvest, for there is an awful lot of straw. It is said that day wages will be three dollars a day. . . .

This time I will try to tell you a little about the Norwegian school here in America. In most places the Norwegian school is held in the English schoolhouse, when this is possible; if not, then farmhouses must be used. In two of the districts where I teach, they have built a schoolhouse especially for the Norwegian school. The last one, which was built last fall, is a really fine schoolhouse. It is 16 by 24 feet and is equipped with blackboards and desks, with ample space for about fifty pupils. The school session is about the same as in the English schools, that is to say, the school day is six hours, the school week is five days or twenty days in a month. We teach approximately the same subjects as are required in the schools in Norway: religion, Bible history, catechism, reading, writing, arithmetic, and singing. We use the same textbooks as in Norway: the older edition of Pontoppidan's Explanation, Vogt's Bible History, and Jensen's Reader. Basically things are not well with the Norwegian school here, and it is difficult to be a teacher. There is too little school time, and the children, big and small, all meet together, just like in the old days with ambulatory schools in Norway. In one district I taught school for four months this year, in the other two and a half, and in the third, where there is no schoolhouse, for two months, as well as in yet a fourth district, which doesn't actually belong to me, for one month. This one month will be all the Norwegian school those children will get in this year, and that amounts to almost nothing.

Now I have told everything that I can about the Norwegian school, and I don't have anything more to write about. It is true you ask me to write about whatever I like, as long as I write long letters, but now I am stuck, as I lack material to prepare another helping of "stew" for you. You wish to know how I am, which is natural, but that is quickly told. I am, praise God! in good health and am doing well. I have a beautiful girl; from time to time I can press her to my breast and I love her with an upright heart, and I hope she loves me in return. . . . You are the only one in Norway who knows that I am engaged, I have not even told my parents about this.

Well, now I better stop for this time. Greet . . . friends and acquaintances from me. Live well, dear Ivar. Find yourself a little sweetheart soon. And now you are heartily greeted from your always faithful,

A. Hjerpeland

P.S. You say that you don't like the girls in Vågå, because they are a bunch of dull clotheshorses. I know that you prize simplicity, and so do I. But yet I dare say that you haven't seen anything of clotheshorses, in comparison to me; and here in America it is very difficult to find a girl who according to your definition would not be considered a clotheshorse. Yes, I have often been irritated by all the vanity and pomp, which the girls here are loaded down with. And yet the girl I love is, to this way of thinking, also a clotheshorse. It's just that each one of these poor people wants to be like all the others, and I can only hope that under the fine clothing beats a humble heart.

Don't forget to write soon!

A.H.

Lanesboro, Minnesota
December 7, 1878

Dear Friend,

A happy New Year in Jesus Christ, my dear friend. . . . I am in good health and am doing well as usual. I am carrying on my old trade, namely schoolteaching, and have kept school for three months since last fall. The wages are the same as before, twenty dollars a month. Actually they tried to put my wages down this fall, as it has been a bad year around here. It looked like it was going to be a really wonderful year until the wheat headed out, but then we had two weeks of high heat and rain. . . . The crop they got is therefore not only small but poor, so they have to sell the wheat for thirty to fifty cents per bushel. So this will be a hard year for cash. But when I said that I would leave if I didn't get twenty dollars a month, it turned out that they would rather pay than let me go.

Right now I will tell you a bit about the schools in America. I agree with you that the Norwegian school here stands on altogether too poor a footing, but then one must also remember that one is not bound to the Norwegian school alone for education. The primary goal of the Norwegian school here is to teach the children the Norwegian language, as well as to give them some religious training. The public school takes care of the rest of the knowledge one needs for this life. Youngsters can attend from the ages of five to twenty-one. Instruction is given in English, arithmetic, writing, geography, and grammar; or in other words, in all the ordinary school subjects, so everyone who has the desire, has good opportunity to obtain an education.

I have no news that could be of any interest to tell you. In addition, I am surrounded by ill-mannered children, so I am getting one blow after another on the table, and it is almost impossible to write. Therefore it is best that I quit. The content for this reason will be somewhat drier than usual, as it is nearly impossible to think in this confusion.

Greet your family and other acquaintances. You are most heartily greeted from yours,

A. Hjerpeland

Lanesboro, Minnesota
July 9, 1879

Dear Friend,

This time I must begin my letter by begging your forgiveness because I have delayed so long in answering your most welcome letter of February 22, which I received in good time and for which I thank you very much. The reason I have postponed writing to you until now is that I had intended to leave here this spring. "Leave here! Are you crazy? Do you really want to leave again?" you must be saying. Yes, I do want to leave again, but not go so awfully far this time. I want to go farther west in Minnesota, where land is cheaper. Land is so expensive here that it would be sheer stupidity to buy any as long as there is plenty of cheap land to be bought farther west. Yes, I could even get land on a "homestead" for as good as nothing, but I have little desire to travel out into the wilderness, even though for the sake of the future it might be best.

But there was no trip this spring, and the reason is that I couldn't collect the money that I had lent out. Therefore I won't leave here until fall. In the meantime I have taken a trip to look around, and have just gotten back. I liked the places I visited very much; the worst thing I could discover about that country is that it is almost completely lacking in trees. There is lots of good prairie land in the settlements, which sells for around five dollars per acre (really cheap, isn't it?). I didn't buy any land now, as I couldn't quite decide where I wanted to settle down. I found a large Norwegian settlement near the small town of Minneota in Lyon County, Minnesota. They had no schoolteacher, and they heartily wished to have one, so they wanted me to come there. As I liked the place very much, it is not impossible that I will travel up there. . . .

I finished up with school the tenth of May and since that time have not had much to do; there is little work to be had here, but now it will surely be busy for awhile during the harvest. . . . Excuse my short letter, next time it will perhaps be longer. Write back as soon as you have time. Greet your parents and brothers and sisters. You are heartily greeted from yours,

A. Hjerpeland

Fargo, Dakota Territory
December 9, 1879

Dear Friend,

It seems to be taking an awfully long time before you get a reply to your last, most welcome letter, which I received a long time ago and for which I thank you heartily. The reason I have put off writing for so long is this: just as I received your letter, I was about to leave Fillmore County and I didn't want to write until I had reached my new place of residence. "Well, left again!" you no doubt say with astonishment, "I believe you must be crazy, who can never be satisfied without traveling about." Yes, I really have left again, but have not gone so terribly far this time. I have only moved to northeastern Dakota, and this will surely be my last journey in America, as I am thinking of settling down here. I have traveled around a bit and looked over the country here in the West; but I came a little too late to see everything I wanted to before winter set in. Therefore I haven't taken any land yet, but there is plenty of government land to be had, and I will certainly take some land this spring. For the moment I am six miles south of the city of Fargo, and am teaching school. I have been teaching for a couple of weeks now, and will continue with the school here for at least two months and will get twenty dollars a month.

You surely expected to hear that I was married by now, but unfortunately I am still unmarried. I had decided to get married this fall, but then I couldn't get my money, so that by the time I could come here it was too late to get together a little home, so again I have had to postpone it until the spring. . . . I still have not told my parents that I am engaged, so you are the only one in Norway who knows that I have a sweetheart.

Please write to me soon. You may send your letters to: Valley City, Barnes Co., Dakota Territory. I have a friend who will send them to me if I can't get them myself. Greet your parents and brothers and sisters, and you are most heartily greeted, in addition I wish you a happy and joyful New Year in Jesus Christ. Yours,

A. Hjerpeland

North Dakota did not become a state until 1889.

Valley City, Barnes Co.
Dakota Territory
January 11, 1881

Dear Friend,

I have misplaced your last letter, so I cannot see when it was written or received, but I know that it is long ago. . . . You must be so kind as to forgive me again for my neglect.

As it is so long since I wrote to you I ought to have a whole lot to tell, but I truly scarcely know what I should write about. . . . The most important thing I have to tell you is that I have finally gotten married. At the end of August last year I was married in my own home to the aforementioned Lina Erikson, to whom I had been engaged for two and a half years. I am in good health and am . . . very satisfied with my new situation. It is really true, as the saying goes: East, West, Home is Best. . . . Yes, it is truly a great blessing to have a home of one's own, and I am now most astonished that I did not try to establish a home of my own long ago, as many times I have been tired of living with strangers.

I must have told you before about the land I have taken and how I have built, and I only need add that I like it very much here in Dakota. It's true that it is often quite cold in the winter; but we have a healthy and good climate both summer and winter. The soil is very fertile; this year wheat yielded 20–38 bushels per acre, which is an excellent harvest. The government land here is mostly taken for many miles around, but there is lots of railroad land, which right now is selling for: prairie for two and a half to three dollars and wooded land for from five to seven dollars an acre.

A petition has now been brought before Congress to divide Dakota into two approximately down the middle from east to west; the northern half would be given the name North Dakota with territorial organization, while the southern half would be taken into the union as a state. I don't think that this will go through in this Congress, as the Democrats have the majority in both houses, and they will not wish to help the Congress be formed with two Republican members, which would be the case, should Dakota be taken in as a state. But next year the Republicans will have the majority in both houses of Congress, and then Dakota will surely be divided, and the southern half taken in as a state. Land here is being settled rapidly, and before too long, Dakota will have the largest number of Scandinavians of all the states of the union.

You are getting a dry letter from me this time, which is the case as often as not. But I know that such dry food is hard to digest, and I am afraid that you have already had enough of it, so therefore I must quit. . . . You have the most friendly greetings from me and from my wife, even though you do not know her.

A. Hjerpeland

Almost eight years have passed since the last letter in this collection. Other letters may well have been sent; however, the frequency seems to be decreasing. A change of address has complicated the correspondence. This letter opens with the salutation "Dear Sir" in English, instead of the usual "Dear Friend" in Norwegian, and is signed "Respectfully Yours," also in English. Hjerpeland has now dropped the H and spells his name Jerpeland. At the time this letter was written, he was about fifty-four years old.

Daily, North Dakota
June 29, 1889

Dear Sir,

I have recently received several letters from you, for which I say many thanks. One letter, the year-old one, has been in Valley City once before, that is just twelve miles from me. I see that you have had a hard time tracking down the "runaway," and I must admire your persistence. Well, that designation doesn't fit me so well this time, as I am now living in exactly the same place as I was the last time I wrote to you. But the fact of the matter is this, we have gotten a new post office, just a few miles from me. You must not think that I have forgotten you, my dear Ivar, for I have surely thought of writing to you at least a hundred times, but it has been put off time after time and thereby nothing comes of it.

I see by your letter that you are still not married, but that you are now an "old and wise" bachelor of 34 years. However, I understand that you have not yet given up hope of getting married, for you comfort yourself with the thought that you are still twenty years younger than I was when I got married. It is terrible how old you make me out to be. According to your calculations I was 54 when I got married. Now I have been married for nine years; therefore you would have me be 63 years old. Well, no way do I wish to be that old, so I recommend that you immediately cut off at least a half score of years; perhaps then you will get a little closer to my real age.

It is such a long time since I wrote to you that I ought to have a whole lot to tell, but there is so much, that I scarcely know what I should write. Since I wrote to you last, I have been in good health and therefore doing pretty well, though I have had to work hard since I put my feet under my own table. As I was an idiot and traveled the world around, I had put aside too little for a good start, so I had to go into debt, which has been a millstone around my neck the entire time. Now I have gotten out of debt, so what little I have is really mine, as I don't owe a single cent anymore. But now it looks very bad again. We have had an unusual drought all spring and summer, so the fields are now nearly dried up and no matter how much rain we get from here on in, most of the fields won't be worth cutting. . . . We have had two bad years before, and this year we will get nothing. Everything one has to sell fetches a poor price and many are deeply in debt, so I think that this fall there will be a lot of bankruptcies.

As I mentioned before, I have now been married for nine years, but have no children yet, and it doesn't look like I will have any, either.

Write to me soon, and please, if possible, send me your portrait. Greet your mother and your brothers and sisters and other acquaintances.

Respectfully yours,

A. Jerpeland

Daily, North Dakota
January 7, 1891

Dear Friend,

I received your letter of November 25 several days before Christmas, for which I thank you very much. I also thank you for scolding me a little for not writing to you sooner, maybe it will help me a little in the future, although it looks as if I am incorrigible.

I see that your brother has decided to come to America in the spring, and you ask me to tell you where he ought to go. But it is difficult, yes impossible, for me to say which place in America is the best, even though I have been here for over twenty years. In the first place, America is so large that I certainly cannot be acquainted with conditions everywhere, and in the second place, conditions are so changeable that a place that has good business and earnings one year can be bad the next, and vice versa. I see that you think that Washington or the Pacific Coast might be the best place to go to, but in this you are mistaken, and I would definitely advise him against going there. If he has a little capital to start a business with, it might be all right, but it is no use going there to look for work. I won't say any more myself about the West Coast, but will just include a little clipping from the newspaper *Skandinaven*, which I believe contains the pure truth.

I presume that your brother wishes to and preferably ought to go first to one of the northwestern states, where the great mass of immigrant Norwegians have settled, for example, Wisconsin, Illinois, Minnesota, Iowa, or Dakota. But which of these places ought he choose? Yes, that is the question. I see that you don't have a very good opinion of Dakota, and I don't wish to say that it is the best place in America. In any case, I will neither praise nor criticize Dakota, but merely tell what conditions have been like in this past year. Those who hired out this spring (to farmers) got 18–25 dollars a month for six or seven months. In the fall day laborers were paid two dollars a day from the time harvest began until the threshing was finished. In the winter there is not much to do here, which is also the case in the other northwestern states, unless one works in the woods cutting timber. This fall there was a labor shortage here, so many had to use both wife and children to get the work done. Day wages have been higher ever since I came to Dakota than they are in the eastern states, and many sons of my friends from Minnesota have come up here for this reason.

I won't write anymore about this matter now. If you write to me again soon, then you can get one more letter from me before your brother leaves.

My paper is almost full now, so I haven't room for more than to say that I am in good health and doing well. You seem to think that I have forgotten most of the people in Gudbrandsdal, but you are wrong, my friend. When I close my eyes I can see them all yet. But unfortunately the sight gives me only a caricature of most of them. I wonder if you are enough like the Ivar Kleiven I once knew that I would still recognize you.

Affectionate greetings,
A. Jerpeland

Daily, North Dakota
September 11, 1891

Dear Friend,

Early this winter I received a letter from you in which you told me that your brother Hans had decided to come to America, and you asked me to tell you where he ought to go. I answered this letter quickly, but as I have not heard from you I am afraid that you may not have received my letter, for I find it difficult to believe that you have suddenly lost interest in me. Therefore I will write a few lines to let you know that if you have not had a reply to your last letter to me, at least this time it is not my fault. . . . We have had a good year over the whole of America this year, and not least here in Dakota. We have not threshed yet, but as the wheat is tall and the heads seem to be well filled, I hope it gives us a little extra measure. This will certainly come in the nick of time, for after plowing and sowing for three years and harvesting little, a great many farmers around here have sunk deeply into debt. I for my part have managed well, for when I haven't had wheat to sell I have sold wood. I can—just to brag a little—say that I am free of debt. I am in good health and am living as usual. A friendly greeting from yours,

A. Jerpeland

Andreas Jerpeland lived until 1916, so, although this letter of 1893 is the last one available in this collection, it is likely that many more letters crossed the ocean between these two lively correspondents.

Daily, North Dakota
February 24, 1893

Dear Friend,

As I have recently received a letter from you, I don't dare wait any longer to answer it. In your letter you order me to write back to you instantly; but that my letter should be six or seven pages long, as you demand, I dare not promise. I don't know what I could find to write that much about.

It almost seems from your letter that you are dissatisfied with your situation, with yourself, yes, with the whole world, and that you are considering emigrating. According to what you say, it might be rather sensible to do that, for such a large debt is no pleasant guest to have in the house. I will not give you any advice with regard to what you should do, for you are old enough and intelligent enough to decide for yourself. I will only say this much, that if you are going to leave, then do it right away; you have put it off long enough.

As you have told me about your circumstances, this time I will do the same, and tell you how *rich* I have become in America. I took 160 acres of land on a "homestead" which I now have gotten the deed to, so it is my own property. I have a pair of good horses, four cows, three two-year-old bulls, one three-year-old heifer, four one-year-old calves—and still another little bull a few months old. I have all the equipment necessary to run a farm except a reaper. For all this I do not owe a cent, yes, if I look really hard, I may even find that I have fifty or sixty dollars to the good. In addition I still have my whole crop (805 bushels of wheat), together with fifty bushels of the crop from 1891. The reason I have so much wheat left is that the price is low (53–55 cents per bushel). So I am waiting for higher prices, but it looks like I am waiting in vain; there still is no indication of a rise. You may understand from this that I have not become a millionaire yet, but that I have had a rather good income, and, if nothing untoward happens, can live free of worry about financial difficulties.

My dear Ivar! If only my dream could one day come true, that I would see you once again. I am almost beginning to hope for that, for if you tear yourself away from home, you will surely come to America, and then you shall visit me, even if I have to send the sheriff to fetch you. I have had letters from your brother Hans a few times since he came to America, the last time was almost a year ago. . . .

I have left the most important thing I have to tell about myself till the end, namely that since you heard from me last I have been in good health except for sometimes being plagued by rheumatism in my arms and legs, as well as headaches.

You will say that my letter is altogether too short, but now I must finish anyway, and go to the post office, otherwise I will get there too late. Write back soon, and say that you are coming—to America.

You are heartily greeted from my wife and from your always faithful,

A. Jerpeland

NOTES

1. Ivar Kleiven, *I heimegrendi: Minne fraa seksti-aarom* (Kristiania, 1908), 111–12.

2. Obituary in *Fram*, found in Norwegian American Historical Association obituary file.

3. Kenneth Bjork, *West of the Great Divide: Norwegian Migration to the Pacific Coast, 1847–1893* (Northfield, Minn., 1958), 483–84, 317.

2

A Single Woman in Illinois

Berta Serina Kingestad, 1885–1893

*B*erta Serina Kingestad, like Andreas Hjerpeland, was single when she came to America. Migration of young, unmarried men and women was quite typical during the period of mass immigration. And, like many of these single immigrants, Berta Serina married another Norwegian-American after living in the United States for a number of years.

Berta Serina was born on June 21, 1863, on the island of Finnøy, near Stavanger. Her parents, Soffie and Svend Bjøravåg, worked as a cook and a carpenter in addition to running a small farm. Four of their eleven children eventually settled in America. Ole, who emigrated first, seems to have lost contact with his family. Tobias and Johannes went to Illinois in about 1885, followed by Berta Serina in 1886. Her brother-in-law Annanias arrived in 1887, and was joined by his wife, Berta's sister Marta, in 1890 or 1891. Berta Serina was following a long tradition of migration from the Stavanger area to Illinois, coming to a community populated by friends and relatives.[1]

In Norway, the Bjøravåg family struggled to make ends meet, and the children all went out to work at early ages, the boys to sea and the girls to work on neighboring farms as servants. In her letters from Illinois, Berta often worries about whether her family at home has enough to eat, and mentions sending money from what little she has. At one point she and her brothers plan to send money home so that her family can purchase a cow. Although she often longs for home and misses her family sorely, Berta Serina feels she made the right decision and does not regret having emigrated to America.

In the years between 1886 and 1891, Berta Serina writes about her daily life as a hired woman on farms in the Fox River Valley in Illinois. She gave birth to a son, Sven, only seven months after arriving in Illinois, and she writes fondly of his growth and antics. Sometime around 1891 or 1892, Berta married Knud (Newt)

The Bjøravåg family home on the island of Finnøy has been moved, and now the idyllic location is used only for vacation cabins. The oldest woman (lower left) is probably the wife of Berta's brother Sven. Photo courtesy Margrete Indrehus and Nils Ladstein Vestbø.

Tuttle and moved to Rowe, Illinois. Their son Grant was born in 1892. The last letter from Berta in this collection is dated December 3, 1893. In November 1894, her brother Tobias wrote that Berta had been ill but was getting better. In August 1895, Tobias wrote to his parents again to tell them that he had visited Berta just before she died. She didn't suffer much pain, he reported, but had wasted away as people with consumption often do. She died of tuberculosis on August 2, 1895, and was buried in Rowe, Illinois.

For a young woman with relatively little schooling, Berta Serina writes well-composed letters with a rich and sophisticated vocabulary. She uses many biblical quotations and allusions, and the sincerity of her religious beliefs shines through clearly. Berta Serina takes her religion seriously, but she can poke fun at herself, as when she sends her family a poem she has written and signs it "written by the famous poet, Bertha Bjøravaag." She has a good sense for stylistic variation, and although she writes fairly standard Norwegian, she sometimes uses folk sayings and dialect for deliberate stylistic effect. The one place where she is inconveniently inconsistent is in the use of names. She refers to the same people by many different names and with several variations in spelling. The issue is further confused by the fact that several people in her circle of friends and relatives had the same name. She spells her own name both Berta and Bertha, and as a last name she uses Bjøravaag, Svendsen, Svendsdatter, Kjingestad, Kingestad, Kingstad, and finally, after her marriage, Tuttle. Her husband is referred to as both Knud and Newt, her brothers as Tobias, Thom and Tom, and Johannes, John, Jan, and so on. Sometimes it is pure guesswork to figure out whom she means.

In this letter to her brother Tobias, Berta Serina expresses her fervent desire to emigrate with him. Prospects looked good for her in America. Her other brother, Johannes, wrote in his first letter home: "Well, you must greet Berta and tell her she did a terribly dumb thing not to have come here before. There is such demand for girls here that someone or other is at Uncle's nearly every day trying to get hold of Lava." By that time, Berta had made up her mind to emigrate, and she left Norway on May 26, 1886.

Bjøravåg, [Norway]
February 8, 1885

Dear Brother,

I will now try my luck at sending you a letter. . . . I am in quite an agitated state of mind today. What concerns me most is all the discussion of that confounded America. It was really too bad that I didn't find you that Sunday evening when I was at home. . . .

Well, now, Tobias, I have not said anything definite to you about America, but the truth is that I have always thought that if you went, then I would go too if it were at all possible. I don't know how it happened that we never got to talk seriously while you were at home, but now that you have left again, I find that I have so terribly much I should have talked to you about. What should I do now, Tobias? Shall I write a letter to Uncle on my own and ask him to send me a ticket as soon as possible, and act as though you had never written a word about me? Then if I get one, we can travel together, whether you get a ticket or travel on your own money. I don't know what I should do. You know it was remiss of me that I didn't tell you anything definite right from the beginning, but the truth is that I am too vacillating and undecided. Yet it has always been my intention that if you went, I would accompany you. It is true that I told Mother I wouldn't go, but you know how she is, and so I thought it wasn't worthwhile to cross that bridge before I came to it, but you know what I always said to you and that was my intention. . . .

Adieu. I wish you a good catch. Write soon! Write soon! Dearest greetings from me, your sister,

Berta Serina

This may be her wedding picture. Berta Serina is shown seated with her husband, Knud Tuttle. The other couple is probably Berta's brother and his wife. Photo courtesy Margrete Indrehus and Nils Ladstein Vestbø.

Berta Serina's first letter from her new country graphically describes the rigors of the journey and the culture shock of arrival, as well as the way new immigrants were cared for by those already established. The Fox River, Illinois, area was an old, established colony, which had first been settled by Norwegians from the Stavanger area in the 1830s. Some of the names she mentions, such as Walde and Grødeim, were among those early settlers. The end of this letter is missing.

June 20, 1886

Dear Parents and Brothers and Sisters,

Since I have now safely arrived in America, I won't tarry but will send some words to you, my dear ones. I will start by telling you a bit about the journey. We departed from Liverpool the second of June and were below Ireland on the third. There we took on board 200 people, in addition to the 600–700 of before, so now we were about 900. You can just imagine what life was like on board. There was gambling and dancing, card-playing and wretchedness. Wherever I cast my eyes I saw nothing but depravity, and certainly no one thought about the fact that only a thin plank separated us from the deep grave. Yes, I thought many a time that it was more like hell than like real life.

As far as the weather goes, it was reasonably tolerable the whole time. We had storms . . . and a little fog now and then, but this was a very poor boat we were on, for we spent thirteen days and nights on the journey. I was sick nearly the whole trip, except for the last two days, when I was well enough to eat a little, though not of the food we received on board, for everyone found it almost inedible. You can well imagine how good I look now, after having fasted for a week and a half. We arrived in Philadelphia the fifteenth of this month at two o'clock, and left on the train at 8:30 the same day and arrived in Chicago on the seventeenth at 7:30 in the evening. There I stopped for just one hour, and then left on the train again, but now I was completely alone, for there was no one going in my direction of those who had been on board. At eleven o'clock in the evening I arrived in Malta, but now came the worst situation of the whole journey. There I stood, completely at a loss. There was not a single soul with whom I could speak a word and I didn't know which way to turn, so I prayed to God, our help in need, that He would save me and help me, and that He did, too, for someone showed me to a house where a Swedish shoemaker lived. I could talk to him, and that was a great relief, but he had arrived so recently that he didn't know very much about the people I was asking for. But he was one of those who will do what he can, and he knew an old Swede living a little ways away who was well acquainted with the Norwegian farmers, and so I left my trunk and he accompanied me to the home of these Swedes—a kindly old couple. I ate dinner with them, and then they took me a little ways farther, to a Norwegian boy by the name of John Walde. I can't say for sure who his parents are. . . . He accompanied me to the station where he rented a horse and buggy and drove me . . . to Per Grødeim and Marta Nordskaar. Here I received a warm welcome and have been here ever since. . . .

Friday I visited my brothers, they live five miles east of here, where they are working close to each other, Tobias for a Yankee and Johannes for a Norwegian. They were both well, and it was a great joy for us to meet. To-

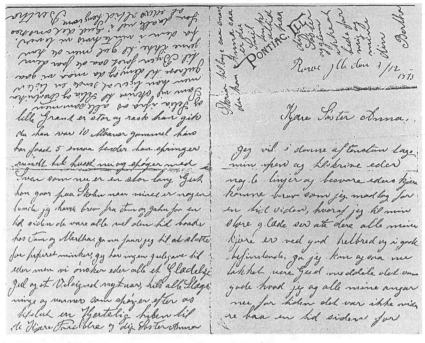

Berta Serina often filled her paper by writing all around the edges.

morrow I am expecting Tom here, he is going to drive to town to fetch my clothing, which I still haven't gotten. Then I will go with him and buy some cloth for working clothes, as Marta has promised to sew them for me. . . . [The rest is missing.]

Malta, Illinois
July 17, 1886

Dear Sister,

Your most welcome and longed for letter of June 15 arrived on the fifteenth of this month. I read it with great joy and pleasure, when I found that all of you at home were well, and I have the same good news to relate from here. I must tell you that I have been out working for fourteen days, and I work for a Norwegian family. The wife is from Stavanger, and she is very well acquainted with our community. . . . They are exceptionally kind, both of them. He is from eastern Norway. I will get a dollar a week to start with.

As far as my own well-being is concerned, it is going better than I had expected. Naturally there are a few heavy moments now and then, that is true for all of us who have recently come over and no less for me. Yes, dear

Anna, there are many trials for a poor greenhorn here in this country. When I left, I thought I knew how to work, but when I got here, I found that I didn't know the least bit, but of course I am not too old to learn. I don't have any especially hard work to carry out, it is just to keep going all day, and that is tiring enough in the long run, so I can truthfully say that I was seldom as tired when I went to bed in Norway as I am here, but I can only thank God that I have the health to be out working. It didn't look good when I first came over, but you know that it is hardest at first until you really get the hang of things.

As far as the weather is concerned, it has been unusually dry and hot here, has scarcely rained for two months, so things look quite bleak. For the most part they have finished haying; it was quite thin, they say. The corn looks good but the oats and potatoes will not amount to much. . . . You have probably gotten in the new potatoes by now. I often wish I were at home and could sit at the table with you and eat those delicious fresh potatoes and fish. Here they eat only pork, and I cannot stand to eat the wheat bread that they use. I got such an aversion to it on board that I almost throw up when I see it. I have not suffered for lack of food, as I am allowed to fry pancakes for myself, though I can't eat much anyway in this heat, but just wait until it begins to get a little cooler. . . . Right now I am eating mostly gooseberries and sweet green apples. There is a lovely large garden here, so I am coddled when it comes to eats.

I am home entirely alone today, the others have gone to visit an old man . . . from Stavanger. They say he is Father's cousin, but I am not sure of that. Well, I have been here for almost five weeks now, and I have not been to church or a prayer meeting yet. So I must say that I am longing to hear God's word proclaimed. . . . It is true that there are many churches and min- isters here, but there are also so terribly many kinds of sects and I don't know yet if I want to go to the church that most people belong to, the Catholic faith. There is a Norwegian Lutheran church west of here, but I don't know exactly where it is. I usually get a little time in the evening after I have done the dishes and then I read in my dear books, and those are, God be praised, the happiest hours I have. You can imagine that there are all kinds of temp- tations here for a poor heedless creature such as me, but God is powerful . . . and with His blessed help I hope to withstand even the worst temptations.

Well, now I had better quit writing. Dear Anna, when you write to me you must tell me many small pieces of news from home. You know I want to hear how you all are, if Father will sell the sheep this fall and buy a cow. . . . Tom wants to send ten dollars this fall, and Jan five, then they said they thought you could get a cow. Tom said he would write and tell Father to do that. In any case, they will send money, that I know. . . .

Loving greetings from Tom, Jan and Uncle Ole and Per and family. We are all well. Greet Sven, Serina, Annanias and Marta and the folks at

Skare from us, but first and foremost our dear old parents and Soffia and Selia. Your eternally devoted sister,

Berta Serina

"Watchout" is the name of the family dog.

Malta, Illinois
September 25, 1886

Dear Sister,

Your dear letter of the twelfth of last month I received with great joy some time ago, and I now send you my heartiest thanks. I had waited for a long time for a letter from you, so it was all the more precious when it finally came, on a Sunday, fourteen days ago, when I was so downhearted that I could scarcely bear it any longer. I had not seen Tom for five and Jan for eight weeks, and not heard anything from home for ever so long, so you can well imagine that I was unhappy. But just then Tobias arrived with a letter from you. . . . I couldn't have been happier if I had gotten all of Illinois that day.
. . .

I can't exactly say that I like it so well here in this so-called marvelous West, as my thoughts dwell among the hills and rocky slopes far, far away, across the prairies and the great ocean. Yes, not a day goes by, scarcely an hour passes that I am not at home with you. It is just as though I imagine that I can see what you are doing. I see Mother standing there cutting our small fields, and then she is no doubt thinking of us here in America, maybe she is thinking of that time I was going to try to use the scythe for the first time and I was so clever that I turned the straw for binding the sheaf backwards. I see Soffi and Selia and Watchout and everyone. I see you out . . . working and sweating. Father is someplace or other using his hammer and saw, but surely his thoughts sometimes tear themselves loose from the surroundings and fly over to the unknown plains. . . . Thus in my thoughts I am often more in Norway than in America. . . .
. . . Now I will break off for this time, with the heartiest greetings . . . to all who ask about me, though that is probably not so many. Finally, you Anna have the heartiest greetings from me, your devoted sister,

Berta S. Bjøravåg

As we read this letter, we are reminded of Berta Serina's seasickness and inability to tolerate the food at first, as well as her remarks about being tired. Berta usually writes standard Norwegian. However, in this letter she uses the English word plenti.

Norway, Illinois
June 20, 1887

Dear Sister Anna,

I received with great joy your most welcome letter, from which I see that all my dear ones at home are in good health. . . . We truly owe our Lord great thanks for granting us this blessing. . . . I hear that Annanias is about to say farewell to his Fatherland. He is expected here soon, if all goes well. Poor Marta, it will not be so easy for her to part with him and remain behind with two little ones, but there is not much to do if one stays at home and I hope that when he comes over here he will get both work and wages.

In any case the crops look rather bleak this year here in our parts, for it has been unusually hot and dry, so that the fields are as bare as if it were February. Many folks must go four or five miles to fetch water for their cattle, and let them into the farmyards so that they won't starve to death. If the Lord does not have mercy on us soon and send some rain, then the cattle will have no winter fodder. . . .

I am glad to hear so much news of things happening at home, births and deaths and marriages and a little bit of everything, as the saying goes. Just think, old Jens Berge married!!! I don't laugh very often nowadays, but when I read that I had to chuckle. . . . But now I also want to know how it is going with all those who were engaged so that the gold rings shone for miles around. . . .

Greetings to Mother and Father from Per Skaar, who lives near here. He was together with them at Selvaag in their salad days, he said. One time he and Mother were at a wedding and he danced so much that he wore out a pair of new leather shoes. He was up here one day, and I noticed that he didn't seem to be capable of wearing out many pairs of shoes with dancing nowadays. He used a cane that was almost as tall as he was and he took a terribly long time to walk a little distance. . . .

I see from your letter that there is a good deal of gossip at home, which unfortunately I can witness to the truth of. I had the honor you see, or perhaps I should say the dishonor—I don't know which word fits the best—to embrace as his mother a little smiling blue-eyed boy on the seventh of February, so he is already nearly four months old now. It would have been proper for me to have told you this before, but I knew that it would not be pleasant news for you and therefore I didn't want to inform you about it until I heard that rumors had reached home. Before I go any further, I want to implore all of you, my dear ones, that you must not despise me or be angry with me as I rightly deserve. I know that by my bad conduct I have wounded and offended the hearts of my dear old parents and brothers and sisters, and also caused sorrow to our dear God, but I hope and certainly know that He, for Jesus' sake, has forgiven me my terrible sin and will never more remember it and so I hope that my dear ones also will forget and overlook my flaws.

You can imagine how my heart was beating fast when I went to Tom last October when I had to quit my job and tell him of my situation. And you may imagine as well how surprised he was. His face turned as white as a sheet and I saw how he fought to control his anger, but then his brotherly love won, as he said to me in a voice choked with tears, "You should try and go down to Aunt, and if you need anything there I will send you money." Yes, now I had fought a great battle, and my heart was lighter, but I had much left to endure. First of all, I had to travel all alone by train, forty miles among only Yankees, and when I finally arrived at the last station, there was the question of how Aunt would receive me, who had come over in this condition. What if she showed me the door? But no, thanks be to God, she didn't do that. They accepted me in a friendly way, these two old folks, and they have been as kind to me as though they were my own parents, and Tom and Johannes have been the same. They have been more than brothers to me. Tom was here when the little one was born and he fetched the doctor and paid him seven dollars and when I was sick he watched over me for six nights and since then they have also sent money to me. Yes, people here are far different than in Norway. People that I had never seen came and looked after me and I can tell you, for example, that I have gotten thirteen pieces of cloth for clothing for the little one. You see, they don't swaddle the babies here in this country.

Well, now I had better close. The boy is thriving and is chubby and fat, and endlessly angry the whole time. He is lying here on the floor now kicking and screaming as hard as he can. His name is Sven.

Well, greet all the relatives and acquaintances, but first and foremost parents and brothers and sisters. . . . And finally you have the heartiest greetings from your eternally devoted sister,

Berta Kingestad

Berta Serina uses many different names for the same person, and the Annas she mentions in this letter is short for Annanias, her brother-in-law. She frequently uses the nickname "Svennemann" for her little boy, Sven. The Marta Prestagaren she worked for may be one of the early settlers in the Fox River area. A woman named Marta Prestgarden married Lars Nielsen Hellen in 1836 and traveled to America on the brig Norden in that same year.[2]

Norway, Illinois
August 26, 1887

Dear Sister Anna,

Today I am home alone, and therefore have taken the opportunity to answer your most welcome letter, which I received on Tuesday. . . . I must not forget to thank you so much for the beautiful yarn and also the crocheted things which you sent to me with Annas. I would really like to be able to send a little something to you, but it is seldom that anyone travels home and I don't have very much either, but if I ever get the opportunity I will remember you with something or other. . . . It must soon be time for Soffia to be confirmed, so I will send my best wishes, Soffia, and hope that you think carefully over the importance of the promise that you will make before the triune God. May you find the grace to be faithful to that promise until the end. . . .

Now I must tell you that I have been in Lee County. I drove there with our cousin Ole Johnsen two weeks ago. I talked to Tom, Jan, and Annas. They were all well. Annas was not terribly satisfied, he said, and that is not to be wondered at, as scarcely anyone is happy here during the first weeks, but it gets better in time as one becomes more accustomed to conditions.

Well, I have nothing new to tell you. I am thinking of going out and working. I can work for an old couple, she is Marta Prestagaren from Hjelmeland. Mother must have known her when she was young. They will give me a small weekly wage and I think it better to work for my bread rather than be a burden on other folk. Svennemann is thriving and he now has two small teeth. I am as pleased with my situation and as calm of mind as I have ever been. It is true that many a tear has fallen since I departed from my beloved home . . . but I also have happy hours in between and so time passes for me as for so many others, alternating between joy and sorrow.

. . . Now I must stop for this time in hope that the Lord will have mercy on you. . . . Greet all our dear ones at home and write again soon. . . .

Berta S. Kingestad

In this letter Berta Serina mentions someone named Christian. Internal evidence from this and other letters seems to indicate that Christian may be the father of her child.

Norway, Illinois
November 19, 1887

Dear Sister Anna,

Today I will take pen in hand and send all of you at home a few words and thank you heartily for the most welcome letter which I received a week ago.

. . . I am now working, as I mentioned before. I have been here for twelve weeks now, and I think it has gone quite well, though little Sven doesn't always get the best care, as I must do all the necessary work in the house, and that as you know is not so little. We are five or six grown people almost every day, but when babe and I have our health then I have nothing to complain about, and I get both food and a small wage so that I can buy a little clothing and shoes for both of us. I have just bought us new shoes and cloth for winter clothing for the little one. I will send you a scrap. I am often over at Aunt Torborg's, she has promised me that I can come back when I want to, and now it is getting so cold that I am afraid I may not be able to stay here longer on account of the baby. He is so big and healthy and good, he can almost walk alone.

. . . I have now and then thought that . . . Christian would perhaps like to come over, but that is probably difficult and I must truly say that in this case I am rather like the bait Lars used when he fished with the dip net. If you understand what I mean.

Yes, yes, dear sister, if you only knew how often I think of you and long to talk to you and Mother and everyone at home but alas, we are too far apart from each other and must be content with some words now and then, but when I get your letters then I imagine that I am with you all, and it is a great comfort to me in my loneliness here among strangers.

Well, now the paper is disappearing, the sun is going down, and little Sven comes creeping across the floor crying mammammamma so I had better quit. When you write you must tell me if Marta has thought about coming over in the spring. Greet her from me and say that she must just come . . . and I will help her all I can. . . . There are better opportunities here than in Norway, I know that now from experience. I have sewed a pretty quilt that I will give her when she comes here and you and Mother will also get one that I will send home. Live well in the name of the Lord Jesus and remember me in your prayers.

Hearty greetings from your humble daughter and sister,

Berta S. Kingestad

Norway, Illinois
February 17, 1888 [?]

Dear Sister,

You must truly forgive me for not writing to you long ago, but it has always been put off, and the main reason is negligence. I thank you heartily for your dear letter which I received a week ago. . . . I am here at Aunt Torborg's again, and have been here since before Christmas, but now when spring comes I must try to dig myself out as soon as I can get a place. Yes, dear sister, you can imagine that my days are not always happy now, as scarcely a day goes by that I don't have to see a cross face and listen to my little Sven be scolded and pushed around. But when I receive the grace to take my refuge in the Lord and pray to Him for patience then it goes a little easier anyway. . . .

Now you all must not be too concerned about me. I hope with the help of God that things will get better for me. If the child and I can only preserve our health, then I think I will find a place and work for my bread when summer comes and will no longer be dependent on the charity of others.

. . . Oh, yes, dear Anna, you can believe that I have wished more than once that I were in Bjøravåg, but it is difficult to know whether I will ever get there again. However, everything is in the hands of the Lord, for Him nothing is impossible. Annanias has been at Ole's this winter and now he is here. He doesn't like it here and talks of going home in the fall. I am supposed to greet you all from him. . . .

Now I must close for today. Excuse me, dear sister, I haven't time for more, but next time to make up for it you will get three sheets of paper. . . . You must all pray for your poor Berta and her little friend; that is what they need the most. You must greet all . . . who remember Berta. Live well in the Lord and receive the heartiest greetings from little Sven and your poor,

Berta Svensen

Lee, Illinois
April 30, 1888

Dear Sister,

I received and read with great joy your most welcome letter of the second of this month, and wish to thank you heartily for the same. I am so happy each time I get a letter from you, my dear ones at home, and to see that you are all well. . . .

I must tell you that I moved to Lee County a month ago, and am now working for old Per and Talleta Trævland. This is a good place for me, for there are not any children, and the old people are very good to me and to my little one. Yes, dear sister, you can never believe how happy I am to be able to eat the bread I have earned myself, even if I have to work rather hard for it.

I am quite close to Uncle Ole and have the opportunity to visit them often. They are quite well, you should just see what a nice house they have and now they have five cows and two calves and a number of chickens and ducks. Uncle goes hunting all the time. He has a very bad cough and often complains of pain in the chest. Annanias is now in Creston, a town close by here, at a tile factory. I haven't seen him for awhile now, but I think everything is going well. . . . Tom is working nowadays for an Irishman. . . .

Well, now I will soon have to stop. Oh, how I wish I were close enough to my dear home that I could come and talk with Father and Mother and you, dear Anna, then the time would not be so heavy and long for me, but now my pen must serve. . . . I hear that Soffia has gone out to work now. Poor little sister, she will find out what the world has to offer. . . .

Well, now I must break off my poor missive for today. I have such a headache that I scarcely know how I have written this letter, you must excuse me. . . . Hearty greetings to my dear old parents and you, Anna and Selia, from your always faithful,

Berta S. Kingestad

In an undated letter to her niece, Berta added a brief postscript in which she again mentions Christian in terms that make it seem that he is the father of her child.

Listen here, Anna,

I am very curious to hear something or other about Christian. Tell me in your letter what you know about him, please. He is probably married now, but tell me who he is married to. I don't think I either could or would want to get anything from him, but I would like to hear who has taken my place in his home as well as his heart. Hearty greetings, your sister,

Berta

The town of "Rasjel" that Berta mentions in this letter is Rochelle, Illinois.

Lee, Illinois
November 11, 1888

Dear Parents and Brothers and Sisters,

I can just imagine how often you have been over . . . asking after letters from me and not getting any, and it is really a shame how my writing has gone this time. You must not believe it is because I have forgotten you, my most dear ones at home, no, far from it, there is not a day or hour when you are not in my thoughts. . . .

The other evening I found out that I simply had to go to town on account of these confounded teeth that had been trying my patience for several days, and so it was decided that I should go to the doctor and get not less than three of them pulled at once. That was rather hard at first, but now I hope I am finished with the toothache for awhile.

I am, thank God, in good health, as are both my brothers. . . . Little Sven is also healthy and growing and happy as a horse. He is beginning to babble and talk now. In my next letter you will get a picture of him if everything goes as planned, for Uncle Tom has promised to go with us up to a town called Rasjel as soon as he is through working, which will be in a few weeks.

I must tell you that I have left the old folks at Trævland and have been here with some people from Tysdal for a few months. I may stay here this winter, but I want to go six miles east and visit Uncle P. Kaada soon now, I haven't been there since Svennemann came into the world. I have worked rather hard since March, so I would like to rest for awhile in the middle of the winter. . . . Sven will soon come sent in a letter, and then you shall see for yourself what a wild American you have for a cousin. . . .

Well, I should have lots to tell you, but my pen has run out. . . . I had better quit, as I am sitting in a cold room and freezing until I am almost blue. I am sending a little scrap from my dress and Sven's. The darkest one is Sven's and the little velvet is from the decoration on mine and the little silk thread is from Sven's embroidery. . . .

So now I will stop in the hope that these lines find you all in the best of health both in body and soul. Greet . . . everyone who remembers me. . . . But first and last, you, my precious old parents, are heartily greeted from your daughter,

Berta Serina

When Berta Serina brags about Sven in this letter, she uses the English word boy *followed by the Norwegian* gutt.

Malta, Illinois
February 27, 1889

Dear Parents and Brothers and Sisters,

Finally you are getting a letter from Berta. If I had been near enough, you could have given me a spanking and I would have deserved it, but now you will just have to let me get off with a good scolding, and see if I can't learn to be a little more faithful than I have been lately. It's true, as the saying goes, people always find an excuse, and that's the way it is with me, too. . . .

But now I will be able to tell you a bit about myself. I am, thanks be to God, in good health these days, as are Svennemann and my brothers and all our relatives around here, . . . and I wish the same to all my dear ones at home. I must tell you that I moved . . . a month ago, and am now working for an old English widower. I have a really good position here, because I can putter about alone with Sven all day as the old fellow has so much to do outside, so there is no one who watches me and counts the crumbs I give to my little boy. He is a kind man, the old fellow, both to Sven and to me, so I don't need to be afraid when I see him in the doorway. I also have quite good wages, so I can only thank God who has arranged things so well for me.

Well, by the time you get this letter I believe Sven will have come home, or more accurately, his shadow, for you see Tom sent two pictures several days ago. . . . Yes, now Svennemann is already starting his third year. As you know, he was two years old on the seventh of this month. I think time has gone rather quickly. When I think back to the time I went about in Bjøravåg getting myself ready to leave for America . . . I can never forget what was said: "Yes, Berta, now you must say farewell to Bjøravåg for the last time." Oh, I didn't believe then that it would be for the last time, and I don't dare believe it now, but perhaps it will be so. I can still see Mother and Marta as they walked away along the shore, and I surely never realized how precious Mother was and how much she meant to me as right in that moment when I saw her for the last time, and it was the same when I parted with Anna and Father in Stavanger. Oh, that parting, how hard it was, and it is not erased by the first tears, no, they return again and again. I think about it more than ever before, now that I am alone so much.

I certainly didn't think, when I left home on the 26th of May, 1886, that by the same time the next year I would have a four-month-old son on my lap, or my ticket to America would surely have gone without me. But remarkably enough, no matter how dark it has been nor how heavily my tears have fallen in America, I have basically never regretted the step I took. . . .

More than once I have wished that you were all here so that little Sven and I could visit you, but the only thing I can do is to wish and long and weep. . . . Sven speaks often of Grandma and Grandpa in Norway, you know I have taught him that. You should hear how he can chatter now, but he doesn't speak good Norwegian, he mixes it too much with English. I have decided that if he lives to get a little bigger, then I will teach him to speak Norwegian as well as I can. You must not laugh at all this nonsense. You know he is all that I have in this big strange country and when nearly everyone flatters me by saying he is a "capital boy," then I can't help being a little proud of him. People might call that seeking honor in one's disgrace, but I can't help it. Well, now I had better quit for this time. . . .

I read your letters over and over many times, until I receive a new one. Yes, many times I sit on the floor next to my trunk and reread the letters I have received since I came here. . . . [The rest is missing.]

Berta Serina writes the words go to bed *in English.*

Malta, Illinois
April 14, 1889

Dear Sister,

As I sit here all alone on this Palm Sunday, my thoughts fly out into space and suddenly stop by a small, red-painted house standing in a bay by the sea. It seems just as alone there as I am here today, yet when I look into the door I find so many wonderful things. There I see the spot where my cradle stood . . . and there I see you still today, dear Mother, with graying hair and sunken cheeks, but I hope and know for certain that the same heart still beats warmly for me. Yet the best thing you can do for me is to pray that we may one day meet again in reality and not just in our thoughts. I also see my dear old Father, grayed and bent with age and with the hard work he has endured to sustain himself and his dear ones, but be comforted by this, dear Father, that soon you will go to rest. Yes, I think I can see you, Anna, and Selia and Soffia and everyone. Alas, it is so far away, and yet in my thoughts so near.

Well, I must tear myself away from this dream and tell you that I am, God be praised, in possession of good health, and Sven too and all our family over here as far as I know. Yesterday Tom was here and he had just come from John's. They are both well and send you their warmest greetings. I am still with the old Englishman and I have a really good position here both for me and for little Sven. You should see how big he is, he runs around outside nearly all day now when it is nice weather, but today it is too cold and now he is lying here sleeping.

Well, dear Sister, I don't have much new to tell you today for I don't go anywhere and the only thing I hear and see are the old man and a little blackbearded man from eastern Norway who works here, so the time often passes slowly and especially on Sunday, for it is so far to church that I cannot walk there. . . . You know I have my dear Bible and a few other good books that I also use, though certainly too little, but anyway it is difficult when I can never talk to anyone about that which is true and when I never hear anything other than raw ungodliness almost everywhere I turn. But the Lord is faithful who sustains the wretched and He has not deserted me.

Both Tom and Jan have written to Soffia that she should come over here and I also believe that it would be best for her to come, the sooner the better. Now is just the time for her to learn both to speak and to work, and when she comes over, then we will all do our best for her. I really feel sorry for her having to work in that ugly barn . . . in big wooden shoes and shovel manure and go out into the fields . . . and do all kinds of hard work. . . . She doesn't need to do that kind of heavy work here for we only have to take care of the house and besides we have so much more freedom here in America than at home.

I tell you, Anna, that here in this country we don't need to sit up and toil and work the long winter nights until we are so sleepy we are almost faint. No, at most places, that is, at Americans' and Englishmen's places, the hired girls have the whole afternoon free, that is to say, after they have washed up in the afternoon until it is time to fix supper, and then when we have washed up for the evening we can *go to bed*, if we want to. Well, if Soffia wants to come, then let her come as soon as she can. You don't need to rig her out much with clothing and shoes. If she has one pair of shoes then that is absolutely enough for I will tell you that Norwegian shoes aren't worth much over here. They are usually too heavy as it is so hot here and the air so dry in the summer that they go to pieces. On the other hand, socks are good to have and then there is one thing I would like to have her bring me if she comes. That is a little bit of black wool and a pair of carding combs. I have been able to borrow a spinning wheel, but there are so few combs here. I have gotten a little white wool . . . and when Soffia comes with black wool and combs, then I will spin gray yarn and knit gray socks for Svennemann for the winter. If she has a hat, then let her wear it when she crosses the ocean. And then I will tell her what she should have to eat, that is, rye rusks and dried mutton, and if you can buy a bottle of fruit wine, it is excellent to mix with water. Grind some coffee and put in a little box, then she will get boiled water on the ship and then she can take a little of the coffee in a tin cup and pour the hot water on it and let it stand for a while and then it is good. A little Naphtha or Hoffmanns drops are good to have, but then she must have a little white sugar to take them in, as the water is quite poor. Have a large towel in her traveling bag and a comb and soap. If she wants to have eggs, then cook them at home and place them in the one part of the pail and sprinkle a little salt on them and then they will keep. Well, now I have written a whole lesson that you must read for her and then I hope she will come. It will be hard for you to part with her, but the day may come that you will not regret that she went. Tell her that she has brothers and a sister here and a number of relatives who will be happy to receive her and do the very best they can for her in every way.

Well, now I had better come to an end for I have written so long I am almost dizzy. I send you all a little remembrance in this letter. Dear sister, it is something that I have made myself, therefore I think it will be precious to you. I thought you could fill it up with dry sawdust and use it for a pincushion. I have one like it myself.

Well, now I must break off for today. . . . Greet . . . everyone who asks about me, but first and foremost may you, Anna, receive a warm greeting from your faithful sister,

Berta Serina

In this, as in other letters where she describes her work, Berta Serina indicates that she does not milk the cows nor participate much in caring for the animals. In Norway, this was women's work. In America, the women worked mostly in the house and the men did the outdoor and barn chores.

Malta, Illinois
May 2, 1889

Dear Parents and Brothers and Sisters,

I wish in this evening hour to answer your heartily welcome and anxiously awaited letter that I received two days ago. I see to my great joy that all my dear ones at home are in good health. . . . We do indeed have much to thank God for. . . . I have now been here for almost three years, and still have never heard anything but good news from you. Sometimes I think you wouldn't tell us if one of you were sick. . . .

Well, I don't have much to write about. I am just here at the same place, and there are no changes. We are having really beautiful weather now, and the trees and fields are green all over. The flowers are also coming out now. I was out in the garden this evening and picked some, which I have in a water glass here on the table beside me, but they don't smell as wonderful as our Norwegian flowers. Today I have been ironing almost all day, and I have also baked bread and cookies and filled a large tub with butter which I churned yesterday—two and a half pounds. You can just imagine how heavy it was to churn. Early tomorrow old Smith will drive to Malta with it and send it to Chicago on the train where it will be sold. . . . He has seven cows that are milking, but I don't milk nor am I outside in the busy time, but I have to prepare the food and skim the milk and churn, and then I have four calves to feed and lots of eggs to pick, and then you know I have to keep the house in order and wash and bustle about. You know I have to do everything myself, as there is no housewife here, but on the other hand, I have greater freedom in some ways. I have the use of the horse and buggy, and can drive to Malta and sell eggs and then I buy things that we use in the house like coffee, sugar, tea, soap and starch, and things like that, you know.

Yes, I often think of you when I fix a little coffee just for myself. I think that if only Mother and Anna were here now, they would get good coffee. . . . And then when I sit and think about you at home my coffee doesn't taste so good anymore.

Well, now I have chattered a great deal, which isn't worth much of anything, but occasionally we must talk about our daily lives, too. On Sunday I am thinking about driving west to Uncle Ole, six miles from here. It is John's birthday and then he and Tom will be there, too, I expect. Well, now I had better quit, as the paper is running out and my eyes are also getting rather heavy. The old man is sleeping in his rocking chair with Svennemann in his lap, also fast asleep, so neither of them is disturbing me now.

Before I stop, I must thank you for the letter and for the beautiful rose you sent me. It is the dearest thing in the world to me when I receive something from home. Please greet all my dear brothers and sisters and relatives. . . . Finally, a loving good night and a warm greeting, dear Mother and Father and Anna.

Yours,

Berta Serina

Malta, Illinois
September 18, 1889

Dear Sister Anna,

I won't wait long to answer your most welcome letter that I received a few days ago. I opened it with trembling hands and fast-beating heart, fearing that something must be wrong with one of you, as it had been so long since I got a letter. I was so happy to see that you were all well. . . . Still, there are several things in your letter, dear sister, that fill my heart with sadness. I believe that things are not well with you at home. I can just imagine how little you are able to harvest this year, when it has been so unusually dry and hot. I always think, when I sit at a well-covered table, what do they have to eat at home now, those poor folks. Perhaps they don't know what they are going to have for dinner, while here there is an abundance of everything. If only I could reach them with some of it. Yes, that is the way I think, Anna, and then I lose my own appetite. . . . You can't imagine how dearly I would love to help you if I could, but unfortunately, my help can't be so very great. Yet I will try, if God grants me health, to send you a little money this fall. I have talked with Tom and John and they will also send some. It will be a little bit to help out when winter comes. I don't have any right now, but when the old man sells some oats I will get something, and then I will not forget you.

I must thank you so much for the letter and for the little bushes you sent. I laid them in water as soon as I got them and watched and hoped that they would begin to turn green. Oh, how I longed to see a small shoot and life, but alas, they are still dead. I have planted a few flowers, which I have here in the window. One of them is blooming now, but they are not as beautiful as the ones we had at home. I have no myrtle or fuchsia or anything like that. How often I wish I had a cutting from each of those which stand in the window at home. I imagine that I can both see and smell them when I think about them.

. . . I think I will stay here with old Smith this winter, too. This is a pretty good place, for he is as kind as he can be to both me and Svennemann, and I have a good deal of freedom and an old horse and buggy to use.

Well, now you must not wait too long before you write to me again, dear Anna. I count the days and weeks from the time I send a letter home until I get one back again. I know that money is scarce back at home, so you can send my letters without paying for them. I will be glad to pay for . . . every letter I get. . . . I haven't seen Annas for a long time. Last time I talked to him, he said that he would send a ticket to Marta, but I don't think he meant it. Well, now I must stop, but before I fold the letter up I will ask you for a small gift, and that is a lock of hair from Father and Mother so that I can have a living memory of them, and also a little scrap of cloth from the last dresses you got. I hope to get your portrait sometime. Dearest Anna, God grant that I may someday see you and everyone in real life. Well, you must greet everyone on Finnøy, both friends and relatives . . . and anyone who asks about me, but especially my precious old parents and Soffia and Selia. Never forget me in your prayers so we will gather every day before the throne of grace. . . .

Finally, loving greetings to you, dear sister Anna,

Your devoted sister,
Berta Serina Bjøravåg

Malta, Illinois
January 7, 1890

Dear Parents and Brothers and Sisters,

I scarcely know how I should begin this letter, I must just say right out that I am ashamed at my almost unforgivable negligence in not answering your very dear letter which I received several weeks ago and for which I now send my heartiest thanks. . . .

Now we have celebrated both Christmas and the New Year again. Just think, this is the fourth Christmas I have spent without even getting to go home. . . . Alas, you would not believe what a sad and cheerless Christmas holiday this has been. Just think, not even to be among Norwegian people, and these English and Americans don't care about Christmas. Around here there were many who went out and plowed on Christmas Day. Here where I work at least we kept the holiday. I am ashamed to admit it, yet it is true, that I went around in an old, worn, and dirty dress, and this is surely the first time in the 26 Christmases that I have lived that I have not washed myself or changed clothes. You must not be angry with me when you read this. I could not help it, and it is so difficult to be among strangers. I thought about you at home where I have spent so many happy Christmas Eves and I imagined that I could see you and hear the lovely old Christmas hymns sung by all those dear voices, and then it seemed that everything around me was so lonely and joyless that I didn't want to do anything. . . .

Well, now, I mustn't forget to thank you so much for the precious locks of hair you sent me as a living memory of my dear old parents. But I bitterly regret that I have lost your lock, Mother, and you must please send me another in your next letter. I had laid them both in tissue paper and put them away in a little box, but one Sunday when John was here I took them out to show him and then I must have lost yours. I have searched and searched, but could not find it anywhere. You must please send me one again. There is something else that we all want you to do, and that is that you— Father and Mother especially—get your picture taken and send us. We will send you money when you need it, if you will just have your portrait taken. It is difficult to know whether we will ever see you again in person . . . so it will be especially dear to see your picture.

Well, I don't have much news to tell you. We are having an unusually mild winter, with almost no snow, and only a little frost, but we have had a good deal of rain and that is almost as bad in this country as snow and frost, for the roads are so awfully muddy here when there is a lot of rain, so it is almost impossible to get anywhere.

Annanias is here now taking care of the animals and it is a great joy for me, for I can speak my dear mother tongue every day. He is very kind and amusing, so the time goes much more quickly for me now and I believe he is tolerably well pleased, too. He and Sven fool around something fierce sometimes. Sven is growing and thriving wonderfully and is as wild as a cat. He seems to be gifted with a good mind and ability to learn. He has now learned one verse of the hymn "Your Name, Oh Jesus, Calls to Me." I started to teach it to him on New Year's Eve and he knows it as well as I do. Isn't that great for someone who isn't even three years old yet?

. . . Well, I had better quit now for Sven is lying in his bed and crying for Mama so loudly you could almost hear it at home. You see it is bedtime now, and he has been asleep for awhile and has woken up again, and then there is no quarter given. Please greet . . . everyone who asks about me. . . . Your devoted daughter and sister,

Berta S. Kingestad

Malta, Illinois
February 14, 1890

Dear Sister Anna,

I now have received your most welcome letter, and this time I will not wait so long to answer it. I can report to you that we are all in excellent health and I see from your letter that the same good news applies to you, and therefore may the Lord be greatly praised and thanked.

We thought it was a terribly hard and unexpected message we received here two weeks ago when Marta wrote to Annanias that our dear beloved sister Soffia had died suddenly of a brain-fever. Yes, I must admit, even though I am ashamed of it, that I was so overcome with grief and despair that I could neither eat nor sleep, until one day Annanias said to me, "Berta, don't you know that it is heathen to grieve as though there is no hope?" Then it was as though a light went on for me and I had to feel ashamed of my lack of faith and ungodly sorrow. . . . Is this not a healing balm . . . that God . . . has taken her to grace? Yes, dear Father and Mother and brothers and sisters, I would so dearly love to comfort you though I am scarcely able to do that, but the God of all grace comfort and be with you all, that is my earnest prayer. . . .

You have now had some unanticipated expenses . . . and therefore we have talked among ourselves, the boys and I, about sending you a little money. . . . So when you write back, tell us if you want it now or later, it makes no difference to us. . . . We would very much like to help you as much as we can.

Well, here we have had an unusual winter without frost and snow, but at the same time a lot of sickness and not a few deaths. . . . Annanias is still here, and both little Sven and I are happy about that. Sven is already into his fourth year. Isn't it strange how time flies? He was three years old last Friday. He is still big and healthy and thriving and growing for better or for worse.

Now it is getting to be evening, and my paper is diminishing, so I had better cut off my writing for this time, but before I quit I don't want to forget to thank you for your dear letter, Anna, and the fine little piece of cloth from Selia's dress. When you write, you mustn't forget to tell me if you and Mother have black dresses; if not, I shall try to send you a little money when I get my wages here, so you can each get a dress. I will go to town as soon as the weather permits and buy one for myself. I have no black dress now. I will enclose a little scrap of my collar and mourning band. That is what they use in this country, and you will get a scrap from my dress in my next letter if we live so long. . . .

Well, now Annanias has sent a ticket to Marta. It will be sad for you to part with her, too, but Annanias says that if it seems altogether too hard, then she may send the ticket back instead. I put a little scrap in with her letter when Annas wrote and asked her to go home and ask for a little black wool for me, and if they have a little yarn it will be very gratefully received, especially gray, for soon all of of our socks will be footless. It is a shame to beg for yarn again, but please don't be angry with me. Father, you must make a pair of wooden shoes and send them with Marta when she comes. You know that Mother's shoes will fit me, and I would also like to have a sheath knife to whittle spoons with. Sheath knives cannot be found in America except one or two that have come from Norway.

Well, now I had better break off my humble writing for this time. . . . Finally, you, my dear parents, and you, Anna, and little Selia are heartily greeted from Svennemann and me, your devoted,

Berta S. Bjøravåg

Malta, Illinois

April 27, 1890

Dear Sister Anna,

Today I will answer your most welcome letter, which I received two weeks ago, and for which I thank you most heartily. It is a great joy for me and all of us each time to hear that you are all well. . . .

Dear sister, you must not be angry with me because I have waited so long to answer your letter. You see, I was sure that Marta would come soon and so I thought I would wait a while, but since I still haven't heard that she is coming, I didn't want to wait any longer. . . .

I don't have much news to tell you from here. I am still scratching around in the same place as before, but I don't know how long I will remain here. I may stay with Marta when she comes, for awhile in any case. . . . Svennemann is big and healthy as before. He can say his Lord's Prayer now and some small hymn verses that I have taught him. If he and I stay in good health, then we will have a picture taken this summer for you. Couldn't Father and Mother get themselves taken? I would so much like to see their dear precious faces again even if only in a shadow. And you, kind Anna, please take a picture of yourself and little Selia and send it to me. I am enclosing a little scrap of my dresses. The dotted I have for Sundays and the black for a best dress.

Now I must stop in the hope that these lines may find you all in good health both in body and spirit. . . . Hearty greetings from Svennemann and me, your humble sister,

Berta Serina Bjøravåg

Folkevennen, which Berta sent to her parents in Norway, was a weekly Christian newspaper published in Chicago in the 1880s and 1890s.

Malta, Illinois
June 25, 1890

Dear Parents and Brothers and Sisters,

In this evening hour, I will take my pen and send you a few lines, which I ought to have done long ago, but it will have to be better late than never. First of all, I can now tell you that we are all well, and I wish the same for you, our dear ones at home. Well, now Marta has finally arrived. I was with her almost a whole week after they had moved to Creston. She is very satisfied with her new home. She says that she wishes all of you were here, and it can't be denied that Berta also entertains that wish, . . . but God alone knows if that can ever happen. . . .

I don't know how I can thank you for everything you sent me. Many, many thanks to you, Mother, for the lovely yarn, and for the wooden shoes you sent me, Father, and you, sister Anna, who sent such lovely good socks for Svennemann. Many thanks from both of us, they fit him perfectly. And not less dear was the little remembrance of Soffia that you sent me. . . . I don't know what I can do for you, who are so good to me. I will pray for you, . . . and then as a little show of my gratitude, I will pay for *Folkevennen* as soon as I go to town, so you will get it again before too long. . . . It was really too bad that we were so careless that we let it stop last year, but I hope that won't happen again.

With this letter I will send a little package of calling cards with my name and Sven's on them. Sven's name is written the English way, namely Sam, but mine is the good old Norwegian, and I have written on the back what it says in English on the front so you can understand what it means.

Well, I should have much more to write to you, but you will have to excuse me for this evening. It is so terribly hot here and the mosquitoes are swarming around me and biting so that I am as bitten up over my whole body as if I had been in an ant hill. Yes, I am sitting here in a thin cotton dress and shirt, that is all I have on, and even so I am covered with sweat as I have been from morning to evening for the last six days, and when night comes it is almost impossible to get a wink of sleep because of the heat, so I hope it won't last too long like this. I must quit soon, for Sven is lying in his bed crying and saying "the bad lice are biting me." He calls flies and all kinds of insects lice. He has never in his life seen a real louse.

My dear old parents and you, dear sister Anna, and Selia are greeted most heartily from Svennemann and me, your devoted daughter and sister,

Berta Serina Svensdatter

This Christmas, spent with sister Marta and her family, was much happier than

previous ones in America. Letters from Berta Serina are becoming less frequent, although some may be missing from the collection.

Malta, Illinois

January 4, 1891

Dear Parents and Brothers and Sisters,

Some time has already passed since I received your dearly welcome letter, and it is surely time for me to send you some lines in reply. We have begun a new year, and I can inform you that all of us here in the distant West were able to begin it in good health and . . . I sincerely hope the same is true for all our dear ones at home. Well, now this is the fifth New Year that has crept by us since I was at home with you. Isn't it strange how time passes? We have certainly had some sorrows and trials in these past years, but the Lord has also been good to us both materially and spiritually. . . .

I must tell you a little about what I did this Christmas. I went to Creston to Martha on Christmas Eve and I stayed there until the Monday morning after Christmas. That is the longest free period I have had since I came to America. Everything was fine with all of them. They have bought a house, so now they have a rather pleasant little home. We didn't have any Christmas porridge, as there was not much milk available down there, but we had plenty to eat. Marta cooked a big fat hen on Christmas Eve, and on Christmas day we had a roast for dinner. Svendine and Andreas and Sven also had a really fun Christmas. They ran around making noise every day from morning to evening and they got some toys for Christmas presents, some small tin horses and wagons. I gave Svendine a new dress and a doll and Marta a pair of china cups. Annanias and Andreas each got a neck scarf and then I got a fine album from Annanias and Sven got a pair of new socks from Aunt Martha. I also got a fine box with paper and envelopes (which I am now writing on) from Tom. You surely know that Tom is married. I suppose he has written to you about it. He is going to build a house this winter in Malta, where he has bought a little piece of land. John will help him build it when the weather is good enough. . . . [The rest is missing.]

Malta, Illinois

March 10, 1891

Dear Sister Anna,

Now I am finished with my work for today. We have eaten supper and I have washed up and laid a good fire in the stove in the living room, and then I went back to the kitchen and strained the milk. When I came in again Svennemann sat sleeping in a little armchair, so I went and rolled down the shades and then he woke up and asked me, "Mama, what are you going to do tonight? I want to write to Grandma and Grandpa and Aunt Anna and Se-lia," he said. I undressed him and put him to bed, and now he is fast asleep again. . . .

I can never thank you enough for your dear letter, which I received together with your many precious gifts. Yes, dear Father and Mother and Anna, you cannot imagine how surprised John and I were when we opened the package and found all those wonderful things. . . . To us, it was worth double what we send home. I could not hold back my tears when I saw all the wonderful yarn and thought that each strand had gone through your hands. . . . And then I found the sheath knife that you sent, Father. You can imag-ine how Sven stared when he saw that. He knows it will be his. You must thank them so much, he said tonight, and a kiss for Grandpa and one for Grandma. He can't use it much yet, because he turns the blade in toward his chest, but I will hide it until he can use it right. . . . When I get the oppor-tunity, I will send you a fine jackknife if you want one. I must not forget to thank you for the carding combs. No one will ever take them from me. I will borrow Marta's spinning wheel soon, and then I will both card and spin.

I don't have so much news to tell you. We have had some really bad weather for a few weeks, with snow and frost, but today it is a little milder, so we hope spring will soon be here again.

Now I will stop for this time in the hope that these lines find you in good health. You must greet brother Sven and family. . . . I have not forgot-ten them. Beg them not to forget me. . . . Hearty greetings to Father and Mother and Anna from Svennemann and me, always yours,

Berta Serina

Berta Serina's flock of nieces and nephews is steadily growing.

Malta, Illinois
October 10, 1891

Dear Sister Anna,

Now it is already a long time since I received your most welcome let-ter, for which I thank you heartily. It is my greatest joy to receive your dear letters and hear that you are all well . . . and I lift up my heart in thanks to God whenever I hear how good He is to you, and likewise to us. I think it is wonderful that you, dear old Mother, are so healthy that you can still partic-ipate in the haying and that Father can still build big houses. God be praised for giving you strength and health to work, as old as you are now. There are many who give up before this time.

Well, now I must tell you that I was at Marta's last Monday. . . . You should see what a sweet little girl she has. I have almost never seen such a beautiful child. You know I was there when she was born and we talked about calling her Soffia, but then Annanias said that they didn't have anything but S's, and now they should name one after themselves, so she was baptized Myrtie Annara. Myrtie is a pretty name, but it isn't Norwegian, you see. We always call Svendine Soffi now, since they live entirely among Englishfolks and that is a real English name. To tell you the truth, I don't think it is always so pleasant for Marta. She seldom sees a Norwegian person, and as near as I understand, he is not the nicest husband either, so it happens that some tears flow there now and then, but don't let this get any farther. She would not like it if she knew that I was writing about such things, but I know so well that she needs your affection and prayers, as we all do.

I was over in Malta with Tobias and Lava that day, too. They are also all well. Little Simon is as chubby and lively as he can be. He has a pair of thick square hands just like Father's. For that matter, I don't know who he is most like, but I do know that he is both beautiful and well formed, and that is what counts. . . . [The rest is missing.]

This short note—written in Berta Serina's hand—from Sven to his cousin Selia indicates that Berta has just married Knud Tuttle of Rowe, Illinois. On the return address, she spells her husband's name Newt. She writes her son's name as Svend Knudssen Levegstad on the top of the letter and signs it Sammy Kingstad at the end. She inserts a parenthetical comment about the name Sven calls his stepfather in the middle of his letter. The list of Christmas presents gets longer each year, indicating increasing prosperity. This letter has no date or place, but must have been written in either December 1891 or January 1892.

Mrs. Newt Tuttle
Rowe P.O.
Livingstone Co., Ill.

Dear Selia,

I asked Mamma to write to you and she will do that. Many thanks for the letter that you sent me. I wish I could write as well as you, then you would get great big letters from me. But you know I can't ask Mamma to write everything that I want to tell you. Well, now I have been in Creston with Aunt Marta a whole week. We had lots of fun, but then Andreas got sick, and so Mama came and got me. Now I will tell you what I got for Christmas. I got new clothes and then I got a fine little cup that said Forget-me-not on it and a harmonica and a little railway with a car and a little horse and carriage. When you write to me, you must tell me what you got for Christmas. . . .

There is a man here that Aunt Marta said I should call Papa, but I don't want to call him that, so I call him Hans. (He always calls Knud Hans.)

Well, I had better quit now. You must greet Grandma and Grandpa and Aunt Anna, but most of all greetings to you, Selia, from Mama and me.

Sammy Kingstad

Rowe, Illinois
January 15, 1893

Dear and always remembered Sister,

As a long time has passed since I received your heartily welcome letter, I will now try to answer it.

I can tell you that we are all healthy to date and wish the same for all our dear ones at home. Our small family has now grown. You see, we got a little well-formed son on December 22 at eleven o'clock in the evening. He is now just over three weeks old. He is growing and thriving, but is rather vexed, so I don't get many free hours, but I have no reason to complain, as I have been quite well all the time. All went well and quickly when he was born, we didn't have the doctor, just one of the neighbor women was here. I was up on Christmas Day and made dinner for Knud and Sam and washed and changed the baby. He hasn't been baptized yet, but I think we will name him after Knud's father, who is dead. His name was Gunder, and we will call the baby Grant. You probably think that is a strange name, but it is much used in this country, and usually if we call them by Norwegian names, they just twist them around to English when they get big.

We are having a really hard winter, with blowing snow and frost almost every day. We keep a fire in the stove all the time, both night and day, but even so the milk freezes in the cupboard in the living room sometimes. Well, I don't have much other news to tell. . . .

Kisses to you all from little Grant. Write back soon, please, dear Anna. Live well in the Lord until we meet, that is my wish. . . . You must greet everyone who asks about me, but most of all a hearty greeting to you, my dear old parents, and you, sister Anna, and Selia from Knud, Sven, and most of all from your devoted,

Berta Serina

This letter, the last full letter from Berta Serina in the collection, was written on fancy stationery that had "Pontiac, Ill" printed at the top.

Rowe, Illinois
December 3, 1893

Dear Sister Anna,

In this evening hour, I will take my pen and write you a few lines in answer to your welcome letter, which I received a while ago, from which I see to my great joy that all my dear ones are in good health. Yes, thanks be to God, I can now also report the same concerning all of us here. It was not so good for awhile, as Knud was sick almost a whole month, so he couldn't do anything. He had pneumonia, the same as he had two years ago, but it wasn't nearly as bad this time, and now he is quite well again, so that he can work outside a little every day.

Now we are finished with the corn. We didn't get much this year, though more than we had expected. Winter is here for good now. We have had some big snowstorms. It snowed and blew all day yesterday and last night, but today it is clear again and very cold. This is the first snow we have had to amount to anything this year.

It will soon be Christmas again. How I wish I were close enough to go home and have Christmas in Bjøravåg and taste your delicious Christmas porridge. What I wouldn't give, Mother, for a few spoonfuls of that porridge and a little of your good pickled pork. . . .

I don't have much to tell you. Little Grant is big and healthy. He could walk when he was ten months old. He has five teeth now, and runs around the house and plays with Sven, who is a big tall boy. He goes to school when the weather is passable. . . . Well, now I will have to quit, as my paper is diminishing. I have no Christmas present for you, but we wish you all a merry Christmas and a blessed New Year. Write back as soon as you can, Anna, please, and think always of your sister and don't forget to pray for me and mine. Greet all the relatives and friends who ask after us. Sam will write. . . . Live well in God, your devoted,

Bertha

NOTES

1. Information about Berta Serina's family may be found in the Stavanger Regional State Archives, together with her letters and the letters from her brothers.

2. A. Knutsen, *Utvandrere fra Rogaland: Utarbeidet ved A.K.* (Haugesund, 1942), 25.

3

An Urban Norwegian
in the Red River Valley

Gunnar Høst, 1883–1905

G unnar Høst is one of the small number of Norwegian immigrants from an urban background. Born in Moss in 1861, he was educated in Bergen. His
father, Ude Jacob Høst, was the district doctor in Kinn from 1863 to 1880. Around
1872 Høst went to Bergen to attend school, and he lived for eleven years with the
family of Claus Hansen. Claus Hansen worked in a bank, and the Hansens were
an upper-class, educated family of scientists, businessmen, and doctors. Among the
children of Claus Hansen were Gerhard H. Armauer Hansen, the doctor who discovered the leprosy bacillus, and Klaus Hanssen [sic], a pioneer in the battle against
tuberculosis. Gunnar Høst was brought up as a son of this household, and he regarded the whole family with great affection. After attending business school, he
worked for a short time as an assistant at Norges Bank, where Claus Hansen also
worked. However, he wanted to seek his fortune in America, and left the Hansen
home in Dræggen (a residential area of Bergen) in May 1883, traveling to America
with two friends, Birger and Henrik Smitt. Birger later became a journalist and
Henrik entered business. [1]

Gunnar Høst writes from the perspective of a well-educated, urbanized person. Spanning the years 1883–1899, the twenty-four letters in this series were all
written to Høst's foster sister, Agnes Hansen, or to Malla, another member of the
Hansen household. They tell of his arrival in the United States, how he started out
as a farmer and then moved into business. He owned a store in McIntosh, Minnesota, and later worked for a firm in Grand Forks, North Dakota. Gunnar Høst
married Ida Olson in 1892. She was born in 1868 in Decorah, Iowa, but grew up
in Minnesota. The Høsts had four sons, Sidney, Archie, Victor, and Edgar, and one
daughter, Agnes. After living in McIntosh and Grand Forks for some years, they
moved to Leeds, North Dakota, in 1901. There Gunnar Høst established a store,

54

Gunnar Høst was an up-to-date businessman. The interior of the Host & Sons Store in the 1930s. Photo courtesy North Dakota State Historical Society.

which he and his sons ran for fifty-eight years. He served as mayor of Leeds from 1923 to 1927. Mrs. Høst died in 1925, and Gunnar Høst died in 1943.[2]

As we would expect from an educated person, Gunnar Høst writes well, using standard spelling and grammar. He gives detailed descriptions of his activities and discusses his feelings openly. His affection for his foster family comes through clearly in these charming letters.

At the time of this first letter, Gunnar Høst and his friends Henrik and Birger Smitt have begun farming in the Red River Valley, near Stephen, Minnesota. The reference to "my friend Bjørnson" in this letter is to Bjørnstjerne Bjørnson, a Norwegian author who held many controversial social and political beliefs. Bjørnson traveled and lectured in the United States in 1880-81.[3] Gunnar jokes about his friend Nikolay Martens and his bread. The Martens family owned a bakery in Bergen.

Stephen, Minnesota
July 18, 1883

Dear Agnes,

Many thanks for your dear letter. I was especially surprised to receive an answer so quickly. It was nice to hear about the wedding and about all of you. From my letter to Malla you can see that we have taken land up here and have begun working for ourselves. We are trying to get our land under cultivation before spring so that we can plant wheat, which is the only crop found in great quantities up here. We can't have much livestock because it is too cold in the winter, but we are thinking about getting land near the river, where it is wooded, then we would move down there in the winter when the prairie is so bitterly cold. If we do that, we might go in for raising cattle. The prairie landscape is not in the least poetic, not a bush nor a rise in the ground can be seen, though it is not so bad here where we are, for we can see the woods in the distance and that immediately makes the landscape livelier. We often sit outside in front of the house in the evening when the sun goes down behind the edge of the woods, and then it is really rather beautiful. One eventually gets used to it. I would never have believed that I would find beauty in a landscape without water, mountains, or forests nearby.

Our work day lasts from six o'clock in the morning until six o'clock in the evening. The most pleasant time is before and after supper. Before supper we sit outside and follow the sun—yes, ask it to greet our dear ones in the east, knowing it will awaken you in a few hours—and after supper we sit and chat over a cup of tea and a pipeful of poor tobacco. You ought to see me do the housework, cooking, baking, and washing. Tell Father that it is coming in handy now, that I learned a thing or two during the time I lived in Dræggen. . . . When you write to Salma you must tell her that I am a master of potato cakes, though mine are still not quite up to the quality of hers. We frequently dine on duck, as there are lots of them around here. We most often serve them boiled, but on Sundays I brown them á la Salma in sour cream and butter . . . and ours taste *almost* as good as hers. We don't prepare anything other than duck, since we can't afford to buy beef or pork, which is terribly expensive. I am best at baking bread. I am certain that my friend Nicolay Martens wouldn't believe that I have baked our bread this week, it is really splendid. As you know, we live rather frugally, flour and water in different combinations, such as porridge, pancakes, lefse, etc. Anyway, now we have gotten two chickens, which lay every day, so our pancakes are superb. You should have seen us one day, we were so fancy that we treated ourselves to soft-boiled eggs for supper, how our faces beamed. No, this is getting to be completely a "food letter" . . . so enough of that for this time. . . .

I have not written before and told that when we got to New York we had to go into quarantine. You see, there was smallpox on board, luckily the first-class passengers got only one day, where the third-class had to stay eight days. The reason I haven't mentioned this before is that I did not want Mrs. Smith to know about it in case she would worry. . . . But now two months have passed, so I am sure we can be regarded as not contagious, which, of course, we were declared to be in New York. The day we stayed in New York was very moving, everyone thought it was sad that we should be parted and so we decided to stay in the same hotel, the whole first class. You can imagine how comical we looked when we came walking through the streets of New York all in a line. There were many good wishes and promises to write when we departed from our friends after having spent a pleasant evening together in New York. On the railway journey we met many friendly people, but since I

Gunnar Høst, ca. 1920s. Photo courtesy
North Dakota State Historical Society.

had gotten instructions from my American friends to take care, I always answered coldly and shortly, so H. and B. often thought I was a bit curt.

Yes, at this time of year it is wonderful in Bergen, we really miss the
long, light evenings. Here it gets dark as soon as the sun goes down. It is
really comical to see America close up and compare it with the reports we
heard. I especially have to laugh when I think of my friend Bjørnson's description of the intelligence, freedom, and equality of the Norwegian-
Americans. Class differences are absolutely as strong here as in Norway. "Big
farmers" keep together and naturally exclude small farmers and workers—and
it isn't the core of the Norwegian nation that emigrates, it is cotters and small
farmers who have difficulty making it at home who seek a new home in
America. Those I have met have been decent and good people, but quite
astonishingly low class. . . . The worst, I think, is that they do not have
enough concern for their children's education, so that they don't have the
opportunity to rise much above their parents' station in life.

I was pleased to hear how you appreciated my letter from the Atlantic
Ocean. I thought I had to write to you before I wrote to anyone else. You
were sister, mother, and friend to me and followed me with interest during
the eleven years I lived with your family. . . . I lived a blessedly happy ado-
lescence in Bergen, and yet I am happy to be in America with a bit of my
youth left. It is good to get out a little, and especially I believe it is good for
young people to come to America. If I had come over here alone, I believe I

would never have been happy, but since there are three of us, then we all get along remarkably well, and yet I always work with the thought in the back of my mind that someday I will return to Norway again. . . .

You must promise me that my letters won't get outside of Dræggen, I cannot bear to have my letters read by everyone. They are for you and Father and Malla. Of course, I don't object if you tell what you want of what is in my letters. . . .

A thousand greetings to Father . . . and all the others in the family . . . as well as any others who ask about me. Live well, dear Agnes, and greetings from your loving,

Gunnar Høst

Christiania (also spelled Kristiania) was the capital of Norway. The name Oslo was restored in 1925. This letter was also sent from the farm near Stephen, Minnesota, in the Red River Valley.

September 11, 1883

Dear Agnes,

I received your postcard from Christiania yesterday, and am glad to see that you have had a pleasant trip. . . . Here we are all still fine. We have had a beautiful summer with quite a bit to do. Now it is getting along toward fall, so we must begin to think about going in to town to seek winter employment. At any rate, we will first go out for three weeks and earn money during the fall work. I am going to work for a Frenchman and will get two dollars per day plus room and board. I believe I will begin to miss this place if I go into town this winter. I have become so accustomed to the landscape now, and will be longing for next spring when I will come up again to begin the plowing. I have high hopes of getting a really good farm up here, if I just have enough money for the first plowing, and that I hope to earn this winter. We have cut a great deal of hay this summer, and have been out working for other farmers. I am finding the work very agreeable, and have been poorly just once. It was my old stomach problem, and went away quickly. . . .

Birger and I were over on the other side of the Red River in Dakota last week to look for work. We thought we would reach the town of Grafton in the evening, but the night became so dark that we had to sleep on the open prairie with our coats around us. But we slept well and fortunately suffered no ill effects from this. Henrik and Birger have both been healthy the whole time and, like me, are very happy here. When we have been gone a couple of days, we take great pleasure in our cozy little home and exclaim, "How nice it is here." As we now have high hopes for the future and good health, I can't think of anything we are lacking.

No, now I have to fix supper. You won't hear from me again until I return from the fall work. Live well and greet everyone. . . .

From yours,

Gunnar Høst

The ink in this letter has faded, and some words are completely unreadable.

October 7, 1883

Dear Malla,

Yesterday I received your dear letter of last month; it is a long time since I had heard anything from you and it was a great joy to hear that you are all well. . . . As I wrote to Agnes, we went out working; we all three worked with a threshing machine in a French colony on the other side of the Red River. We got two dollars a day and free board. Now we are home for a few days before going out again later in the week. It is pretty hard work with the machine. We had to get up at four in the morning and work until seven in the evening with one hour for dinner. The food was remarkably good; you see, the machine went around from farm to farm, and as the farmers over here help each other with the threshing, the one Mrs. would outdo the other in the matter of food, which was very fortunate for us. I like the work, but there is one drawback: it is beginning to get rather cold here now. We have even had several nights with frost; but I hope we will still have some good weather in October so that we can earn enough money to be able to go down to a larger town, where we could get work through the winter.

We got a real fright when we returned from our work. We had been told that the whole prairie on this side of the Red River had burned. Of course, we had taken our best clothes up to our neighbor, but the thought that our cozy little home should be burned up was most unpleasant. Great was our joy when we caught sight of our little house and our two stacks of hay. We found all as we had left it, but to our sorrow, heard that our neighbor had lost two haystacks in the flames. As he has a family and cannot get anything off his land before next year, we decided to give him one of our stacks of hay — the fruit of many days of hard work. In return we got lots of potatoes and frequent invitations to his home. Lately our kitchen has been very poorly provided for, mostly flour and water in the form of bread, porridge, pancakes, and potato cakes.

It is strange to live so completely cut off from the civilized world. I have only seen newspapers a couple of times since I came out here, so I have no idea how things are going out in the world. So please write a bit about political conditions at home, as well as what new things in literature have

come out since I left. Greet everyone and . . . write often to your faithful son
and brother,

Gunnar Høst

Stephen, Minnesota
October 28, 1883

Dear Agnes,

Well, now I am about to change tools. I am sick and tired of darning
socks, and will therefore take up my pen to write a few words to you and
thank you for your dear letter, which I received the other day when I came
home from a trip to Caledonia. You see, I have been on an errand down to
Mr. Jacobsen, the man we came to last spring. You can believe I had a good
time down there! Mrs. Jacobsen did everything she could for me, and I just
enjoyed myself. Yesterday Henrik went down to wait at Jacobsen's for Birger
and me while we get ready for our trip to Chicago. We are thinking about
spending the winter in Chicago, you see, or possibly St. Paul. Later this week
Birger and I are going to take a trip over to Dakota to sell some hay. Tomorrow we are going hunting, as we are out of food—this time it's prairie chickens that will fall to our sure aim. They taste splendid and are about the size of
regular chickens. We make soup out of them and brown them in the pan. At
the same time as we go hunting, we hope to get a small pail of sour cream, so
we can fry pancakes with sour cream and live like kings. . . . We have been
busy lately washing and repairing our clothes, which isn't much fun.

I don't need to tell you that I get along with my two friends remarkably well. . . . Henrik is unusually practical and clever with his hands; Birger
has enough energy for all three of us and is the noblest person under the sun.
They both like the country life best of all, so it is with sorrow that we think
of parting from our dear home on the prairie, but that must now be done.

All summer I have been collecting butterflies, and had a nice collection. Unfortunately, the other day the wind almost completely wrecked it for
me. I had intended to send them over to Malla, but now I will have to owe
her until next year. There are some beautiful specimens here.

This evening we are going to have porridge, as we got a pailful of sour
milk from a farmer because I wrote a letter for him. Dear Agnes, you must not
be angry with me because my letters are so dry and short, but there is little
here to write about, as we are so isolated. Greet the family and others from
me. . . .

Gunnar Høst

*The end of this letter was written around the edges of the paper, and was quite faint
and difficult to decipher. It was most likely written in 1884.*

Grand Forks
September 24, 188[4]

Dear, dear Agnes,

I received your wonderful letter of August 25 just today, and want to thank you so much for it. You have no idea how wonderful it is to get your letters. . . .

I came to Grand Forks four weeks ago as wages here were higher than close to the farm. I was lucky and got a job for $2.50 per day, but after four days of work I had to come into town as I had gotten a bad case of jaundice. The doctor forbade me to take any kind of work until I was completely cured. You can well imagine it costs a pretty penny to lie here with doctor bills and medicine to pay for. Yet one must simply accept it. It is hard to lie still now at the best time of the year, when one should be earning for the winter. If everything had gone well, I would have earned about $100, and that would have been enough for the winter. The other day I felt strong enough to go out working again, and then they put down the wages and all the workers went on strike. Now it's like this here in America, you have to go along if you don't want to risk getting shot, and therefore I also had to strike after having worked only a few days, even though I would rather have worked for $2.25, as it is always difficult to get a good place again, and besides, it's a waste of time. I am still not well, but will just have to keep at it. The jaundice has worn me out, and in addition, I have a complaint in my chest. I don't know what it is, but it bothers me when I am working. I hope it will soon get better, otherwise it looks dark for me.

I have not decided what I will do this winter, but most likely I will stay up here. I may be able to work for a doctor. He has a farm six miles from town and wants a man out there to take care of the cattle and the farm. In the spring I am planning to go down to St. Paul where I can get work for the government for $100 per month, as well as everything, including clothing, free. It's true that I have to bind myself to stay for three years, but there's no help for it. The work is easy and only eight hours a day. Most likely I will be sent west to the Pacific Coast. When the three years are up, I intend to come to Europe again, to look around. If I could find something at home in Norway, I don't think I would come back here again, but much can change in that time. Don't talk to anyone about this, as it is still undecided if anything will come of it. . . .

As you probably have heard, Henrik has gone to Watson, Minnesota, where he has gotten a position in a business. . . . Thus our partnership has been broken. We are having wonderful weather here, and the harvest work is going well, but it is hard to work from five in the morning till nine in the evening and then lie in a shed without bedclothes. In four weeks I think most of it will be finished and then we will creep into our dens for the winter; that's what's so bad up here, for seven months of the year everyone goes completely into hibernation.

Live well now, my dear Agnes, and heartiest greetings to all in the family. . . .

Your always grateful brother,

Gunnar Høst

In this letter, Høst begs Agnes to send him the latest book by the great Norwegian playwright, Henrik Ibsen. The Wild Duck *came out in 1884.*

Grand Forks
November 13, 1884

My dear Agnes,

Many thanks for both letters, which I have now received. You have no idea how pleasant it is for me to get your letters. I become like another person just by receiving them. The letters from home are always more depressing, as I am not spared from hearing about my father's rather poor economic circumstances. You can imagine how that discourages me, as I am under great obligation to him, yet am still not in a condition to do anything. Every time I get a letter from home, I open it with fear, and as often as not I am in rather low spirits when I have read it.

As you probably already know, Birger is no longer with me. He went down to St. Paul three weeks ago. . . . Since then I have been out working, and have done quite well. We have gotten snow now, and intense cold, so all work is stopped. I took a trip down to the Norwegian settlement near Mr. Jacobsen to see if I could get a job as a schoolteacher down there this winter, and was lucky enough to be hired. First I must travel up to our land to pick up my things and then I will go down to begin the school. It won't be any great wages, but one must be glad to have something. As far as comfort is concerned, that too will be sparse, as the farmers down there live anything but comfortably, in my opinion. Still, I am quite happy, and will just have to take pleasure in my books and the children this winter. Most of the time I will teach in Norwegian, giving instruction in religion as well as arithmetic and writing. . . .

I am now free of my jaundice. Thank goodness it went away quickly, and since then I have been well. The other day, when I stopped at a hotel in a little town by the name of Fisher Landing, I was served with—potted meat—made just like you used to make it. Then I couldn't help thinking about the pleasant fall and winter evenings in Dræggen, and it cannot be denied that tears threatened to flow. I often become quite melancholy when I remember my life with you, many times I wish I could make myself invisible and fly home to you even if only for a few hours. And yet even though I often miss good care and pleasant family life, I have never regretted that I came to America. I feel so strongly that I could never become a *man* at home.

If you should see Miss Kjeding, you must tell her the following. I came into the hotel here after having been out in the country working for four weeks. As soon as I came into the kitchen (I am always good friends with the kitchen personnel) I was told that a terribly fine lawyer from Minneapolis had come in. I was very curious to see this fine gentleman, and met him then at the supper table. He condescended to speak to me, and it turned out that the fine lawyer was a Mr. Boyesen, one of Gina Kjeding's good friends from Chicago. He had been watching me and wondering what kind of a fellow I was, of the "better class" and yet wearing working clothes. Since then, Mr. Boyesen and I have become good comrades. He dupes people with his fine exterior, while I stick to my working costume, though in the evening we discard our masks. . . .

I am ashamed of what I am going to serve up next, but the matter is this: I have read in the newspapers that Ibsen is coming out with a new book in time for Christmas, and my dearest wish is that you and Malla will send it to me. I know it is terrible to beg, but I am just about crazy when it comes to good Norwegian literature. Ask her please not to be angry with me—ask her to imagine herself exiled among people without a trace of interest in anything other than their farms and then to understand my joy over receiving a little intellectual nourishment! Finally, my own dear Agnes, many thanks for the paper and envelopes. How wonderful it is for me to receive a sign of your affection. Greet everyone in the family . . . from your devoted,

Gunnar Høst

Grand Forks
November 25, 1884

My dear Agnes,

If you are to get a Christmas letter, it is time I took my pen in hand. Since my last letter I have been up to my land and gotten everything there in order for winter. I had a rather hard trip, as it was terribly cold. This afternoon I will go down to take over my post as schoolteacher, which I told you about in my previous letter. But I didn't tell you that there was a student who also wanted the position that I got. He was going to teach in another district a few miles from there, and he wanted to have both schools through the winter. However, the farmers thought it best that we divide it, and so, as I said, I got the post. In the meantime, I had not met the student and didn't even know his name, but I was a bit anxious that he would eliminate me from the competition, for as a student he would naturally have far greater knowledge than I. When I got to Crookston, I found out from an acquaintance that this student was none other than—can you guess?—Fredrik Mohn—Uncle!!! I was told that he had been seen that day in Crookston. I went downtown immediately to look for him, but unfortunately he had already left. However, I hope to meet him either this evening or tomorrow in Fisher Landing or Sandhill. Then I can relay greetings to him from his parents and brothers and sisters. Isn't it remarkable how people can meet up with one another. You can imagine how I am looking forward to seeing him. . . .

Well, now Christmas is fast approaching, and then, you know, my thoughts fly over the Atlantic Ocean. I am wondering where you will all be on Christmas Eve. Klaus has first priority, of course, but on the other hand, Sofie would surely like to have you together with her family. . . . I have already been invited out for Christmas Eve, to Mr. Jacobsen, as well as to Grand Forks.

My dear Agnes, I send you my dearest greetings and wishes for a blessed Christmas holiday for all of you, and do not forget me when you sit in your pleasant family party.

> Your gratefully obliged,
> Gunnar Høst

> Caledonia, Dakota
> December 10, 1884

My dear Agnes,

Well, now I really must write to you and tell you about my meeting with Fredrik Mohn. You can just imagine how surprised he was to meet someone from Bergen who came with greetings from home, even if they were rather old. I was together with him for two days in Fisher Landing, and we had a really good time. He thought that everything I told him about Bergen was so pleasant, and I am never happier than when I can talk about Bergen and my dear ones there. You can imagine how surprised I was to find Fredrik as a totally healthy, noble, and vigorous young person. The fact of the matter is, I thought that by studying theology, if I may say so, he would have become intellectually crippled, but quite the opposite, he is imbued with a true, inner, healthy Christianity and is an outstanding person. I have not heard him preach yet, but from others who have heard him I know that his sermons are supposed to be very good. What he most lacks is self-confidence; he is almost too modest. In the old country modesty was supposed to be the greatest virtue a youth could possess, but here in America it doesn't do to be too modest.

I went up and visited him the other day. You see, his school is about five miles from here—and then I brought some photographs along, and you can imagine what a pleasure that was for him, as he recognized old familiar faces. I had planned to make a short visit, but ended up staying the whole day. I think it is so pleasant to have him nearby, as I have become very fond of him.

This Christmas we are going to have a Christmas tree for our pupils; we two are going to go together to make a pleasant celebration for the children. Yes, now I have started as a schoolteacher, and think I will like it. I don't know yet if I will be any good at it, but I hope everything will go well. I have been offered a teaching post at twenty dollars a month starting this spring at a place four miles from here—I don't know yet if I will take it.

Christmas Eve I will be with Mr. Jacobsen and I have also been invited out on the other days of Christmas. The young people are going to have a sleigh ride and I have been asked to go along. This will no doubt be the last letter you will receive from me in the old year, so . . . thank you for each loving thought and for all your dear letters in the past year. . . . Greet everyone . . .

From your devoted,

Gunnar Høst

Høst has received a copy of Alexander Kielland's novel Fortuna, *which came out in 1884. Kielland's novels were sharply critical of contemporary Norwegian society, and in* Fortuna *he concentrated his attack on hypocrisy in business. Høst refers in this letter to "Christmas Fools." The Christmas Fools, or Mummers, traditionally dressed up in masks and went in groups from house to house, demanding treats at Christmastime, rather similar to the American Halloween tradition.*

Caledonia, Dakota
January 14, 1885

My dear Agnes,

Well, now, it was really kind of you to write to me again. I had been waiting for a letter all week, and it finally came on Saturday, just as I was about to go north to hear Uncle preach on Sunday. I also received *Fortuna* in the same post. . . . I threw myself over *Fortuna* at once, it is very well written, and the descriptions surely true, but I found it all terribly depressing. When I was at home, such books didn't make as strong an impression on me as they do now. I don't know the reason, but I believe that I now need a different kind of literature to feel satisfied. Perhaps it comes from my changed life circumstances, perhaps I just don't understand contemporary literature, as I have already spent too much time in the wilderness.

I have had a most pleasant Christmas with dancing and other fun, yes, I have even been out Christmas Fooling. What do you think of the worthy schoolmaster as a Christmas Fool? Fredrik Mohn and I had a Christmas tree for the children last Saturday. That was also very pleasant. I like being a schoolteacher, and believe that I am well suited to the profession. The other day, one of the most respected older men in the settlement came and asked if I was the one who was so unusually good at teaching the children reading and arithmetic. You see, my reputation is growing. Well, if only I can succeed in getting something into the heads of these children, which is truly not so easy, as instruction on the whole is quite neglected for most of them. Their dear parents believe that a schoolteacher can, in the course of one or two months, teach them all the wisdom of the world. I work with the children five or six hours a day. My free time I spend studying, together with a little outdoor work and sport, namely rabbit hunting. The people I am living with are unusually pleasant, so I am getting along fine. Mail days are a real holiday for me, and I usually get quite a few letters, but my greatest joy is when I hear from my dear old home in Bergen. However, most of my mail comes from my friends here in this country. . . .

"Uncle" speaks enthusiastically of Malla; she is his ideal. On the whole, he is happiest when I go up to him and stay overnight. We disagree on a number of issues, so we have a lively discussion from the time I come until I leave. In the morning I am awakened by him as he reels off all the arguments he has thought up during the night, and so we start up again. He very much wants to have me as his sexton during church services, but I don't want to. What do you think of that, Uncle as minister and me as sexton? Ask Salma what she thinks of Høst as a sexton! I had better quit here for this evening. I am supposed to play with the children, and they are getting impatient. . . . Greet . . . everyone who asks about me.

Your grateful,
Gunnar Høst

Caledonia, Dakota
February 6, 1885

Dear Agnes,

Just a moment ago I received your dear letter . . . and it was a great joy to hear from you! . . .

I am now working hard trying to get some knowledge into the heads of my pupils, and I believe that it is going rather well. They all like me so much, that sometimes it is almost too much of a good thing. If I have a free hour, they compete for places on my lap, around my neck, and on my shoulders, and I must tell stories. Unfortunately, I can't remember so many fairy tales, so I often have to make them up myself, and everything appeals to my grateful listeners. The little girls vie to stand high in the favors of the schoolmaster.

. . . Yesterday we had a lovely sleigh ride with my pupils in crisp, cold moonlight, which you can well imagine was lots of fun.

Next week I am going to a wedding, and for that occasion I have written two songs, they were created in ten minutes, so you see it doesn't take long to make a "verse," but you can imagine how they turned out. Nevertheless, they are the best ones people around here have heard! So the poet has every reason to be satisfied.

I am very busy teaching, chopping wood, sawing, as well as taking care of the animals, so have little time to read anything for myself. . . . Is Miss Kjeding coming back to America? If she does come, there are a few small things I would very much like to have her bring over: wool jackets and underclothes. What you get over here is such poor quality that it can scarcely tolerate washing. I will send money if she is willing to bring them over with her. . . .

Live well, dear Agnes, and greet everyone. How is Salma? I think of her almost every time I eat a meal. With loving greetings,

Gunnar Høst

Caledonia, Dakota
March 24, 1885

Dear Agnes,

My last two sheets of paper must be divided between you and my parents in Moss. Yesterday I got your letter . . . and I read it over and over again and seemed to see you and the others so vividly before me. I have also had a letter from home, and it was the nicest letter I have had from them since I came to America. They would very much like to have me back again, but as you yourself can understand, it isn't possible for me to go back to uncertainty; it would be different if I had a position to return to. If I can earn enough this summer and sell my land profitably, then I might take a trip home, either in the winter or next spring, to fulfill my parents' wishes. As for myself, I both want and don't want to come home. If I were to live in Norway, I could not imagine any other city than my beloved Bergen, and times are so bad there now that there is no future for a man without capital, though it would be wonderful to come home and see all my dear ones. But there is no place for these thoughts, they are too disturbing.

I quit teaching several weeks ago, and have now begun working. . . . I am sawing and cutting from morning to night. It is quite strenuous, but pays well. When sledding conditions break up I may possibly begin teaching school again if nothing more advantageous comes along. I talked with Fredrik Mohn the other day and he . . . is holding an evening school three miles from here. He was a bit downhearted yesterday when I talked to him. "You have made a hit here," he said to me. He has not got the ability to get along with people that I have. . . . Poor Fred, he isn't suited for the practical life, and is having a hard time fighting his way through to becoming a minister. I like him so well, and try to "push" him a little, if only it would help. . . .

Greet all friends and loved ones from your devoted,

Gunnar Høst

Gunnar Høst dreams of eating such Norwegian delicacies as ptarmigan (a wild bird, similar to a grouse) and cloudberries (a delicious arctic berry).

Caledonia, Dakota
April 25, 1885

Dear Agnes,

Many thanks for your dear letter, with the news that you have sent three sets of wool clothing with Miss Kjeding. I will send you the money as soon as I receive the package. It was more than kind of you, dear Agnes, to go to this bother for me. They will no doubt be expensive, but it is worth it for the durability.

As sledding conditions broke up some time ago, I had to look around for something to do this summer. At first I thought of farm work, but wages are so low, I decided to rent a house out on the Dakota prairie and advertise a school. So I came out here eight days ago, well equipped by all my farmer friends with all kinds of good foodstuffs, such as pork, bread, potatoes, eggs, etc. I rule the roost all alone in a house with six rooms, have nailed together a school table and bench, which is all the furniture I have. I started school on Monday and have fourteen pupils, which is really good at this time of the year, as parents have use for the children at home during planting. I predict that I will get more than I can handle once that is finished, though there are not so many families here with big children. However, they come from a long ways away to seek *the great master*!!

My hands have been terribly sore from cutting wood, and now I have a badly swollen finger. I took my departure from Fredrik Mohn two weeks ago when he went to Crookston. What he is going to do there I do not know. He was rather shocked that I was cutting wood. He, the refined Fredrik, almost threw up his hands the first time I presented myself to him in my working costume.

I hope to be able to send you a proper letter soon, now my finger is bothering me too much. . . . Greet everyone at home and in the family. The other night I dreamt that Salma was standing there crying because Høst hadn't been home on Sunday and we had ptarmigan and cloudberries (yum! yum!). I especially think of Salma now that I am taking care of myself. I wonder if I will ever again eat food prepared by her. To me, hers is the best of all food. Greet her so much from Høst. My greetings to . . . all the others, but first and foremost to you, dear Agnes, from your brother,

Gunnar

Grand Forks, Dakota
August 17, 1885

Dear Agnes,

Now it is a long time since you have heard anything from me. As you probably know, I have been working . . . at the county treasurer's office. When that was over I became a juryman and now tomorrow shall begin as a clerk in a large dry goods and grocery store. I expect that I will live with my employer, who has an unusually pleasant American family. I have been with this family quite a bit, and together with the daughters and a son I sing in a quartet in church. Yesterday I sang two solos, which earned me lots of praise. Americans are not fussy when it comes to music.

I have finally gotten the underclothes from Miss Kjeding, and they are absolutely wonderful. I will send the money as soon as people get their wheat threshed. You see, money is tight here right at this time of year, but it looks like it is going to be a good year, and then people will have cash. In a few days I will send you a photograph. I have shaved off my beard so I won't frighten you, but as you see, I have gotten old in these two years. I still have my farm, and will keep it until times get better. It looks like Grand Forks will be my place of residence in the future. It is a bit sad to give up my outdoor life, but on the other hand, one must think of the future, and for me it is more certain in town than in the country.

Live well now, dear Agnes, and many greetings to all my dear ones in Bergen . . .

From your,
Gunnar Høst

This letter is the first of many on letterhead from the Gotzian & Christoffersen Dry Goods Store. From the opening paragraph of this letter, we can infer that Gunnar Høst has had a trip to Norway. In a later letter, he mentions having visited Bergen in the spring of 1887.

Grand Forks, Dakota
December 2, 1887

Dear, dear Agnes,

Christmas will not go by before you hear from me. It is wrong, I know it is wrong, that I haven't written before, and I have no excuse other than that I have been terribly busy and that I have been waiting and waiting to hear from you. I don't know if you are aware that I am no longer working at the old place, for Mr. Griffiths. I started working for a new firm when I got back. I like it, but have terribly much to do. I had an absolutely delightful journey over, wonderful weather and pleasant company. I met up with three ladies from Christiania, who were more than happy to place themselves under my protection. I stayed in Chicago for eight days and had a most pleasant time with my old friends and acquaintances. . . .

We have had unusually nice weather this fall, still no snow though rather cold. Now you must think about me a little this Christmas, Agnes, and write to me. I miss your letters. Best wishes for a Merry Christmas and a blessed New Year to you and all in the house. . . . Hearty greetings from your devoted,

Gunnar Høst

This letter consists of loose pages, which may not all belong together. The beginning is missing. Høst mentions celebrating the seventeenth of May, which is Norway's Constitution Day.

Grand Forks, Dakota
1888

Several times I have been offered positions in other firms, but I don't think it looks good for a young man to change places too often. Besides, I have good prospects of getting into a business here, and then my future will be assured. I could have come into this firm some time ago, if I had put in some money—but it is terribly expensive to borrow money out here, so I decided to work for a monthly salary until fall in any case. . . . [The top line of the next page is missing.] to be taken into the firm without very much capital in the fall. Thus one builds castles in the air. If they stand, all is well, and if they fall down—well, you can just build new ones. That is what is so delightful about America, one has such rich opportunities for building castles in the air—here nothing stands in the way.

Well, you can believe that I have got a nice situation now—when it comes to food, that is. A widow here, of a Doctor Monsen. . . . [The top of the page is missing.] As you can imagine this is very different from eating at a hotel. It is Mrs. Monsen's greatest joy to see us eating well and she seems to have devoted her life to preparing good food. The others who eat at her place are Boyesen the lawyer, Berg the pharmacist, Lohrbauer from Christiania, Mr. Sanness, and me. Mrs. Monsen reminds me a little bit of you when you smiled in great satisfaction every Tuesday as you watched me empty my plate of rice porridge.

[The top of the page is missing.] I have been waiting and waiting for the life and action that comes with spring. However, my expectations have not yet been fulfilled. Only in the last few days have we had any warmth, and with that a little bit of green on the trees. You cannot imagine how dreadful this winter has been, cold and long, though I really have nothing to complain about as I have my work indoors where I certainly do not spare the wood and coal . . . [pages missing].

Salma doesn't need to worry about me, I am getting plenty of good food. The 17th of May our Choral Society was up in a neighboring town touring from five in the morning to six in the evening, when we returned to sing in the festivities here. As a result of the singing and shouting I am so hoarse I can scarcely talk, though I expect it will soon pass. It looks like we will have good times this summer and fall and that will be wonderful, doubly wonderful if I could set up in business for myself.

Everything would be wonderful out here if we only had a little more feminine company. I hear about so many young women who go out in the world to try their luck. It astonishes me that none of them think of Grand Forks, where we have a very respectable collection of young Norwegian gentlemen.

My best to you, dear Agnes. Greetings to all . . . and write back soon to your devoted,

Gunnar Høst

Grand Forks, North Dakota
February 22, 1890

Dear Agnes,

Now it is really a long time since you heard anything directly from me. . . . I recently had a letter from Malla—Did I say letter?—I meant a telegram. Yes, she is incredible, she can tell more in a six-page letter than most people can manage in twelve pages, but then sometimes you have to guess a little at the meaning. As you have probably heard from my family, I am very well and contented in all things. I had a letter from my mother the other day, in which she maintains that I could join in with Jacob in Christiania if I could contribute 10,000 crowns and could then work in the office. But I am afraid I have been in America too long to be satisfied to work at home. I don't know very much about the . . . business either. I hear reports from home that it is going splendidly, but one cannot always trust that kind of information.

I have worked up to a good position here and have a pleasant living situation. Three . . . gentlemen, Lohrbauer from Christiania, Boyesen from Lillehammer, and I live with a Norwegian doctor's widow, a Mrs. Birmann from Christiania, and she really knows how to make things pleasant for us. At this time of year we finish a little earlier in the evening, and then it is extremely nice to come home to a pleasant house. We have had an unusually mild winter this year, hardly cold at all. Greet everyone I know . . . from your always devoted,

Gunnar Høst

Gunnar Høst now has his own letterhead, which reads "Gunnar Host, Dealer in General Merchandise." In this letter, he uses the English word business *but encloses it in quotation marks. There are no letters in this collection between 1890 and 1892, so some of Høst's letters are probably missing, including those telling of his marriage in October 1892 and of starting his own business in McIntosh, Minnesota.*

McIntosh, Minnesota
December 5, 1892

Dear Agnes,

Many thanks for your exceptionally pleasant letter. Ida was overjoyed to receive it. The first thing she asked, when I said I had a letter from Norway, was whether it was from "that one who looks so nice." You see, she had just remarked a few days earlier on your photograph. I am very happy in my home, and Ida is an unusually excellent housewife. My business is going very well, and yet it has caused me many agonizing moments. There was a man who was going to invest $2,000 in my business, but when it came time to pay, he couldn't get the money—he had sold his farm but couldn't get the cash. However, I had organized my business in the expectation that I would get the $2,000, and there I stood! My business has, as I said, gone very well, but it is almost too much to manage. It is nearly impossible to borrow money out here, as it is so expensive. A loan of $1,000 would cost me $100 in commission plus twelve percent in interest, and that is backbreaking. If one could only borrow money at a reasonable interest rate! But what am I thinking of, writing about business to Agga? It is just that I am so concerned about all this that I have no peace, either day or night.

Well, now it is getting close to Christmas, and this was supposed to be a Christmas greeting to you. I sincerely hope that this letter finds you and all my dear ones healthy and hearty. Best wishes from both me and Ida for a very Merry Christmas. Hearty greetings,

from Ida and Gunnar

In describing his home, Høst uses the English words for parlor *and* bedroom, *but the Norwegian word for* kitchen. *At least one page is missing from this letter, and one page included here may actually belong to another letter.*

McIntosh, Minnesota
October 21, 1893

Dear Agnes and Malla,

No, now I must write to you and tell a little about how we are. I have been waiting and waiting for better times — it is so difficult to write when something is weighing one down — but in vain. It just gets worse and worse. The only ray of light is in my home. And now I must let you know that I have become a papa; on September 22 Ida gave birth to a large boy (eleven pounds). It went well and both she and the boy are fine. I would rather have had a little girl — yes, I had even picked a name for her. She was to be named after you, Agnes, and my mother: Agnes Lorentze. What kind of name we will give the boy I don't know yet. Norwegian boys' names don't sound good in English. . . .

Oh, I guess I didn't tell you that I have built a little house. It went up in nine days, and consists of three rooms — parlor, bedroom, and kitchen. That's right, Agnes, will you please send me your recipe for potted meat, as well as for Salma's pork pancakes and rice cakes? I am longing for some Norwegian homecooked food. As you probably know, we are living in a period of monetary crisis, a crisis that I don't see any end to. God knows how it will go — one must do the best one can and let come what may.

Ida's sister was here for a time while Ida was sick, but now we are alone. It wouldn't be possible in Norway to take care of one's baby, do the wash and all the housework, but I couldn't convince my wife to have a girl to help for anything in the world. Here one is respected and admired for the work one does, be it physical or intellectual labor. Let me hear from you soon. The large picture is a great joy to me. I chat with you all now and then. Greet everyone from yours,

Gunnar Høst

In describing his baby son, Høst writes the word bright *in English, but puts it in quotation marks.*

McIntosh, Minnesota
December 4, 1893

Dear Agnes,

Many thanks for your most welcome letter. It is so nice to get your letters telling about everything. Today we are coming for a Christmas visit—my little son and I. It is not such a good picture of the little boy because he wouldn't sit still—and the light was too strong for his eyes—so he doesn't look as "bright" as he is. But for a not quite two-month-old baby it isn't so bad. I thought you would like to see how we looked, but don't give it out for public criticism. You can get another one when he is a little bigger. Unfortunately I have no photograph of Ida. She should have had one taken with the little boy, but to tell the truth, she didn't have a decent dress to use, since all her old dresses have become too small and she hasn't had time to sew any new ones. I can't get her to have any made, she wants to do it herself.

Many thanks for the recipes, a little bite of "Dræggen" food will surely taste good. For Christmas we are going down to Grandmother's house, and Ida and the boy will stay there all of January for her to rest and get her strength back. Here we are still fighting bad times. They are trying to get people to believe that better times are in sight, but it doesn't look good. God knows how it will end. Our little boy still has no name. He will be baptized at Christmas time down at Grandmother's house. He is chubby and fat and seems to be doing well. He is already ten weeks old and weighs eighteen pounds.

We are now in the midst of winter with snow and biting cold. But life goes on as long as one has a reasonably warm house.

Christmas is approaching fast—if only we could peek in on you—but that is not possible, so we will just send our best wishes by letter. . . . You won't forget to greet Malla and Salma, as well as anyone who cares to get a greeting from me.

Your brother,
Gunnar Høst with wife and son

McIntosh, Minnesota
February 2, 1894

Dear Agnes,

The other day I sent a picture of Ida, so that you can have some idea of what she looks like. It isn't a good picture, as she has a melancholy expression that is not natural for her. . . . I have never liked this picture, but thought just the same that now I had to send it or else you would think I was ashamed to show off my wife. She is no great beauty, but nevertheless prettier than the photograph shows, tall, with an attractive figure.

We spent Christmas down with Ida's parents, where we had a very pleasant time. The intention was that Ida would stay there through the month of January, but after I had left, she began to get homesick and came back on January 4th. We baptized the boy while we were down there, and named him Sidney Clifford. You probably think it strange that we didn't give the boy a Norwegian name, but the reason is that he will no doubt live his entire life in America, and so he will get a name that fits.

Many thanks to Malla for the Christmas greeting, it was wonderful. . . . I began to be quite homesick for the mountains and the ocean. I always used to think it was an affectation when anyone talked about longing for the sea, but one who has grown up near the sea and then comes out to America's plains certainly will feel it — and I have felt it, too.

Our little Sidney is getting along very well — growing big and strong and he is very good.

This year we have had an unusually mild winter, which is a blessing in these bad times. You can have no idea how terrible it is in America right now. Millions of people without shelter and food. What the end will be is a common question, and no one can answer it, no one can give hope and comfort to the hungry masses. No, let me stop before I get too far into this sad theme.

Tell Salma that the potted meat was excellent and that I am now eating pork pancakes and rice cakes every week.

Greet everyone in the family and others who remember me. Your brother,

Gunnar Høst

The "Sigurd" mentioned here is probably Sigurd Scott Hansen, a member of Fridtjof Nansen's expedition that drifted in the polar ice on board the ship Fram from 1893 to 1896. The expedition members were brought safely to Vardø, in far northern Norway, in 1896.[4]

Grand Forks, North Dakota
September 1, 1896

Dear Agnes, Malla, and all,

Well, it is a long time now since you have heard anything from me. First and foremost I must report that we have a little daughter, born on the 9th of June. Her name is Agnes Lorentze, after you, Agnes, and my mother. So many wonderful memories are attached to that name, that I thought I had to have it in my own family. We are all very well. Ida and the children are visiting her parents right now and having lots of fun.

Times are very bad in America, though I cannot complain as I have a good livelihood. I was surprised by a visit from Birger Smith a week ago. He came up here on a survey. He might settle down here as an illustrator for a newspaper. You must all be very joyous over Sigurd's happy homecoming. People here thought I was crazy when I broke out in cheers upon reading about Nansen's and Sigurd's arrival in Vardø.

Now I must quit. Greet everyone, don't forget Salma, and let me hear from you.

Sincerely yours,

Gunnar Høst

Grand Forks, North Dakota
May 24, 1899

Dear Agnes and Malla,

Lude has just arrived and has been down here with all the gifts. I don't know how I shall begin to thank you enough, I was completely overcome. You are certainly more than kind to think of us. Little Agnes was so proud of her beautiful Norwegian flag—and believe me, Agnes, it will always be held high in honor and remembrance of Aunt Agga. Rolfsen's reader is excellent, and I have had all I can do to tell the boys about the many wonderful pictures. It was so nice for me to get the book about Bergen, with all the wonderful, well-known faces and the biographies. I don't know how long it has been since I have had such a pleasant evening as yesterday when I read it. Many many thanks for all the wonderful books. You can't imagine how nice it is to get something from home. And then the pictures of Lorentz and Sofie's children! I have been sitting with them in front of me for many hours and never tire of looking at them. What marvelous faces and all so different. . . . You must greet Lorentz and Sofie and thank them for the gift. I cannot describe how much it means to me. Lorentz has always been my boys' ideal. I have told them about him and his ship, and that is something that appeals to a child's imagination. They always want to show off the picture of Uncle Lorentz who has the big ship.

Here we have finally gotten summer and it feels good after a long cold winter. My three little ones are outside playing all day long and enjoying life very much. They are all healthy and hearty, if not always as nice and well brought up as we could wish.

Everything is going well for me, I have a good income, that is to say, I have a salary of $25.00 per week and can earn a little extra and that is not so bad. Two years ago I bought a house with a small yard, so we live in our own home and have all reason to be satisfied. Today I am sending you the program from a concert we had a while ago, together with a description of our

17th of May celebration. You must show the program to Tommy Hagerup so she can tell Edvard Grieg that we are trying, even out here on the outer edge of civilization, to interpret his wonderful melodies to the best of our poor abilities.

I see Pastor Hovde now and again, but our Norwegian ministers out here are so shortsighted that it is almost impossible to have anything to do with them. We have three different Lutheran congregations here in this town. They all have a monopoly on heaven, and they all state boldly that they can prove by the Bible that all the others will go to hell. Pastor H. thinks I am taking a great responsibility upon myself by sending my children to the American Sunday School instead of the Norwegian, but since my children don't understand a word of Norwegian and there is never a word of Norwegian spoken in my home, then I certainly don't understand why they should have their religious instruction in Norwegian. Of course my children will learn Norwegian, but first and foremost they are Americans and shall be brought up as American citizens. And as far as religion is concerned, I am quite certain that Our Lord understands English as well as Norwegian, even though one of our honorable pastors up here assures me as to the contrary!

. . . You must excuse me for not writing sooner and thanking you for the Christmas letter, but it is so hard for me to write, especially to answer your letters. I feel my own incompetence and am ashamed. You know I never write Norwegian except for a few words home now and then, so I get completely out of practice. I never dare to read my letters through, for then they would go right into the wastebasket. Excuse me, and take me as I am. It is all well meant.

Greet everyone within the family and the others, too. If only I could see you all again some time. Don't forget Salma. I think of her often and pray that things will go well for her in her old age. Thank Lorentz and Sofie. I don't dare to write to them, but you may be my interpreter. Hearty greetings from,

Ida, the children, and your brother,
Gunnar Høst

Grand Forks, North Dakota
October 8, 1899

Dear Agnes,

Well, what do you think of me, letting your dear letter go so long unanswered, though I hope you will excuse me when you hear that it is work that has taken up my time. I have been working from seven in the morning until ten in the evening for a long time now, and then I don't feel like writing when I get home at night. However, this evening my employer decided to quit at nine o'clock and therefore you have me here this evening. My letters can never be as interesting to you as your letters are to me, for everything you write about I absorb eagerly. Every name and every event reminds me of my own dear old Bergen.

Now I will begin as usual to write about "myself." You already know that I have an exceptionally good position. I like it very much here, and just the other day had the pleasure of hearing from my employer's own mouth the most flattering comments on my business acumen. It is always pleasant to work for someone who recognizes that one is striving to fulfill one's work obligations as conscientiously as possible, and especially when this recognition takes the form of a raise in wages. We are having extra good times here right now since wheat prices are rising. My only regret is that I have not broken up more of my farm, as it would be a gold mine if war should break out in Europe. And it looks very much like that might happen. Even so, if times remain this good, I will earn good money on my farm.

I have heard nothing from or about Fredrik Mohn. We parted as not very good friends, as he could not tolerate my criticism of him, although he asked my opinion. Likewise, he got angry when I encouraged him to give up theology, as there were a number of things that seemed to make him unsuitable as a pastor, especially in a time like this. He became very offended, even though it came after he had repeatedly asked my opinion. He was peculiar and terribly stiff. . . .

It is beginning to get quite cold here now, winter is knocking at the door. But I am well in all respects so I have nothing to fear. . . . My heartiest greetings to you and to all, don't forget my old Salma (I'm sure she remembers me), from yours,

Gunnar Høst

Six years after the last letter from Gunnar Høst available to us through this collection, we have another brief glimpse into his life in this charming letter from his sister, Louise, written while she was on a visit to the United States.

Prairie Farm, Wisconsin
March 11, 1905

Dear Agnes,

I promised myself that when I had seen Gunnar I would write and let you know a little about him as I know you are always interested. I especially wanted to do this as I know how seldom he writes. Well, he has been down here in Wisconsin on a very quick trip—from Saturday evening to Monday morning was all the time he could spend down here. His journey otherwise was to St. Paul and was a business trip.

I must hasten to say that it was really a joy to see him again after eighteen years have gone by. He looks like a happy man, and as far as I can see, has a healthy outlook on life and is in all ways content. It must be said in his honor that he has managed to preserve the mark of an educated man—his appearance as well as his opinions astonished me. The fact of the matter is, it is not so easy to keep oneself up, and when one succeeds without apparent difficulty, that must be remarked upon. It was truly pleasant to see him again. Naturally, I will also go up and see his wife and children, but that will probably not be before this summer, about the time I will be turning my face toward home again. My leave of absence from the school is valid for one year, and I must say that such a year in exile is very fruitful in more than one respect. . . .

When I spend some time with Gunnar, I am looking forward, through his children, to getting some idea of the schools up there. Gunnar, together with a partner, has now bought the business that he has been running lately. He expressed his hopes for the future of the business and regarded himself as one who is coming along well. His four boys are his pride and joy. They are all musical, even his little daughter, Agnes Lorentze, who he has warned me is a self-willed little thing. I take it as a given that he is a bit of a patriarch in his own home, and that his wife waits on him more than we are used to. But he speaks of her with great affection and says he is more in love with her than ever.

She is dreading a bit having a visit from a sister-in-law from Norway, but when I have lived in America for over half a year, then I am somewhat able to understand and appreciate how the free America sees fit to bring up and develop her daughters. It would be sheer foolishness to expect to find a European lady. And anyway, such a one would be ill-suited to manage the demands made on a wife and mother here. But if I have understood Gunnar correctly, then his wife is a genuine daughter of the West, working for herself and her loved ones from morning to night.

I don't need to tell you how everything I see here interests me. The land around here is rather new, the forest has given way to farms and only in a few isolated places are there any woods left, but one is not, as in Dakota, forced to burn coal. It is very pretty here, as the land is quite hilly and rolling, but water, the sea—oh, no. One has to get along with a little lake every now and then, and you know that is nothing. . . . But Gunnar, who is used to the ugly, endlessly flat Dakota prairie, thought it was really beautiful here.

I read your memoirs this summer at Jacob's. They brought me such living memories of the time I spent with you in Bergen. . . . But people are so much more than books and possess a strength that surpasses time and place. I felt some of that now, when I found Gunnar again, so unchanged. He was fortunate in his youth to be surrounded by all of you, who encompassed him with love and care, just as if he were one of your own, and the character that this gave him has become his for life.

. . . Dear Agnes, stay well until next year, when I can come and greet you in person.

Your devoted,
Louise Høst

NOTES

1. Information on the Høst and Hansen families may be found in Chr. Brinchmann et al., *Hvem er hvem* (Kristiania, 1912), and in the University of Bergen Library manuscript collection together with Gunnar Høst's letters.

2. The North Dakota Historical Society's Historical Data Project Files contain a biographical account of Gunnar Høst. Further information on the Høst family may be found in the two Leeds area histories: *Our Heritage, Leeds York, 1886–1986*, and *Seventy-five Years, Leeds York, 1886–1961*.

3. For more information on Bjørnson's visit to the United States, see Eva and Einar Haugen's book, *Land of the Free: Bjørnstjerne Bjørnson's America Letters, 1880–1881*.

4. Jon Sørensen, *Fridtjof Nansen: En bok for norsk ungdom* ([Oslo], 1942), 88–124.

4

An Unhappy Immigrant Returns Home

Hans Øverland, 1887–1893

*H*ans Øverland was born in Nedstrand, near Stavanger, in 1864. He came from a distinguished and politically active family. The position of lensmann, or sheriff, passed from his grandfather to his father, and later to himself. Both his grandfather and father served in Parliament and held local offices. Hans was educated in the local school, where he studied German and mathematics in addition to the ordinary subjects. His sister, Marta, went to school in Stavanger and emigrated to New York, where she became a lawyer and wrote a book on American business law. His brother, Orm, also emigrated to the United States, where he called himself Tom Øverland. Tom worked as a journalist for several Norwegian-American newspapers and became editor of an American newspaper, The Industrial Age. Hans never came in contact with his brother or sister while he was in the United States, aside from exchanging a few letters and receiving copies of Tom's newspaper.

Hans Øverland came to Minneapolis as a young man in 1887. He failed to find his brother, and after working briefly in Minnesota he went to Montana, where he worked on the railroad and held a variety of unskilled jobs. He was not happy and longed to go home, but the kinds of jobs he held, together with intermittent periods of unemployment, did not allow him to save enough to pay for the return trip. Help from his father finally allowed him to make the journey home in 1893, after six years in America. There are no letters in this collection from the year 1892, but something must have happened to him during that time, for he writes in his last letter "when I got out among people again" and implies that someone had been telling lies about him. He must have written at least one other letter to his father, because he refers to his "begging letter," but it is missing from this collection. There is no record of Hans Øverland in the Montana State Prison or the Warm Springs State Hospital, but he may have been ill during that year. Although Hans Øverland was economically and socially a failure in the United States, he was fortunate in being able to return to

Norway, where he led a successful life. Such return migration was actually fairly common.

After coming back to Norway in 1893, Øverland worked in Stavanger before returning to Nedstrand in 1902 to help his father. When his father retired in 1907, Hans became sheriff. He was well liked as sheriff, and retained that position until his death in the fall of 1923. Throughout his life, he was active in Liberal party politics and in the temperance movement. He married Inger Johanne Bustad from Nedstrand and they had seven children. [1]

It is clear from the political references in these letters that Hans Øverland and his father belonged to the "pure" or radical wing of the Liberal party. The moderate wing, under Prime Minister Johan Sverdrup, formed the government, and included members of the conservative state-church clergy. One of these clergymen-politicians, Lars Oftedahl, is often mentioned in Hans Øverland's letters in tones of great scorn. Oftedahl had taken over the seat in Parliament held by Øverland's father.

Hans Øverland was educated and literate. His spelling is standard and error-free, and he uses sophisticated vocabulary and literary allusions. His style of writing seems modern, with short sentences, abrupt changes of topic, and many abbreviations, giving at times a feeling of impatience. He mentions being ill or unhappy, but does not dwell sentimentally on his homesickness. His letters convey a warm and affectionate relationship with his father. He is sometimes funny, often ironic, and uses many analogies and figures of speech that are difficult to interpret. These letters were obviously written by a young man with a keen mind and broad interests.

Torbjørn Ubøe, who also later returned to Norway, was a cousin of Hans Øverland. The Lafayette Hotel was built as a resort in 1882. It was a sprawling building with five acres of floor space, and was located on Lake Minnetonka, near Minneapolis.

Minnetonka Beach, Minnesota
August 3, 1887

Dear Father,

I am writing this first letter now, sitting in my bunk during the midday rest. Arrived here Saturday the 30th. Orm is not to be found. He was in Minneapolis the whole time, until the day before we arrived, but since then no one has seen him or knows where he is. Sunday I came out here to Thorbjørn and found him at once. Was out here all day, and got work together with him. Get $25 a month plus board, not too bad to start with. Everyone in Minneapolis said I was lucky to get it. Thorbjørn drives and I break out ice, take care of the horses, drive sometimes, and so forth. This is a very large

Hans Øverland. Photo courtesy Regional State Archive, Stavanger.

hotel called Lafayette. There are about 800–900 travelers or vacationers here. I am busy, and the work is somewhat hard, especially in the forenoon, but it will be all right for a month and a half, then the hotel closes. It is very hot, thunderstorms every night.

The train trip was monotonous. Stops for several hours where we had to change trains. Stopovers took approximately two days. J. Hovda and the others caught up with us in Chicago. We left from N.Y. Tuesday evening 7:30 and they left Wednesday at one o'clock. That's how great the difference was. We changed trains eight times, they had the same car from N.Y. to Chicago. Well, I don't have any more to tell about. I am eighteen miles from town, and therefore I know nothing from there. Maybe Tom has shown up again. I suppose that in the winter I will go there again and come back in the spring. Don't really know. Perhaps the man I am working for will give me work in Minneapolis or St. Paul during the winter. Torbj. sends greetings. Don't know when I'll write next time. Greet all friends and acquaintances. And most of all greetings to you from,

Hans

Some letters written by Hans Øverland are missing. They may have gone astray, as he suggests in this letter, or they may not have been preserved.

St. Paul, Minnesota
March 21, 1888

Dear Father,

I had actually decided not to write to you anymore until I got a letter back, as I have not received a word since your last at Christmas time, whereas I have written three letters, of which it would be remarkable if all had gone astray. Still, I will try one more time, as I wish to hear something or other from home. . . . I have been laid up just about all winter. Have now worked for Tom Ubøe for eight or ten days. He has had the measles.

Three or four weeks ago I had a trip down to Mower and Rice Co. . . . I was received with great joy wherever I went. Old Osmundsen had to get up out of his sweet sleep at 11:30 at night, but when he heard who was knocking on his door, he was not *too* angry. We sat up until 2:30 that night and chatted. He asked me to tell you that he very much wished to hear two or three words from you, as it was a long time since he had heard anything. Jonas W. has grown a beard like yours. Good-natured and lively, well off, he has let his sons and son-in-law take over his land, and sits like a pensioner with a fine house and two acres. He is going to Norway in June and then you will see him. Bjørn is going to Dakota, just had an auction of his cattle when I was there. Tonnings were the same. All of them worked for a rich German who has a 1,600-acre farm. There was full employment for four men. . . . [The rest of the letter is missing.]

There are several rather cryptic references to Norwegian politics in this letter. Lars Oftedahl was a charismatic preacher, a member of the moderate-conservative wing of the Liberal party, with a large following in the Stavanger area.[2] He was a member of Parliament in the 1880s and 1890s, having defeated Øverland for the seat. When Hans hopes that some "pure" ones will be elected from other parts of the country, he is a referring to the radical wing of the Liberal party. The reference to Jacob Stang as prime minister is a bit odd. Jacob Stang was a Liberal politician who was a member of the Sverdrup government from 1884 to 1889. Johan Sverdrup was the prime minister during this period. He was soundly defeated in the election of 1888 (probably what Hans is referring to in this letter), and was replaced as prime minister by the Conservative politician, Emil Stang, in 1889.[3] The "Fatso" in this letter is probably Lars Oftedahl. Skandinaven was a Norwegian-American newspaper published in Chicago. This letter is written on letterhead from Montana Hall, "the best lunch establishment at the Depot."

Hans Øverland was working as a night cook in Helena in 1888.

Helena, Montana
September 6, 1888

Dear Father,

Just quit working at 7:30 in the morning, and decided I should write to you. I get almost no letters from anyone. . . . I work as a night cook in a little restaurant here in Montana Hall. Began yesterday evening—but today as I was about to sling myself down in a chair, I got such a terrible stomach cramp that I was almost unconscious. It is over, but I must hold myself straight up and down, just like God created the heron.

From the enclosed pieces from *Skandinaven* I see that you had to retreat at the Stavanger meeting. The Oftedahl folks no doubt will dominate the election this year, too. That is all right, if only some pure ones get in from other parts of the country. I suppose the election will take place a few weeks from now, and I hope you will write at once. I wish I were home again, and will come as soon as I can raise the money. From the West Coast I ought to have a chance to get to Europe one way or another. I hate to go eastward. The conservatives have set up a fine Oftedahl program. They are fishing with long lines, and no doubt the fish will bite well. For we have Jacob Stang, "the gauntlet thrown in the face of the Norwegian people," as prime minister. O. Olson as cabinet minister, the whole thing so well mired together that the followers of Fatso don't bother to [unclear]. We all are sitting pretty, said the cat, as he sat on the pork, and shat on his lordship. Phooey.

The man I am working for is kind, and I am thinking of staying with him as long as possible. He said that I could work here as long as he keeps the restaurant, and I hope that will be awhile. Just these few words. Write often to this same address. I have fallen asleep five times on this page. Greet everyone at home from son, uncle, cousin, and brother,

Hans

On the back of this letter, Hans wrote, "The devil take the Oftedahl and Sverdrup folks."

Avon, Montana Territory
November 4, 1888

Dear Father,

Here it is over a week now since I got your last letter, and it is bad of me not to have answered yet. I am still well, and am still working on the railroad, suppose that I will stay here as long as possible. I hope it will not be too long before I get a better job. It is starting to get cold, but we have not had any snow yet. . . .

What else should I write about?—Nothing—. Don't hear anything from anyone. Well, Ola Stuvig writes often from Omaha, where he works and is well. . . . He wants to go west, he says. There will be lots of work on the railroad here this winter, and besides one can go to Washington Territory. I am thinking about going out there and starting a saloon near one of the new railroads. That is a good way to earn money here in the West. I'll send a Swedish comrade of mine out first to check it out, and in the meantime I'll get together a few more bucks.

Who got elected to Parliament? Who were the electors from Ned-strand? Naturally you don't say anything about these matters. I wonder if you get all my letters. This is the second from Avon. Now it's late, and I must quit for this evening. Another day gone. It has snowed all day, and with that winter has begun in Montana. Nothing more. Write about everything and everyone. Get someone to write to me. Little Marta, for example. Greet every-one at home from the gandy dancer,

Hans

Hans's birthday was April 1. The end of this letter is missing, just where it appears he is going to relate some juicy bit of gossip.

Avon, Montana Territory
February 11, 1889

Dearest Father,

Thanks, and thanks again for your letters, which I received Sunday. I don't understand how one of them could have been in Helena, as I am in the same place I was where your letter of last summer reached me. It must have had the wrong address on it. . . . In the meantime, I was delighted to receive it, as I have waited a long time.

We have had a break on our section, a freight car loaded with wood went in the ditch Sunday, and one axle was broken in the wheelbox. Now we have been out for two days with a work train and unloaded sleepers along two sections, and gotten some things up out of the wreck. Today I have worked like a horse, as the roadmaster always called on me when there was anything to be done with block and tackle or cables. He couldn't get anyone else to understand him, he said. I have had a good winter. We are three men on our section and all we have to do is to go over the line with a handcar and see that everything is all right. In the spring I think I may get a section to myself, and then I can soon come home again. This life does not suit me. But what won't the German do for money. . . .

Christmas—worked every day—no Christmas for me. I was in Helena two weeks ago and talked to Jacob (R. Norem's boy). . . . I suppose that you have gotten a birthday card from me, I am expecting something back from you for my day. Marta and I correspond rather regularly every week. She is fine. Orm has his own newspaper now in Duluth, it seems to go well. He is president of the "Knights of Labor" lodge there, and is a candidate for election as alderman in his district (a kind of chairman). He never writes to me, but regularly sends me his newspaper, which is a good paper, by the name of *The Industrial Age*.

I knew a lot of what you told me. . . . In addition, I could tell some other amusing things about some of it, but I won't. It was fun to relive a sailing voyage again. I will never forget the sea and the boats, even though I now travel in a far different vessel. . . . What is Holger Bjelland doing? Was America too hot for him? Thought I heard something about lynch justice. . . . [The rest is missing.]

Avon, Montana
March 30, 1889

Dear Father,

Received your letter of the eleventh today. It was most welcome to me, alone out here in the wilderness, as I might say. Still working in the same place. Earning only a little bit, believe I must go farther west if I can't get a section for myself. I wish I were home again, that is all, but I don't dare think too much about that, or I'll get sick from it, like I was at Christmas time.

Marta writes now and then . . . she seems to be getting along well. Orm sends me his English paper, and that is all I hear from him. O. Stuvig is in Omaha and working now. I haven't been in Helena lately. I haven't seen Peder more than once. What more should I say? I am like everything around me, empty and sullen. There is no more peace in the house. We are now twelve men, six on each section. Perhaps twenty before long. I have a new foreman. My old one, who I worked for for six months, went to Garrison, where I followed him, to work at the station. Then he began to drink again, so I went back. He was as angry as the very devil, completely forgot that if it hadn't been for me, he would have been dead many times this winter, the old drunkard. I took care of his work for three months. Now our new roadmaster has given him the sack. About time. I have never seen a worse life than here in this house this winter. However, it is not suitable material for correspondence, and will have to wait until we see each other, when we can tell some stories. I have enough of them. Railroad life around here is too strange. In the East they pay less. There is more civilization near the coast. Met an engineer Lyng out here, who knew you from Christiania.

Montana is a state now, as are Dakota and Washington territories. I see that you are going to visit our acquaintances again. That pleases me. If only I could go along. I could cheer up your company with hair-raising lies about the railroad. Just wait til I come home again. Spring has come. One summer, fall, and winter more, and then? If I live. I never earn money, it goes, even if (as now) I don't drink. It's all the same, I'll live until I die. Write back soon, immediately, like I have done, otherwise I will fine you. I have forgotten how to write from learning to pound spikes on the railroad.

Greet everyone, don't forget anyone, but especially you and yours, from brother and son,

Hans

The end of this letter is missing, breaking off right where Hans begins expressing a rather strong opinion.

Warm Springs, Montana
July 7, 1889

Dear Father,

I received your long awaited and greatly welcome letter with great joy today. I was about to send you another scolding letter. I feel so endlessly alone sometimes when my thoughts turn toward home, which I should never have left. As you can see, I have moved, but only a few miles. I am on a little road that goes from Butte to Garrison, just 52 miles long. Montana Union is still the best road here anyway, pays better and is in beautiful surroundings in Deer Park Valley, a fertile valley inhabited by many farmers. Where I am there are warm springs, after which the place takes its name. There is an insane asylum here, run by an old German doctor. That is about all. It is far better than the place I was last winter. I am working for a Norwegian now, the best section foreman by far around here. We have the same roadmaster here as on N.P. [the Northern Pacific]. I am in better spirits now than I was last winter. Everything here is lighter and better. The farmers are suffering from drought on the grain and hay. There won't be any grain. Besides the fact that they must irrigate the pastures every year and often bring water for a mile or more in long ditches, now the rivers and streams around here are drier than they have ever been before.

Today—Sunday, I was up and visited a Danish farmer whose sons I have gotten to know, and spent the most pleasant day I have had for a long time. Next Sunday I am going to take a riding trip to Anaconda, where I think the world's largest smelter is. On the Fourth of July I was home all day. We had a little beer and the rest of the time I lay on my bed and read novels. The world's largest circus will be here around the nineteenth. Let them, I don't care. Tomorrow John L. Sullivan and Jake Kilrain are going to box, first to see who is the world's best boxer, second for $20,000. It will be a hard fight, as they are about equal. Though John L. is supposed to be the best. I wish I had that meat, so that the dogs could fight over it. . . .

It will be fun to get home sometime. If I come, I will never travel here again. I don't get any letters except from O. Stuvig. . . . I think that he will come up here now, as there is nothing in Omaha—strikes everywhere, last in Duluth, 1,500 workers laying streets. The Italians are driving day wages down around here. New railroads are being built, but a white man can't get work. On a sideline of the N.P. there are now only 500 workers. A sideline or double road is being built in sections here. Thirty men who were ordered out here from St. Paul by contractor Kilpatrick were turned away without work, and so our men went to the judge and he is doing something or other. All contractors ought to be shot. I have a good six-shooter—44 caliber . . . [The rest is missing.]

The beginning of this letter is missing. The letter is undated, but it is probably from 1889. It is written on railroad company letterhead.

Montana Union Railway Company

I don't think I will go any farther west. I am longing for home and must try to save up a few hundred for that. I have almost nothing now, a little bit coming from last month. The tenth is payday. Are people still pietistic at home—or have they changed their minds and no longer roam all around the country like they did three years ago? Here there are mostly Mormons— Smith's Morm.—I promise the Mormon who runs section number five that I will become a Mormon, too, and we are good friends until I begin to find fault with everything that goes with the faith. He preaches—I listen, and then everything is fine again. He thinks he has won a new brother. I know nothing about Orm, and don't care either. So to bed, and greet everyone from,

Hans

The E. Vullum mentioned here is Erik Vullum, a Norwegian Liberal party politician, journalist, and author.

Warm Springs, Montana
October 12, 1889

Dear Father,

I received your letter two days ago, and the newspapers this evening. Thanks so much for everything. I plowed quickly through the Stavanger newspapers and saw lots of news. I am still well and working steadily on the railroad. I went in to Butte Thursday with the railmaster, and he said I would get a section next week. I fell off the handcar one day and injured my left side, so I couldn't work for several days, but now it is fine again. I get paid for all the days in the month. The weather is still nice here, but it's beginning to get a little cold going out at seven o'clock.

We had an election. The Democrats won except for a congressman who is a Republican. They used the Australian system. From one of three election judges you get a ballot with the names of candidates from both parties, and you prepare your ballot in a separate room. That is to say, you put an X by the man you want to vote for and then you turn it in to one of the judges who puts it in the box. It seems to work very well, but even so there have been a few complaints of fraud. Here in W.S. there was a four-to-one majority for the Republicans, and the Democrats said that if there had been one more asylum in Montana, the election would have gone Republican.

Tomorrow I am going on a trip to Anaconda, where the world's second largest smelter is. I met a son of clerk Thomson (from Stavanger) in Deer Lodge, where he worked at the same kind of job as I have. He has left, but I don't know where to. Everyone out here travels around from one place to another, works a few months, and then takes off again. But I find it best to stay in the same place. I have it good here. I spend every Sunday with Nielsen (a Danish farmer) and run down there sometimes during the week, too. I almost have a second home there. They hardly want me to leave.

I see that E. Vullum is coming to America on a lecture tour. Do you think he'll get out here? It would have to be to Helena. It was nice of Lars to write to me before he went to sea again. I don't understand that no one has a spare half hour to write a letter to me. Out of sight, out of mind it seems to be for my friends in the old country. I will repay them in kind, those rascals. . . . I don't know anything more to tell, and am sleepy. . . . I am so tired. Coming home next winter. And so loving greetings to all from,

Hans

Warm Springs, Montana
January 30, 1890

Dear Father,

I received your letter this evening, and am now answering it. Your letter was quite old, 77 days. It usually takes only 19-20 days. Anyway, thanks for writing so often. It is the only news I get from Norway. . . . I am hale and hearty and still working on the railroad. I was up in the woods a few weeks, but the water froze and we got sick from melted snow. So I came back again and got in at my old place. We have quiet days, out at 8:30, home at dinner time for a few hours and quit at 5:00. Of course it's only in the winter that we do it this way. My "service," as you call it, doesn't keep me tied down. The pay is the same even if I'm gone for a day. . . . This summer there will be lots of work here, I think. Perhaps competition between two lines.

There is not enough snow here in Deer Lodge Valley to use sleighs, but round about us the trains are blocked for days at a time. In Nevada the snow is as high as the telegraph poles in some places. It hasn't been cold either, just "fun and games" on the railroad this winter.

So you are in on the township board again, yes, I thought as much. . . . You said in your last letter that you would send me newspapers. So far, I haven't seen any, but hear that Marta has received a few. Send me some when you get this.

You can hardly imagine the uproar in the young state of Montana. There are eight Democrats and eight Republicans in the Senate. Voting is decided by the lieutenant governor, and he is a Republican. So when any of the Republicans are away, the rest refuse to vote, and likewise Dem. They were supposed to send two senators to Washington—the Democrats elected and sent two, the Republicans likewise. All four had insufficient credentials. The two Democrats had the signature of the governor (Democrat), the two Reps had just the seal of the secretary of state (Rep.) on theirs. Both the governor's signature and the seal of the secretary of state are necessary for a full credential. It is a circus every day, to read about their meetings in Helena. They do nothing, just quarrel and revile each other. In North Dakota there are about twenty Norwegians in the legislature, here there is only one.

The Russian influenza is raging everywhere in America. People are dying of it in this area, too, but we have been untouched by it right here. But the weather is just right for getting a chill, it can easily change in half an hour. I will come home as soon as I can. I ought to be able to find something to do. This country and I are so heartily sick of each other. Nielsens are going home this summer or fall. He has about 200 head of cattle that are nearly unsalable now on account of several years of drought and therefore little hay. Delivered to the place it now costs from $15 to $20 per ton here in the valley, and will probably go even higher. But now the ground is bare, and the young cattle can manage outside. And outside they are, especially the horses, no matter how cold it is. . . .

It is getting late, and I have little to write about. The prairie wolves are howling terribly, we will surely get more snow. Yes, that's right—we have a debating society here in the W.S. schoolhouse. You should have heard how well I debated fourteen days ago for immigrants here in this country. The topic: An immigrant should be able to read and write the English language before he has the right to vote. I spoke in English, of course, and our side won the debate. We wanted to have the right to vote also for those who didn't know English.

Well, now it's time to quit for this time. Dearest Papa, write again soon. Greet everyone from,

Hans

Written on Northern Pacific Railroad Company letterhead. Martin is Hans's youngest brother. Normanna was a Norwegian-American newspaper in Minneapolis.

Avon Station, Montana
May 3, 1890

Dear Father,

Your most welcome letter was finally received a few days ago. But if I have to wait so long another time, then I won't write back. It was fun to hear from home after such a long time. As you see, I am back at the same place I was a year ago, and am working here again. I had to leave Warm Springs because I couldn't work for the damn Irishman who came there. I am working for an Irishman now, but he is a nice fellow. So you understand that I am content here, as I always am at this place. I can't tell you much about my relatives here in America. It seems as though they have made a pact not to write to me, with the exception of Marta, who writes every week. . . .

The devil will no doubt get hold of Oftedahl sometime if he doesn't already have him. And then I believe that politics will go a little better for the Liberals than it has up to now. I read a little bit every week in *Normanna* from Minneapolis. I get it for nothing, if Marta isn't paying for it.

. . . You are getting old, you say. Perhaps I should come home and help you. It looks like I can't get anywhere here. Still, I don't want to come home for a few years yet. My friend Nielsen from W.S. wants to go home this summer. I helped him (as a witness) to get a piece of land he had taken up over there. I am about 35 miles from there now. A sawmill has been put up next to the station house since I was here last, and now we are going to lay a side track for them. There is lots of timber here, but just hill after hill, and impassable terrain.

I have little to write about, as usual. Martin must be quite a fellow, to walk to Næsse alone already. Tell him that there is no one around here who could walk that kind of distance. Things are just beginning to sprout around here, after several days of thunder and rain. It's been cold until now. An early spring was expected after the relatively mild winter, but it hasn't shown itself until now. Snow has been the order of the day until the last few days in April. They really felt the winter in Idaho. A company that owned two or three thousand head of cattle — had only 200 left two weeks ago. A man was seen in a town down there offering a large steer for sale for a bottle of whiskey. You have no doubt read about the hard times in Dakota.

Are you going to get the eight-hour day in Norway? It sounds as though it has won out nearly everywhere over here. But we will no doubt labor ten hours for the damned railroad companies for awhile yet. We can't even manage a strike.

So this will have to be enough. Write again soon, dear Papa, and greetings to everyone from,

Hans

"G.C." is Grover Cleveland, who was elected in 1892 to a second term in office, after Benjamin Harrison had served an intervening term. The two presidents differed strongly on the issue of tariffs. Hans was visiting the Nielsen family, and recounts the activities of everyone in the household at the end of his letter.

Warm Springs, Montana
December 25, 1890

Dear Father,

In spite of the fact that I am in town several times a month, sometimes even more, I came within a hair's breadth of missing your letter of November 30. However, a friend informed me that it was there, so I got it last Friday. Must ask for forgiveness for not writing sooner. But now Christmas is here, and there is always something going on. I am tired and sleepy after having danced all night, and I was also at a dance two or three nights ago. But now that will have to be enough of that for a long time.

Drove a crazy mare yesterday afternoon, and was almost thrown out of the gig. But I got her to hold herself inside her skin. I am going to break some colts now for awhile. I am hale and hearty, and am glad to see that you are the same at home. We are having d— —weather, blows like the very— — — all day long, and the dust swirls high in the sky. You see, we haven't had snow or frost to amount to anything and it never rains, so the dust is just as dry as in the summer. There are many here in the valley who haven't fed their cattle a single straw of hay yet. But they will feel it next summer. If we don't get snow, the farmers can just as well forget about planting grain.

As far as the elections go here in America, you have no doubt seen that the whole country went Democratic. That will mean the reelection of G.C. in '92, I suppose. It was the newly adopted high tariff law that did it. A large firm refused to pay import duty on some goods that were included in a clause in the law but that had been left out when Harrison signed it. It is in court now, and if the firm wins, the whole law will go up in smoke, which it will anyway in the next Congress. . . .

My letters, as you know, are never very substantial, and this one will be worse than all the others. But where shall one find bread in the desert? It doesn't look like we'll get any Indian war, at least not until spring. The old rogue is dead (Sitting Bull) and with that the worst villain of them all. Now and then a few men appear who claim to be the coming Indian-Messiah, which some Mormon missionaries had convinced the Indians of and thereby started the worst craziness. They may rise again in the spring, but they are weak, and the Canadian Indians won't support their madness.

Yes, tomorrow it's herring and old clothes again. That is to say, I have had my old clothes on all day today, too. Holidays here never last more than one day—and even that one is sad enough, by heaven—but we can't have fun all the time. And besides I'm getting so old that such pleasures can soon go to the devil. If T. Ubøe comes home, don't be nice to him on my account. I don't think I'll ever speak to him again.

Anna is playing the accordian. Peder and Christian are playing euchre, Nielsen is sleeping, Mother is doing nothing, and I am writing. There you have the activities of the entire household at the moment. And I will go up to the depot with the letter this evening. And as I have no more to write, I will stop. Greet everyone from,

Hans Øverland

The newspaper Vestlandsposten *was founded by Lars Oftedahl, the preacher and politician mentioned in many previous letters. "A.G." is most likely the Norwegian author Arne Garborg, who did not get a government author's stipend until 1898. In the United States, McKinley was in Congress. His support of high tariffs led to his defeat in the 1890 congressional election. He won the 1896 presidential election, running against William Jennings Bryan. In this letter, Hans begs his father to send newspapers from Norway. He mentions* Verdens Gang, *a liberal paper published in Oslo. There was also a weekly paper in Chicago by the same name. He gets both* Normanna, *a Norwegian-American newspaper, and* Den Danske Pioneer, *a Danish-American paper.*

Warm Springs, Montana
February 7, 1891

Dear Father,

I received your letter today, and since you did not delay in answering my last, I will also not delay my reply. I am glad to hear that you are all right now. Marta told me after Christmas that your knee was out of order again. You scold me a little for my letter, but what in the name of common sense should I write about from this one-horse town? Nothing happens here — nothing more than the same thing over and over. Since Christmas there has been a change in the weather. We have had quite a bit of snow and a little cold, but it doesn't last long here. They have predicted a hard snowstorm, so we'll wait and see if it comes. Minnesota is having 45 below zero. I haven't done anything since November except help a little with feeding the cattle, hauling hay, and so forth, but soon I will start working at the same place. . . . Well, I can and will come home some time in the late summer or fall, but first I want to make use of as much of the summer as possible. It will be a good summer for work, I am convinced of that. . . .

Now I am stuck again. American politics — yes, perhaps. But politics can be described with the same word A. Hauge used to describe Vestlandsposten — rotten. I take a daily paper and follow along, but in the Senate and Congress they don't do much except fight. The Republican administration is going to hell. The next Congress will be Democratic. The president, too. McKinley has destroyed the party with his tariff law. A new party has been formed here, "Farmers Alliance," which mostly holds to the Democratic side. They are a complete minority in Montana. This year there is a little bit of sense in our state legislature and senate. The majority are Democrats, and the Republicans have to knuckle under. They will be able to do a little this year, smooth out the wrinkles from last year. But our two senators in Washington will take the seats that they won by plotting and bribery—just like the Conservatives back home. Norway is in its childhood when it comes to politics. Will soon be given away to Russia or Germany, if they don't look out. A man came here one day and asked if Norway didn't belong to Germany now. Such nonsense.

The newspapers haven't come. Send some if you haven't already done so. Stavanger papers, *Verdens Gang*, and the like. I have forgotten everything of Norwegian literature. Never see anything about it. Get *Normanna* from Minneapolis, but its news from Norway is restricted to a few old wives' tales from Christiania and the like. *Den Danske Pioneer* has something in Norwegian once in a while, the last a laudatory article about A.G., well written on the occasion of the denial of the stipend. But—send newspapers, it doesn't cost so much. Have been sick for a few weeks, almost well again. Greet Laura, she never writes, and I return exactly what I get. She has enough damned time to scribble lines to others. Whether this is good enough or not, it will just have to do. Greet everyone, most at home, from,

Hans

Warm Springs, Montana
April 3, 1891

Dear Father,

Well, now it's quite some time since I received your welcome letter and the newspapers. Lately I have been so busy that I haven't had time to write. This evening I am a little better off, as you can see. I have worked now for one month for little pay, feeding livestock—about 200 head of cattle and 100 horses. It takes time to get around, even though we feed them hay in the fields. I also had a badly abscessed hand, which made writing impossible. The snow is nearly gone and spring work is beginning. Here on this place, 3,000 acres, there is no farming, just cattle ranching. Where I work is close to Warm Springs.

So you finally have a liberal cabinet minister. But you ought to have been there, too, and I can't see why you don't take it if he wants to have you there. . . . My 27th birthday went as usual. Marta writes often. Have had two letters from Tom. He wants me East. Don't know yet. I still haven't gotten the money from the company I worked for last summer. Probably never will. There was a Norwegian here today who went crazy and was put into the asylum. He has been there before, came out last October, but will no doubt stay there longer this time. I knew him well—and so he came over to a stable where a friend and I were sleeping, at four o'clock this morning, and called to me. I didn't answer. One way or another he got in, and I could see he was completely crazy. I soothed him and advised him to go home, which he did. Later he went to the asylum himself. . . .

What else can I write about? The taming of wild horses is something that wouldn't interest you, and not me either especially. But I must do it. I was just five or six inches from the hooves of a large black horse this evening. He kicked toward me higher than three telegraph poles on top of each other. Then he got a beating and food. We have thirty calves, get one almost every day. I have a place for forty dollars a month assured for the summer and fall if the farm doesn't get sold. A quartz mill will soon be in operation in Deer Lodge, and I may get a job there. The big smelters at Anaconda have shut down, as well as the mines that send quartz to them. About 3,000 to 4,000 men are thereby out of work. The reason was a battle between the railroad and the company and may end with the smelter company building its own railroad. Nothing has been heard from New York yet, where the magnates live—the head men in both the railroad and the smelters. It is bad for Montana—no, for Deer Lodge County. This must be enough for this evening. Loving greetings from your son,

Hans

When Øverland calls Oftedahl a "Catholic," he is being sarcastic, not literal.

Warm Springs, Montana
August 7, 1891

Dear Father,

I received your letter last Sunday, but haven't had time to answer yet. But today I got fired from the place where I worked, so now I have plenty of free time. I was hired for forty dollars a month, but then the man heard that some others paid only 35 and when he didn't want to pay more, I told him to go to hell. Haying is going strong, but the weather has been rather wet. Thunder all the time, night and day. A man and his wife were killed by lightning two or three miles from here three weeks ago. But a child sleeping in the same bed was uninjured. The newspapers are always filled with reports of lightning strikes, hail storms, and floods. About 35 miles from here all the grain and hay were destroyed by hail. The mountains around here are snow-covered today. I will ride up to the station today with this letter and take the opportunity to see if I can get something to do at the asylum. They have a large farm. I have to come home soon. This country is slowly killing me. Maybe I'll be home for Christmas, perhaps even earlier. I have no money, and cannot save any up in this way, work for two or three weeks, then two or three weeks of nothing. I have tried to get steady work—but there is none—and then one must take what one can get. My job as a timber driver just disappeared. The roads became impassable and the sawmill had to shut down for a while. After that I injured my back by lifting an 8 x 10 x 16, and couldn't get up the next morning.

Other than that, I am hale and hearty. I see that folks at home are now as before "fiddling around with marriage." Well, then there will be more who will curse the day they were born. I think there are enough people in the world now. The day will come that there are too many. And I believe that emigration over here will be stopped in a while. There can't be many emigrating from Norway now. I am certain that it is better at home than here.

. . . We had a fine 4th of July in Deer Lodge. A parade with exhibits in wagons from all the stores in town. One had a regular house, another a living room, restaurants where a couple sat at a food-covered table, and so on. Everything driven around to the accompaniment of terrible music. A dance in the courthouse yard in the evening ending with fireworks. There was scarcely a drunk to be seen. But my back hurt and I didn't have much fun.

I am at Nielsens again. They are thinking of going home this fall, and in that case we will all come home to you, after which I will go with them to Denmark. That is the arrangement at this time. Do everything you can for a pure liberal election. Hold public meetings, give speeches, and open up people's eyes so that they can boycott Oftedahl's Catholicism. For he is a Catholic.

Greet all acquaintances and loving greetings to all of you from Hans. Tell Martin that when big brother gets home we will see about fastening all the stakes so that they won't fall on his legs. But we always want to be where we aren't supposed to be. That was my way, and I suppose the way of all little boys. Your leg will heal up again, Martinius.

Your brother

This letter is the last one preserved between 1891 and 1893, just before Hans left the United States to return to Norway. What happened to him in the intervening year is unknown.

Warm Springs, Montana
October 8, 1891

Dear Father,

Your letter came some time ago, but I have been both lazy and for-getful and therefore have done nothing about answering it until this evening. I am happy to see that you are all well. . . .

I am all right. Working on a farm, hauling manure and plowing, but it won't be too long before it will freeze and then the work will be over. How-ever, the big smelter in Anaconda will be starting up again and then it may be possible to get a place there. The fall around here has been good. However, the farmers' earnings will stay about the same, as the high prices of the last few years will naturally go down on account of the quantities. But when the smelter starts up again, prices will go up. Potatoes are selling for forty cents per 100 pounds and here in the valley there are lots of them. I have been out helping the neighbors with the threshing. All the oats on our farm are being cut for hay.

I have seen in the Chicago newspapers that the election over almost the whole country went to the Liberals. Well, one could predict which way Oftedahl's kingdom would go. But Bergen and Stavanger-Haugesund will no doubt be pure. Waiting with anticipation to see what kind of asses Stavanger County sends in, and will find out in *Verdens Gang* from Chicago. Send some newspapers with election news. No wonder that the stargazers went crazy when all three electors were from Nedstrand. But what the devil does that help? They made their own bed. O. Dalva must have taken a turn for the better again, and I am happy about that. We have had many a dispute. Though he was an Oftedahl supporter once, as far as I remember. Still, they are fewer and fewer.

You say nothing about sister Laura, and she never writes either. How is she? Marta is the same; she writes every week. I saw in *Normanna* today that Tom had been in Minneapolis. He has a good position now, and has written to me a few times. Maybe I'll head up there this winter. . . . Now I have run off at the mouth with enough nonsense. . . . Greet the sheriff when you meet him. We were always good friends. Tell him that I always treat my horses well.

Now this must be enough for this evening. Greet everyone, especially at home, from,

Hans

The last letter from Hans Øverland hints at some mysterious trouble. He refers to a begging letter, which his father has apparently answered by sending funds for him to return home. At the end of the letter he returns to one of his favorite topics, Nor-

wegian politics. Johan Sverdrup, the former prime minister, was elected to Parliament from the Stavanger area, but died shortly thereafter. When Hans quotes the king (who was Swedish), he writes the words with greatest satisfaction in Swedish.

Warm Springs, Montana
April 14, 1893

Dearest Father,

Two letters from you today. The one was legitimately sent, the other sent immediately upon receipt of my begging letter. Oh, thank you, Father! But it is not nearly as bad now as I thought before. When I got out among people again, I found out that nearly everyone had turned their backs on him and found out that he was a devil of a liar and mostly I can thank my friend Charles Strømberg (a Swede) for that. But let that nonsense go to kingdom come. I don't remember anything about a promise to come home in August. It would have been hard without help. In the meantime, I will now come home earlier. But don't tell anyone about it. It will be so damned awkward when I get home. So I must be allowed to walk when I come home — yes, to church at first. But that will be about all. I get tired quickly and sore of foot. My hand is unsteady. Worked two horses on the drag all afternoon. We haven't seeded yet, but all the seed grain is ready for next week. But it is still cold, freezes every night, and so we can only work in the afternoon. It has been snowing on and off for a week. . . . I am a tramp, you see. But better a tramp with honor than money without.

Politics is rotten. . . . Never mind about Stavanger County. People there are in their childhood and the result will no doubt be an extra insane asylum, which the king will doubtless provide "with greatest satisfaction." One can't expect anything else since Johan Sverdrup was elected. He himself was so astonished, it was the death of him. They eat too much fish in Stavanger County. More tomorrow evening. Mail on Sunday — no, Saturday — no, we'll drive to Warm Springs today (Friday), and so I'll finish this letter. It froze last night. This may be the last letter from here. With loving greetings, yours,

Hans

NOTES

1. Personal communication from Berge Øverland, son of Hans. See also *Nedstrand herad i hundrad år: 1837–1937* (Stavanger, 1937), 14–17. The 1988 yearbook of the Rogaland Historical and Genealogical Society, *Ætt og Heim*, includes a collection of letters between Hans Øverland and his father covering the years 1882 to 1884.

2. See Einar Molland, *Norges kirkehistorie i det 19. århundre*, 2 vols. (Oslo, 1979), 1:220–22.

3. For a brief overview, see T. K. Derry, *A History of Modern Norway, 1814–1972* (London, 1973), 142–52. A lengthier discussion may be found in Per Fuglum, *Norge i støpeskjeen, 1884–1920*, vol. 12 of *Norges historie*, ed. Knut Mykland (Oslo, 1978), 23–88.

5

A Family Moves to Wisconsin

Barbro Ramseth, 1888–1904

*B*arbro Ramseth was born Barbro Ivarsdatter Gammeludstumoen in Tynset, Norway, on August 21, 1838. She worked for a number of years as an upstairs maid and later as a cook at a country inn in Tynset. She married Paul Ramseth in 1868, and they bought a farm called Lindjordet, living there for about ten years before moving to a home in the village of Tynset, where Paul Ramseth worked as a baker. Barbro was already fifty years old when she emigrated to America in 1888 with Paul and their five children. They lived on a farm in Vernon County, Wisconsin, for the first two years, after which they moved to Shawano County, Wisconsin, where they farmed shares with Barbro's cousin, Tollef Olsen Øien, for two years. There were many other immigrants from Tynset in the area, and they formed a closely knit community. Barbro frequently mentions sharing her letters with these friends from home, and relates news of their doings as well as of her own family.

In 1893 the Ramseths moved to the nearby farm of an elderly couple, Alice and Christian Larsen. Paul ran the farm, and Barbro cared for the house and nursed the old man and his wife; in return, they were to get the forty-acre farm after Larsen's death. This turned out to be a difficult situation both economically and personally, as the old man was reputed to be very mean. The Ramseths' son Ivar was acquainted with Ole Rölvaag when they were both students at Saint Olaf College in Northfield, Minnesota. According to descendants of the Ramseth family, Rölvaag heard the story of Barbro's difficulties with Christian Larsen and of her kindness and deep religious faith. He is supposed to have used this as a basis for the characters in his novel Paa glemte Veie (On forgotten paths). Barbro Ramseth died on December 21, 1913, and Paul died on October 6, 1918.[1]

Barbro wrote long, complicated sentences, with minimal punctuation. Her letters were also long, and contain extended religious passages with many biblical

The Ramseth family photographed in Tynset, Norway, ca. 1882. In front: Ole, Berit, Ivar, Einar. In back: Paul, Karen, Barbro. Photo courtesy of Rolf Erickson.

quotes. I have tried to retain enough of these passages to be true to her personality and give the reader the flavor of her style of writing. Barbro Ramseth's letters reflect her loving concern for family and friends on both sides of the ocean, as well as her religious faith. Even though life was hard in America, she remained optimistic and never regretted coming to the United States.

Bristow in America
November 6, 1888

My often remembered dear old Father,

I hope that these lines will find you in the best of health, and will let you know how we are faring. We are all in good health and like it here quite well, it is getting better and better all the time, so we must just hope that everything will eventually be fine. I often think of Tynset, and of you, then I long for home, but now, thank goodness, things are much better. I am fully convinced that it was best for us to come over here, for our experience shows that it is easier to earn money here, and fight our way through, but it is a painful process, many losses for a newcomer. The trip itself is a great hardship, but all things pass. People have been very kind to us. Before we got our cows, they gave us milk, as well as butter and eggs and fish, so they are very kind and helpful to newcomers, yes, God be praised and thanked for *everything*. We bought a three-year-old heifer, which had calved in the middle of August. . . . He was eight-weeks old when we got him and we slaughtered him. It was delicious meat. . . .

I am sitting at home alone now, the three youngest are at English school, and Paul and Ole are gone, so it is quiet and nice. It is nice for me to have only ourselves to take care of. It is marvelous the way the Lord does things, He does all things well. These words come to me so often: the Lord is my shepherd, I shall not want. . . .

Hearty greetings from all of us at home. Karen is in Chicago. We meet daily in prayer before the Throne of God. Today we have beautiful weather. The sun is warm and no snow.

Your devoted daughter,

Barbro

Dear Sister Marit,

I would like to add a few lines especially for you. We may never meet again in this life, as we are so far apart. Not a day passes that I do not think of you. . . . God's way with us is remarkable. . . .

Karen went to Chicago on the 30th of July this summer. There was no suitable work for her here in Bristow, so she went back to Chicago to her uncle Severin who lives there. He is married and has five children, and has been here in America for nine years. She was with him for one month, and then went out to work for a rich tailor named Dahl. They are Norwegian but live completely like Americans. She takes care of a little two-year-old boy and does the housework. She is just fine, she says, and likes it pretty well. She makes two and a quarter dollars a week. She is learning the language very fast, she says, for they speak only English, all of them. The cook is Irish and

The Ramseth family photographed in Wisconsin, ca. 1895. Seated are Karen, Paul, Stanley, Barbro. Standing are Einar, Ivar, Ole, and Berit. Photo courtesy Rolf Erickson.

is Catholic. The last time she wrote, she said she had never imagined that she would work together with an Irish girl, and least of all a Catholic. Karen says she makes the sign of the Cross in the evening when she goes to bed, and asks if Karen wants to do it too. But she is very kind and speaks only English.

Berit is taking confirmation. There are not more than six confirmands, and they meet once a week at different farms, won't be confirmed until summer. Last Sunday we went to church and were godparents for a little boy. . . . I was also the midwife there, and for that I got a very nice shelf clock, an eight-day clock, a very fine clock.

Around us here, nuts grow in great abundance. The children have gathered lots for the winter. They have also found hops, I use them to make yeast from. We each bake our own bread here in America, and make yeast too, which is very good. We use only wheat for bread. I bake a little flatbread now and then. Soup isn't used much here, but we think we have to have soup. When we can get grapes, we take sugar and make a little wine and a little juice too. But jars are scarce now, there is so much to buy all at once.

My paper is telling me to stop soon. Please greet everyone . . . who would like to have a greeting from us. . . . Live well in the fear of the Lord.

Your always devoted sister,

Barbro Ramseth

This letter consists of loose pages, with no opening or closing. The fragments may not even belong together. One fragment indicates that the family traveled on prepaid tickets. The Ramseths arrived in Bristow, Wisconsin, on July 30, 1888, so this must be one of Barbro's first letters.

[1888]

. . . We moved here on the 30th of July, we live right next to a mill. Uncle Syver and two of his friends have the mill together, and we live in a house that belongs to the mill. It is actually his son Jan, he was the one who sent us the tickets, and he is not married, but lives with his brother Andreas, who is together with him in the mill, which makes lots of money. People come from a long ways away to grind wheat and corn. Here in Wisconsin they had a very good year, lots of hay and wheat. . . .

The bluff is heavily wooded with leafy trees, oak and aspen, nut trees and more. We are well supplied with water, a vein runs close by. There is a businessman close by, and the mill, and Uncle Syver and three buildings that belong to the mill. We live in one and close by lives a big farmer, otherwise the farms are far apart in America. Here in Bristow nearly all the settlers came from Lyster twenty years back and even longer ago, there are exceptions, a few from Valdres, Hallingdal, and Sweden, and Germans also. . . .

Yesterday there was an election here (not for the president, but for the men who will choose the president). They call it "lection." There have been so many meetings now, they are battling each other, the Democrats and the Republicans. It is about the same here as in Norway, except that those who want to be elected to the "Parliament," so to speak, travel around themselves, and ask for it. I think it very strange, but that's the way it is here. . . . [The rest is missing.]

The recipients of Barbro's letters knew perfectly well what she meant by "an uproar day and night." We, however, can only wonder. Nysted was the place where she worked in a country inn for the Tangen family. Barbro introduces some English

The Ramseth family home, ca. 1910. They doubled the size of the house with an addition after they took over from Christian Larsen. Barbro and Paul with their son, Ole, his wife, Lena, and their children Borghild and Paul. Photo courtesy Rolf H. Erickson.

words into the text of this letter. When she brags about Ivar winning a spelling contest, she first writes the English word spelling and follows it by the Norwegian word, staving. She uses phonetic spelling to explain that an English storekeeper is called "staarkjipper."

Bristow, Wisconsin
August 7, 1889

My dear ones, often remembered all at Gammeludstumoen,

Grace and peace in Christ. It is a long time now since you have heard from us, and likewise we from you. In a way, we can imagine how you are, as long as you stay well, but I . . . do not find it strange, if you are now wondering how we are, since it is such a long time since you heard anything from us. How quickly time passes. . . . Just think, it is already the 7th of August, and we have been in America over one year already. It has gone remarkably fast, so when I think back, I am astonished, and can scarcely thank God enough for all His mercy and goodness. . . .

I must now report that we are in good health, and have been almost all the time. . . . We are still here in the place we came to. This spring, in March, Paul went to the city of La Crosse, intending to get steady work there, either with a Norwegian baker or at a sawmill, but at the bakery it was mostly night work, and at the sawmill people were simply flooding in, so we saw that it wouldn't be possible to get anything, even though he waited for a long time, so then he went farther north, to a little town, Menomonie, where there are many people from Tynset. . . . He tried to get into something there, too, but it didn't go any better there either. So as you now can understand, everything is filled up here in America too, with people looking for work. Well, he was gone nine whole weeks, without earning the least little bit, and you can imagine it wasn't easy for us at home either, as he wrote so seldom, still, he came back here again, and both Ole and Paul are working for Uncle Syver. Ole worked there the whole time while Paul was gone, now they are working around here; they finished haying long ago, and are nearly through with the harvest too. There was lots of hay and the oats and wheat did well too, so it will be a good year for everything.

We have been eating potatoes, beets, carrots, and onions for a long time. We have had lovely weather during the days, but at night it gets quite chilly, though not so much that it freezes. I think the climate here resembles that of Tynset quite a bit, although you know it is much hotter in the summer. This last winter we had rather mild weather, so our cow was able to be outside and get her own food nearly all the time up until Christmas. Though they say this was an unusual winter. Now we have two cows, two pigs, and a number of chickens, so we are coming along a bit, as you can see. We have been allowed to cut hay free at Uncle Syver's, so we are assured of enough for our two cows. We are intending to stay here this winter. Paul and Ole don't know exactly what they will do. They have talked about going to the woods and working as cooks, for the cook gets good pay, especially the head cook. If they can only get in some place, then they will do that.

I want to thank you so much for the long letter I received from you sometime before Christmas. You know it interests us to hear from you in dear Tynset. . . . I really must follow the rule that I will answer first those letters I receive first, and that way I can expect a reply, and when you get the letters, you can share them. . . . I would not want to be at Nysted again and have the same situation I had there. I have enough to do, but it is peaceful and good here, praise God. It is better to live without such anxiety as I had there, and so much uproar both day and night. The Lord does all things most well. . . . You know there were many things here that were difficult at first, but one gets used to it. Now I am getting along very well, and the children too, and they already speak just as good English as the others, especially Karen, for where she has been they use only English in their everyday speech, so the children have learned very quickly.

Berit was confirmed on July 21, there were only three boys and three girls, but Pastor Nilsen held an excellent confirmation service, so I was very moved . . . and thought of all of you and of Tynset. He gave the children a Bible verse to take with them throughout life, it was: "Whom have I in

*Frazes i Wis Nord America.
den 26 September 1898.*

Mine Kjære godtfolk, der alle
paa Gamlustumom!

Först vil jeg
da takke dig kjære lille Erik
for dit sidste saa kjære brev,
som det er altid en Glæde at mod
tage i fra Eder. Det er saa inder-
lig kjært at faa höre fra Eder.
Dog faar de undskylde mig, at
Jeg ikke har skrevet igjen för,
men! naar man begynder at ud
sætte, da har jeg ondt for at be-
gynde igjen. Sommeren har
altid noget trabelt med sig hele
tiden. Jeg kan berette, at vi alle
har og ere friske og vel, hvilket
er et stort gode. Her hvad Avl-
ling angaar har vi faaet god-
ablling, meget Hö og ellers godt

Barbro Ramseth usually included North America in her return address.

heaven but Thee? And there is none upon earth that I desire besides Thee."
. . . Berit worked for the pastor for awhile, he had no housekeeper, and Berit
got a beautiful Norwegian hymnal with gold edges and a silver clasp, and
three dollars for dress material from him for confirmation. So you can see that
he is a very kind pastor. He is an old bachelor, and she may go and stay with
him as long as she wants to. . . .

 The last mail day, I had a letter from Tollef O. Øien, where he offers
us his farm on shares, with a half share of everything that is produced, and it
would include a team of horses, a mower, horse-drawn rake, plow, harrow,
wagon, and all the tools and eight or nine milk cows. . . . He also says we
could buy a piece of land there, but still run his farm as long as we wanted to,
and have lots of animals, sheep, pigs, chickens, all kinds of animals. We must
think it over, he says, for they are getting old and poorly and would like to
quit working so hard, and at the same time he would help us, and would in no
way try to trick us into something that wasn't good. Paul should come and see
for himself this fall sometime, he said. Barbro Bakhaug lives there, and Erik
Brækken. . . . It is a little over 200 English miles away. It's not supposed to
be such good soil there, for they have pine forests. We have neither pine nor
spruce here.

 Karen came home for Berit's confirmation and is now at home. She
has to fix up her clothes again before she goes out. She had a good place, and
everyone in the house was fond of her. She got many things from them, and
Karen has earned lots of money since she came here, for servant girls do well
and ordinarily earn good money both winter and summer. We had intended
that Berit would accompany her to town and get a place, but Karen says she
is much too young, and so we think she should go to John Øien, as he is a
businessman, "staarkjipper," as they call them here. Ivar and Einar have also
gotten big, and are doing well in school. Ivar got a prize for spelling, or "staving." June, July, and August there is no school, but then it starts up again.
. . .

 If only these lines would find you all in the best of circumstances, then
I will hope, dear Bersven, that you will write back right away with a very long
letter, for you are such a good writer. Greet everyone . . . from us all and say
I am expecting a letter from them. . . . Hearty greetings from all of us, but
most of all from me. Yours in the Lord,

Barbro Ramseth

Tollef Øien's wife, Kari, died in 1893.

Bristow
December 14, 1889

Dear Bersven and wife and family,

The grace and peace of God be with you. I received your letter some
time ago, and thank you heartily for it. It is always a joy for me to get letters
from you, so we can hear how everyone is. . . . I often feel rather melancholy, as I surely believe that I will never more see you, for this life is so short,
it flies like a weaver's shuttle, and runs like a stream of water. . . . Thank you
so much, Bersven, for all the news. I want to compliment you a little, for you
are such a good writer.

We are all fine. Paul, Ole, and Berit left here last August. Paul and
Ole went to Tollef O. Øien, and Ole is with him this winter helping him in
the mornings and evenings and going to school. The schoolhouse is on his
farm. We are going to take over Tollef's farm in the spring and run it. It is a
big farm. Paul worked for him until the first of November, then he went to
Michigan to a little town called Crystal Falls. . . . He will stay there for the
time being, as long as he can work. It isn't so easy to get work in the winter.
He had thought about being a cook in the woods, for that is supposed to pay
well, but nothing came of it, but perhaps he can stay where he is until the end
of March. Then he will come back here again and we will move to Tollef
Øien's. Tollef's son Ole is in Crystal Falls where he runs a big hotel that
Tollef bought for him, because he didn't want to go into farming. Tollef and
Kari are quite weak now and are often sick.

It is not so easy to get into a business either, as long as one doesn't
know the language, and we old ones don't learn it readily, so it takes a long
time. But the children are already good at it, especially the bigger ones, and
they get to go to school and learn. Karen speaks English so well, for she was
at a place where they spoke only English. She came home from Chicago this
summer in July, and was at home for awhile. Then she was gone for awhile
again, with a Doctor Bean for six weeks, and then she came back home, and
now I can tell you the news, that she was a bride on the 6th of November.
The groom was John L. Ramsett, a very fine man, twice as old as Karen. He
must have thought he was old enough, so he didn't want to wait any longer.
Neither Paul nor Ole nor Berit was at home, so they didn't have any wedding, as is the custom here, unless one absolutely wants to. But even so, it
was very ceremonious and quiet and pleasant. She was well married, he is
both clever and rich. It is his house we are living in, and now they are staying
with me this winter. We are doing the housework together.

I am doing well, and am glad that we came here, this is the future for
the children. Ivar is unusually smart at school, so if he remains healthy and
continues to progress, then something will become of him. Einar isn't too bad
either. So far we have not earned so much that we could buy some land for

ourselves. Paul has been traveling around, and railway fares are much more expensive here, so a lot has been spent on travel. We hope things will improve later. He will try to earn some money this winter.

I have two cows, one calving in the summer and one in the fall, and a number of chickens and a pig. I slaughtered one pig and an old calf. We still have not gotten any snow here. The animals can be outside, and there is good weather now. It was colder earlier this fall. They had snow where Ole is. . . .

May these lines find you in the best of health, and I wish you a good and fortunate New Year. God bless you richly with spiritual and earthly goods. Loving greetings from Karen and John, Ivar and Einar. Please greet everyone. . . . Greetings from Paul, Ole, and Berit too. Oh, our thoughts will surely meet and cross, especially now at Christmas time. Loving greetings. . . . yours in the Lord,

Barbro Ramseth

There is a five-year gap in the letters preserved from Barbro Ramseth to her family in Tynset. The family has moved from Bristow to Frazer and is no longer working for Tollef Øien but, rather, for Christian Larsen. Karen is now a widow with a young son, Stanley.

Frazer, Wisconsin
December 3, 1895

Dear Sister and Brother-in-law and all at Gammeludstumoen,

I will now write you a few words so that you can know how we are. We are all in our usual good health except for Karen. She has been sick since the month of April, and has been bedridden in pain. She has an inflammation almost all around her hip . . . and now she has the pain in her other hip, so she is truly a child of suffering. It is two years since she came home, and it looks like she will have to stay at home, as she cannot be alone with Stanley in Bristow, and she has rented out the mill. . . . It's doubtful whether she will ever be well again. . . . Ole has been working with a carpenter this summer, and we are expecting a farm this summer, so Ivar and Einar have been at home. Ole and Ivar are in the woods now. Berit was married on the 18th of September, she married Mr. J. Jacobsen. He is the son of a farmer. His parents came from Drammen. They don't live here, but went to a place near Milwaukee, called Delafield. He is a businessman there. She made a very good match, as he is well off. We had a nice little wedding, which they helped to pay for.

I think of you often. The other day Barbro Bakhaug was here. Her daughter Anne came too. Embret N. Gammeludstumoen has been there this summer. He is supposed to be engaged to Anne, and we have been expecting a wedding, but nothing yet. When we are together, we always talk about Tynset, and who has last gotten a letter, and so on. . . .

Before Berit left we had our pictures taken, as we have talked of doing for a long time. We are sending you one. I wonder if you will recognize us. Stanley is there too. I have not gotten along very well since we came here, as the old folks are not kind. She is bedridden, has been since the first of September. I have often regretted that we came here, but God will give the strength to endure patiently, and I must believe that it will come to an end. . . .

I hope that these lines find you in good health. Remember us in your prayers. Hearty greetings from all of us to all of you. It would mean so much to hear from you.

Your always devoted sister,

Barbro Ramseth

Bersven, Barbro Ramseth's nephew and chief correspondent, died at an early age; however, his son, "little" Erik takes over the letter writing. The English words chore boy *are written phonetically as* kjorboy.

Frazer, Wisconsin
October 25, 1896

All my dear relatives at Gammeludstumoen,

I thank you, little Erik, letter-writer, for your very dear letter dated September 7 and received here at the end of last month. Well, well, it was certainly an unexpected and sorrowful message for us, but especially for me, to hear that Bersven is dead. . . .

So often this summer I have wondered how he was managing with his artificial foot, wondering if he could work a little, but I knew that he could do many things without having to walk, and I said a prayer to God, dear God, help him in the best way possible. . . . And you, little Erik, are . . . a very good writer, that I can see from your letter, and you must be kind and obedient to your dear mother and grandparents, for now you must take your father's place, and may God teach you and lead you. Think of your Creator in your youth. . . .

Oh, how often my thoughts are with you, and I can see every single place there at Gammeludstumoen, and I remember Bersven following us to the top of the field by the gate the last time I was with you, and I can see him on the platform, as he stood there when the train left. . . . Oh, how I wish I could have been near him in his illness and in his hour of death and at his funeral, but that was not to be. However, I do not regret that we came to America. I am now content in my position. . . .

I must think back a bit to last winter, and tell you about it. The old lady was bedridden all winter last year, and died the 3rd of May. She was completely helpless at the end of her life, so there was a lot of work with her, but thank God, we managed. Karen was also bedridden much of the winter, but now she is fine and has been quite healthy all summer, and has gotten chubby and round. She has been out on a visit to Bristow, where she has the one mill and where she has rented out her part. She sold a number of her things and brought some here, and then she visited Johannes and Berit in Delafield and stayed with them for awhile. Berit had a son on the 6th of August, and all went well. Johannes's mother stayed with them for awhile, and then they came here and had him baptized. He was named Norman Carl after his grandparents, Nils and Katrine. They were godparents together with Ole and Karen. They only have four godparents here.

Ole is working with a carpenter and Ivar went north this spring. He has been a "chore boy" at a mill, and has gotten thirty dollars per month. Now he is home for awhile, but will soon go out again. Einar went to Delafield on Saturday the 24th and will work in the store for Johannes. Einar has gotten tall, he is the biggest of them all. Ole is the shortest, but both Ole and Ivar are quite heavy. Kind and intelligent sons, all of them. Stanley is a good little boy, but he hasn't grown very fast until now. He is about to start school.

We are having hard times in America right now, it is a crisis before the election, which will be held in November. Some predict that it will get worse than ever before. As far as this year's harvest goes, we can say that it was a reasonably good crop, more apples and berries than usual, and tall oats. Wheat and corn are good, potatoes vary quite a bit, garden produce was good. Although here in America there are many destructive insects that ruin the crops while they are growing.

I can greet you from Tollef O. Øien. I went over there right away with your letter, and it was painful for him to hear the news. . . . Brækkens . . . also got to see the letter. I should greet you from Barbro and Klemmet and from Embret Gammeludstumoen. He is there with them, and may possibly remain there. Bersven Haugen has been completely uncontrollable this summer, half crazy. Now he is stuck in jail in Shawano. . . .

Did you have the minister at Bersven's funeral? And was it a big funeral? I suppose you do things the same way as before? Here we meet at the house and everyone goes to the church together where the pastor preaches a sermon, with no refreshments. There have been many funerals here this summer, young people have been dying of tuberculosis.

I must stop for this time, and send you all, both young and old, a loving greeting from all of us. Your always devoted,

Barbro Ramseth

Frazer, Wisconsin
March 6, 1897

My dear relatives at Gammeludstumoen in Tynset,

Many, many thanks for your last dear letter, and especially you, little Erik, the letter writer. . . . It is always a joy for us to hear that you are well. You must miss Bersven very much. How strange are the ways of the Lord with us humans. . . .

I will tell you a little about us now. We are all in the usual health, and have had a mild winter, with no snow, occasionally a little hard cold. At the end of February we finally got some snow, so it was possible to use sleighs, and now folks are busy hauling timber to the sawmills. Ole has been driving some too. Both Ole and Ivar are at home this winter. There is nothing more in operation in the woods this winter, so no more earnings. But Ivar has been going to school since New Year's. He has gotten it into his head that he wants to graduate and become a school teacher in the English school. People predict that he will manage that easily. And now he is working hard and studying, so he may well succeed. Greetings from Berit and her husband, they are healthy and are doing well. Einar is with them, working in the store. They have a little one, and are very fond of him. His name is Norman and he is very chubby and round. We just got a photograph of him.

I have good reason to be thankful to the Lord, for He does everything so well for me, I am always healthy, and that is one of the greatest gifts there is in life. . . . Things are going well for Berit, and they have a good income. It was lucky they could use Einar this winter, otherwise he would have had no work. Better times are expected now, the new president took office the 4th of March, and now people believe things will take a turn for the better. There is terrible hardship and misery in many places, especially unemployment. God grant that it will now improve. . . .

Please greet Mrs. Aasland from me and from Karen. Say that I would not want to be back there again, but am satisfied to be here where I am. . . . Brækkens were here one Sunday . . . and also Tollef Øien, and heard your letter. They all think, little Erik, that you resemble your father in writing good letters and giving pleasure to those who hear them read. . . . Embret is still at Klemmet's. No doubt they intend to have a wedding, perhaps this summer. I won't wait long to write again this time, we see that . . . death is certain. . . . Now I am approaching the end of my paper, and so must close for this time. I commend you all, young and old, to the care of God. Greetings from us all. Write again soon. Your always devoted,

Barbro Ramseth

Barbro writes in this letter that she does the milking In Norway women milked, but

it was not the usual practice in America, where the men normally did all the barn chores.

Frazer, Wisconsin
December 6, 1897

Dear good people, all of you at Gammeludstumoen,

Many thanks for your last dear letter, which I received in October. It is always a joy to hear from you and know that you are all well. . . . God be praised and thanked, we are in good health as usual. This winter none of the boys is at home. Ole is working as a carpenter, Ivar has become a teacher in the English school, and Einar is the cook's helper at a boarding house. Karen and Stanley are at home. Christian, our pensioner, moves around but doesn't do anything. He is 81 years old. Paul does all the outdoor work and takes care of the animals and I do the milking. We have a cow that calves in the fall, so we have milk and butter for household use.

This has been a good year, good crops and prices on cattle have been high and on wheat, but oats are low-priced. Times are improving in America, and things are looking brighter for farmers too, but it has been hard for a time now. In the middle of September I went to Delafield and visited Johannes and Berit. They have a little boy named Norman Carl, a fine little boy. Karen paid for my trip, and it was really a pleasant trip. I saw much that was beautiful, I have never seen such prettiness. Greetings from Berit, she is just fine. They live close to the big city of Milwaukee. We have already gotten full winter, with good conditions for sleighing. We don't usually get snow this early. . . .

Little Erik, you shall have many thanks, because you are so kind and good at writing. . . . Greetings from Tollef Olsen. He is sick and bedridden. He fell under a horse and it stepped on his leg. . . . In October we had a 25th anniversary celebration here, 25 years since the congregation was founded. Many people were gathered together. This summer there have been three big weddings, which the young folks have participated in. Our minister is so enthusiastic about singing and music. He has music practice often. The boys are basses, Karen sings alto, and Einar plays the violin very well. While he was in Delafield, he took lessons from a musician.

Live well in Jesus' name. Merry Christmas and a Happy New Year. Don't forget to write again soon. Please greet all relatives and friends . . . from all of us.

Barbro Ramseth

Barbro is a bit uncertain of the spelling of her new granddaughter's name, and writes "Blanche" as "Blains."

Frazer, Wisconsin
September 25, 1898

All my dear good people at Gammeludstumoen,

First I will say thanks to you, little Erik, for your last dear letter. It is always a joy to receive them. . . . You must excuse me for not writing to you sooner, but once it gets put off, then it is hard to start up again. There is always something going on in the summer. I can inform you that we are all in good health, which is a great joy. As far as crops are concerned, we have had good crops, lots of hay, and others also good. We haven't threshed yet, but they're working hard on the threshing. We can hear four machines close by, as they are competing with this as with everything else.

Karen is quite well again. Last winter she had two operations. Two doctors were here, but the wounds are not completely healed yet and perhaps they will never heal, but she can just be happy that she feels as good as she does. She works a lot here at home. Stanley is quite big now, and goes to school. Ole and Einar are carpenters. They have built big houses for two neighbors. Ivar is a teacher, though he doesn't have school in the middle of the summer. This winter he will have his school post close to the Jacobsens, so he can board with them. Berit, whose name is Jacobsen, had a little daughter a month ago. I was there for a week, and now today, Sunday, she has been baptized and gotten the name Blains Palma, named after me and Paul. We were godparents, so I held her for the baptism. You probably think that is a strange name, but there are many things here in America that are strange for us Norwegians. But the Americans will not have to rename her, and we can agree with the old saying "What's in a name?" Johannes and Berit have taken over the farm down here now, as old Jacobsen couldn't run it any longer, and it is so nice to have them close by. It is a big farm too.

I can tell you that this spring, on the 4th of June, we had our thirtieth wedding anniversary. We were so surprised when about sixty people came here after eight o'clock in the evening to celebrate the wedding, if I may put it like that. They brought all the food with them. Karen and the boys knew about it, but we didn't have the slightest idea, so they had prepared coffee and so on. It was very nice, and we got lots of presents. . . .

I can greet you from the Brækkens. Last Sunday we were over there. They are fine, and also Tollef Øien. . . . Klemmet and Barbro are the same as always. Embret Nilsen is still there, we have been expecting a wedding between him and Anne, but it is just quiet, there must be some disagreement.

. . . I don't have any more to write about this time, but will stop with all our best greetings. . . . Live well in the Lord, all of you.

Barbro Ramseth

Frazer, Wisconsin
February 26, 1899

Dear good people at Gammeludstumoen,

Many thanks for your last dear letter. I am so happy to hear that you are all well. It is good that you old folks are so healthy. Yes, few experience such a great age, it is really rare, therefore dear brothers and sisters, thank the Lord, for He is good, and His mercy endureth forever. . . . Thank you, little Erik letter-writer, for all the news.

We have had a very cold February here in America, unusually cold and snowy, so that many have lost their lives. We have had fire in the stove both night and day, in order not to freeze. I haven't done any outdoor work except for the milking, and that I have dreaded. We can only hope the worst is over for this winter. It is Sunday, and is snowing and blowing something terrible out. Karen and Stanley went out today, so it is quiet and peaceful with only we three old folks.

The "old man" is not very well, he thinks he has "La Grippe." He is now 83 years old, but moves about and takes care of himself. The boys have scattered, each in his own direction. Ole is up north in a lumberyard. Ivar is teaching English school and living with Berit. Einar is in a town called Racine where he has been working in a furniture shop. As far as we know they are all well. Berit is just fine. She has two chubby, pretty children, a boy and a girl, and she is always well and in good spirits. Karen is also quite well. We old folks are in good health, and do our work every day.

At Brækkens everything is as usual. . . . Their son Ole resigned from the congregation. They have been reading some books that have heretical teachings in them, so they are opposed to the pastor and everything churchly. They practice Rational Christianity, and are opposed to baptism and communion. One of Tollef Øien's sons-in-law has also resigned from the congregation. I have been thinking of the old folks at Brækkens, but I haven't talked to them since this happened, because it has been so cold. But they are certainly angry about it, of that I am sure. . . . Everything is the same with Klemmet, Barbro, and Anne. Embret Nilsen has been there for two or three years, but this fall he went to the woods and worked, as many do. . . . Bersven [Haugen] had a tragic death. Just before Christmas he drank too much alcohol and died of it. He had been disturbed this summer, so his wife wanted to divorce him. . . . I don't think he intended to do it. He was operated on by two doctors, it was really a tragic affair. In any case, he lived by himself. He was too brutal to both his wife and his children, for he had lost his reason, poor thing. . . . Ingeborg is completely mixed up now, and is bed-ridden at Tollef Øien's house. They get paid by the county for taking care of her. Well, now you have heard about all the folks from Tynset. . . .

I hear that our old home has been fixed up. I would not have wanted to live there anyway. I had so many sleepless nights there, but now I want to forget about that, as everything is so much better for me here than it was there. Greet all our acquaintances. . . . Hearty greetings from Paul and me and all the children.

Your always devoted,
Barbro Ramseth

[Another letter is attached to the above.]

We can say that we are having rather good times in America right now, with good prices on what we are selling, so the prospects are bright, but we see in the newspapers that there is unemployment in Norway and times are hard. Greetings from the boys. Ole is now at Jacobsens'. . . . I stayed down there a few days too. I wanted to have a little free time before the cows start calving. . . . Karen and Stanley are just fine. Ivar and Einar are away at school, Ivar at St. Olaf College, and Einar in Scandinavia [Wisconsin], where he was last year. Ivar is studying languages, Greek, Latin, and so on. After Christmas there will be 375 students there, altogether too many, I think. It is good when young folks want to go to school and learn what they can. I hear you are also going to school this winter. . . . Tynset is making great strides forward. . . .

Now I will stop my letter for this time, hoping to hear from you soon. Greet everyone from us. Your old aunt,

Barbro Ramseth

Newspapers as well as letters were sent back and forth across the ocean. In this case, the Ramseths sent copies of the Chicago newspaper Skandinaven *to Tynset, and received copies of* Fjeldljom, *a newspaper from Røros.*

Frazer, Wisconsin
August 9, 1899

My dear good people at Gammeludstumoen,

Many thanks for the letter written on July 21. It only took fifteen days for it to get here to America. And the message of sorrow about the death of your sister made a strong impression on me. Oh, how I partake in your deep sorrow. How strange are the ways of the Lord with us humans. . . .

Now I will tell you about us here. Karen went to the post office and got your letter, we sat on the steps outside the house, and I said, Open the letter and read it, so I don't have to go in for my glasses. She opened it and cast her eyes on it, and then she said, someone must have died, she said, but then she read it, and we wept and wept for awhile. Do you have a photograph of her so we could see her, as she was now? If you do have one, please send it to us. The following day, which was yesterday, we went to Tollef Øien so that he could hear it, and then I went to Klemmet and Barbro, and while I was there, Tollef got a letter from you, so I got to hear that.

The harvest is in full swing now, it will be a good crop, lots of hay and good grain, so we have reason to be satisfied. You must have gotten the issues of *Skandinaven* that we sent? It hasn't been sent for some time now, which is simply due to carelessness, but I say that it is only empty reading. Religious reading is more worthwhile, nourishment for the soul. But we will send it to you again later. Paul received nine issues of *Fjeldljom* from you this fall. Don't bother to send any more, it isn't worth it, but thank you for the ones you sent.

Einar is home now. He came home from Racine where he has been this winter. He got sick, couldn't stand working in the machine shop, his chest didn't tolerate it. Ole and Ivar have gone to northern Michigan to work as carpenters, wages for carpenters are good there, they just left recently. Karen is well now, as is Stanley. And everything at Berit's is fine. Her two children are nice, pleasant children, and kind. They were here last Sunday after church. It's only about seven miles between us. And when I want to, I take the horse and buggy, and Stanley and I go over there. We're going down there to pick blackberries to can. We make preserves out of them. We have picked lots of raspberries, and preserved them with sugar for the winter, which we use for sauce, as we call it.

Please greet friends and relatives and acquaintances from us. . . . Write again soon, and hearty greetings to all of you from us all and especially from me, your devoted,

Barbro Ramseth

Frazer, Wisconsin
January 27, 1900

Dear Relatives,

Many thanks for the letter that I received from you early in November, and many thanks for the photograph of you, little Erik. It is a shame that I have not written to you sooner, but when one begins to put things off time after time, then that's the way it is, especially for me. Anyway, you will just have to excuse me, please, and I promise to be better next time. . . .

Here we are all well except Karen, poor thing. She is in the hospital. . . . It started up again, and ached so. She has a bad gland disease, so she wanted to try an operation again. There is an older Norwegian doctor who has such a good reputation. She had the operation three weeks ago, and is doing well under the circumstances, but we don't know when she can come home again. If only it would help, that would be fine. Stanley has also been sickly this winter, so he hasn't gone to school for a long time. . . . I am just afraid that he might also have this gland disease. Now he is pretty well. . . . We oldsters, Paul and I, are well. Einar has been home now and again this winter. He is healthy, and has been pressing hay. They are through now, and he is going to work for Berit's husband for awhile. Ole has said that he wants to come home for awhile in February. He has been far north in Michigan this winter working as a carpenter, and Ivar is going to go to school all winter. We have had a mild winter until now. It was cold at Christmas time for a few days, and again now, but we don't have enough snow so that we can use sleighs. . . .

The old man is still living, but his wife died four years ago this spring. I don't wonder that you ask what our position is. We are in debt, for we went into debt in order to build, and we pay the old man $25 per year. We can't get any farther, but I think of you and promise to send it to you as soon as we can. The old man is 83 years old, but healthy and spry, and so mean, he doesn't do anything.

Erik and Marit, I wish you luck with the New Year. God be with you this year as in other years. . . . We send you all our best greetings. Your always devoted,

Barbro Ramseth

Ivar, who is frequently referred to as "the smart one," is attending St. Olaf College in Northfield, Minnesota. Barbro writes "Minneapolis" instead of "Minnesota." President McKinley was assassinated in 1901, and was succeeded by Theodore Roosevelt.

Frazer, Wisconsin
December 8, 1901

All of you, often remembered, at Gammeludstumoen,

I will now write and thank you so much for your last dear letter. It is always such a pleasure for us to receive letters from you. . . . I hear that the old ones are still living, at a very great age, . . . so it is not to be wondered at that they are getting frail and need to be helped and waited on. . . . Now it is getting on toward Christmas, and we wish you a Merry Christmas and a Happy New Year.

We are all well, praise God. We are having good weather, still no snow to speak of. We have just been fixing up the house, for it has been so cold. Ole finished his carpentry job, and then did some things here at home, and I was surely happy to get them done. Berit and her husband and three children were home today. I should greet you from them, and tell you that they are all well. They have lively and good children. Karen is well, and Stanley too. He is going to school. Einar has been out traveling with some business this summer, but it hasn't gone very well for him, so he won't be going to school this winter. He will probably come home for Christmas. . . . Ivar is at St. Olaf College, a big school in Minneapolis. There are 280 students there, and everything is going well with him, he says.

Times are not so bad in America right now; prices on grain and pigs are high. Cattle haven't been so good, but there are good prices on hay. You have surely heard that our dear president was murdered. Oh, what a sorrow over all of America, for he was excellent in all ways, but we must hope that the one who takes his place will be just as good. He is a Republican, and has said that he will follow in the same path as McKinley.

Things are not going well at Tollef Øien's. Marit, his wife, is sick. He took her home from the hospital, but she will not speak. I went over there and tried everything I could to get her to talk, but no. Once she said she would rather die, but that is all I could get out of her. She mostly stays in bed. They have a servant girl. Everything is as usual at Klemmet's. Embret is there, but it looks as though there won't be any wedding. . . . Just think, Tollef told me that Erik Brækken was thinking of going to Norway for Christmas. I told Erik that he must absolutely come over before he left. I couldn't get over to see him, as it is five miles between our places. Well, Paul told him he must move [his wife] Johanna's body to the cemetery, for he buried her on Tollef Øien's farm, all alone there, as he had lost the right to use the churchyard cemetery when he resigned from the congregation (I told you about that before). Johanna herself believed she would be buried in the church cemetery. She told me that the last time I visited her. Now they say he has already left, and we are quite angry about that. He couldn't reach a settlement with [his son] Ole, and has given his demands to a lawyer, which Ole didn't know anything about, so all of us from Tynset are deeply ashamed. While Johanna lived she mediated between them. . . . We can't understand what is happening with him. . . . He must have heard that we said he should move Johanna's body, and that is why he didn't want to meet us. I am telling you this, but don't tell anyone else, for I don't wish to hurt him, that is not my intention.

Greet your mother and brother, but special greetings to you from me,

Barbro Ramseth

Frazer, Wisconsin
February 22, 1902

My dear relatives at home, especially our letter-writer,

Many thanks for your last dear letter. You surely surprised us with your news, not that such things don't happen and will happen as long as the world shall stand. I wanted to reply as quickly as possible and congratulate you with these lines. Yes, dear Erik, if you only knew all the good I wish for you. . . . God be with you and bless your engagement. . . . I don't know her, but I remember her mother. . . . However that may be, you love her and she loves you. That is the best of all, for faithful love is something beautiful and wonderful. I wish you all happiness and prosperity in your undertaking. . . .

Thank you for all the news you give us, it awakens old memories. . . . So you have had a visit from Erik Brækken. Well, well. We didn't get to see him before he left, for he didn't come here even though I sent several messages to him. But he never came, so one day I said to my folks, Oh, dears, hitch up a horse and drive me to Brækken, so I can meet Erik before he leaves. Oh, no, they said, when he doesn't want to come here, then it isn't worthwhile to go over there, and that might be so, but I didn't see it that way. Everything changes. . . . When I think back to the first time we came here, how pleasant it was to visit the Brœkkens, and we were together with them a lot, but now both Erik and Johanna are gone and I miss them both, for they were so well intentioned and charitable   . . When you meet Erik, you must greet him. Greet all our relatives and friends from us. . . . [The end is missing.]

Frazer, Wisconsin
December 1, 1902

Dear oft-remembered relatives at Gammeludstumoen,

A long time has now passed since I received your letter, which I want to thank you so much for. Time after time, all summer, I have thought of writing, but nothing has come of it. Time goes so incredibly fast. But now I will try to write a little, so you can hear how we are doing. God be praised and thanked, we are all well. We have winter now, just a little bit of snow so far. We have had an exceptionally good fall with nice weather, but the summer was cold, there was hardly any heat all summer, even so, here in Lessor we got quite a good crop, so we shouldn't complain. Only the corn was poor. There hasn't been much sickness and death either.

I can tell you that Karen has remarried. She was married on May 16 this spring. She didn't have much of a wedding, just a few guests. . . . He is a widower with two small boys just a little older than Stanley. They have been engaged for a long time, but as you know, Karen has been sick so much.

But now, thank God, it looks like she is healthy and happy. He is a neighbor to the south, not very far, so it is nice to be so close to each other. We old folks didn't like it that she got married again, we thought she should live for Stanley, but it's no use to oppose what is going to happen. Well, if only she stays healthy, then everything will be fine. She is now selling her share of the mill in Bristow. They have a good farm. His name is Hans Eriksen.

Ole and Einar have been working as carpenters and are still doing that. Ivar has been home this summer and worked for a farmer here, but went back to school again this fall. He is at the same school, there are almost 300 students there. . . . He still has two years left before he graduates, for he is learning several languages, Latin and Greek, and so on. He really likes it. Everyone is fine at Berit's, three lively little children.

Tollef Øien is not very well, he has gotten so shaky and poorly. Marit is still crazy, but is at home. . . . Everything is fine at Brækken. Ole was here for dinner one time this fall when some members of the school board were here to settle up with him. Ole had worked on contract on the school, building an addition with a tower and hallways. Tell Erik Brækken this when you meet him. Otherwise we don't see much of them, as they don't go to church, but both Ole's wife and Martin's wife have had babies, so everything was fine there. You must greet Erik Brækken from us. We miss him. Isn't it strange, things change all the time, Brækken used to be the dearest and pleasantest place to go, and now, I haven't been there since Johanna was buried. I have thought of writing to Erik, but nothing has come of it yet. . . .

The Lord be with you all. Greet relatives and friends, and all who ask about us. . . . Most of all, greetings to you from all of us, your devoted,

Barbro Ramseth

The Ramseths received photographs of Erik's wedding party, and Barbro comments extensively on the people in the picture.

Frazer, Wisconsin
March 7, 1903

Dear good folk at Gammeludstumoen,

Many thanks for your last dear letter, and for all the photographs. It was a surprise and delight, so thank you from us all. We see from your letter that you are married. With these lines, I congratulate you. May God's rich blessings pour over you. . . . It was really fun to get the picture. Many are easily recognizable, but there are also many we wonder about. Your grandfather is natural as he sits there. Just imagine, to live to such a great age and still be spry. . . . Your mother looks just the same, she carries her age well. . . . I recognize your wife's mother easily. . . . We can see Erik Brækken. Is it Kari Haugros in the middle in front of Erik Jørgensmoen? It looks like things have gotten very fine in Tynset, for many have gold chains. . . . You were clever to think of taking a photograph of the wedding party. We were so happy to get all the pictures, and you and your bride are standing there so fine and happy, and it is truly a joyous occasion. The whole group is in a festive mood, some laughing and others smiling, so it is really a pleasure to look at. I see you had an old-style wedding, well, why not, the old ways are the best, I think. You can imagine how I would like to have been there with you, to witness your happiness. I have dressed two brides at Gammeludstumoen. You have a very fine bride, I see, and so young, both of you. . . .

Now we are having nice weather, but still have snow. We have had a rather cold winter. We don't have a warm house, it takes lots of wood. They have been busy cutting and sawing and splitting wood for awhile, so we have never had this much wood. Ole has bought land a mile and a half from here. It is very wooded with maple and birch, nice wood. So you had a complete crop failure in 1902. That is terrible. There is so much in the newspapers about famine in Finland, Sweden, and Norway. All over America, I believe, help has been given, and lots of money has been sent. Do you think it gets to the truly needy? So you are going to stay at Gammeludstumoen. You must have gotten some money with your bride too. That is good. . . .

I can inform you that we are healthy as usual. Ole and Einar have been home for awhile, but they will be leaving soon. Ivar is still at school in Northfield, Minnesota. He is well and continues to study. Karen and Stanley are both well, and are happy and satisfied. Everything is the same at Berit's, they are all well and busy with their work. Berit hasn't been home since I got the photograph, but she heard about it, so she is longing to see it. . . . Now I will close with a hearty greeting from Paul and me. Your devoted,

Mrs. Barbro Ramseth

Frazer, Wisconsin
1903

Dear Relatives,

Many, many thanks for your last dear letter, and also for the previous one. It certainly made a strong impression on me when I got the last one, with the black border on it, for I knew what that meant. Oh, yes, Erik, you are an up-to-date man, you follow along with the times, and you are kind to write to us, for which I am most grateful, and you know how we like to hear from our relatives in Tynset. God be praised that my half-sister, Marit, has passed away, and has been allowed to lay down her wanderer's staff. She had a long life, and we may hope she has fought the good fight and received the victor's everlasting crown, for then she has not lived in vain. . . .

I will tell you a little about us here. Thank God, we are all in good health. . . . We old folks, you know, are feeling our age more and more, but when we are able to do our work, then we can only be happy. We have worked very hard since we came to America, and there is no other way here. If you want to get along, you have to do it yourself, you can't hire help on a little farm. But when the boys are close by, they help out when we're in a pinch, for they are all so kind. Ole and Einar are now building a church for the Germans. Ivar has started school again at St. Olaf, Northfield. This summer, during vacation, he taught Norwegian parochial school for three months in the city of Milwaukee. I don't know if he will study theology, maybe he will go that route. He doesn't want to be a minister, but he can certainly become a learned man, bring honor, glory, and usefulness to himself and for others. I hope so, for he is a very good son, is Ivar. . . . Yes, they are good children, all of them, and are doing well. Karen is healthy, it is nice that she is close to us. Ole and Einar have built a veranda in front of her house and painted it white and green. Everything is fine with Berit. She has been home twice this last week with the children, and Norman stayed with us for a few days, because he is so babyish, and they wanted him to get used to being away a little. Stanley is growing and getting big. He is a good boy. As far as the crops are concerned, we have gotten lots of hay, but there won't be much grain this year, they say. We haven't threshed or cut the corn yet. It has been a cold summer with lots of rain, so we didn't think the corn would ripen, but now we are getting some sun and wind, and then it ripens quickly, so we think we will get something.

If you had been as close as you are far away, then you would have gotten apples from us. We have gotten quite a few apples this year, even though it has not been a good year for apples. We came here ten years ago this spring, and then there was not a tree here, but now we have over twenty apple trees of different kinds and other trees, so we have a nice little garden. There wasn't much in the way of buildings either, but we had to build, you know, if we were to manage, and then we had to go into debt, for we had to borrow money, there was no other way, but it is so hard to catch up. Old Christian is still living, will be 87 in October, hasn't worked since we came here, even though he could, as he promised us, and many a time I have regretted that we came here, for he is so mean and nasty, and has no ordinary manners. But patience is needed, it says in the psalm, and that is surely the case here. It will no doubt continue as before. If we live and have our health, then we have what we need, for this is a very good little farm.

I sent greetings to Tollef Øien after I got your first letter. He is now staying with his son-in-law, John Reitan. He couldn't manage at home, for he is very poorly, very shaky. Marit, his wife, is staying with the widow of Bersven. Marit is just as crazy as before. It is terrible how hard things are for Tollef, poor thing. You know, he gets good care at Reitan's, but he isn't in his

own home. He has rented that out. The other two daughters went to Nebraska this summer, and are still gone. They are such strong Rationalists, a
really crazy teaching, just like at Brækkens and others too. Embret Nilsen
also never goes to church. He is at Klemmet's, but is still not married. It is
strange, and shameful for both Norwegians and people from Tynset, for you
can be sure that other nationalities notice such things. Living together without being married. It may be that they live right, but the example is poor.

So Erik Brækken is coming back. That was what we told him, that he
wouldn't like it there, and he gave up his rights, so now he has to live on
charity. Oh, I have thought so much about him. We think that Ole will be
reasonable. . . . While I am sitting and writing, John Reitan came in, he is
going to get the doctor for Tollef Øien. He is worse, so heaven knows how
that will go. He took your last letter with him. Now I will break off for this
time. Greetings from all of us, but especially greet Grandfather from me. . . .
[The rest is missing.]

*The new address is due to a change of post office. This is the last letter in the col-
lection. Barbro died in 1913, at the age of seventy-five.*

Rose Lawn, Wisconsin
September 29, 1904

Dear Relatives,

Many, many thanks for your last dear letter. It is always a joy to hear
from you. And you, Erik letter-writer, are so good at giving us all the news, so
that's the reputation you have with all of us. I am the one most interested in
hearing from you and Tynset. Yes, time goes quickly here, and we follow
along with all the changes and different kinds of tasks. New generations are
born and the old die, that is the way of the world. . . .

I can tell that we are all well in our family. Paul and I are in good
health and working as hard as we can. Ole is at home and helps us when we
need it, and little Stanley comes too when we need him, so we can manage.
As you know, Ole is a carpenter and mostly works at that during the summer.
The first thing he worked on this summer was a creamery a mile from here.
The farmers built it, and it looks like it will be advantageous for them. Karen
is fine, she is healthy now. Berit is also well, she has four little ones, two boys
and two girls, so she has enough to do. Their names are Norman Carl, Erling
Rolf, Blanche Palma, and Ester Marian. Ivar has started school again in
Northfield, Minn. There are over 300, almost 400 students, a very large and
good school. This is the fourth year Ivar has gone there. Einar is a store clerk
and postal clerk eight miles from here, he comes home on Sundays. Ole has
bought land about a mile from us. And I can tell you that they are engaged

now, all three of them. We have been to three weddings this summer, big weddings. Einar was the groomsman in one of them. I will tell you who they are engaged to another time.

I can tell you that Tollef Øien died on April 23 this spring. . . . He was bedridden all last winter, completely helpless. He was lame on one side, but was completely clear the whole time, and gave testimony that he died believing in Jesus Christ. . . . Marit, his wife, is crazy, but the widow of Bersven Haugen has her, so she has good care, much better than at the asylum, for Tollef took her home from there. . . . Embret Gammeludstumoen is at Klemmet's, but Klemmet is in the insane asylum. It is a mystery why they don't get married. We have gotten tired of asking about it. . . .

The harvest here in Lessor is about middling. We got lots of hay, but grain was poor, and the corn was poor too. . . . We have had some nights with frost, so the potatoes and grass froze. Now it is very nice weather, maybe it will continue. We had lots of berries and apples. We had a visit from two Chicago girls this summer, a niece of Paul's and her friend. They were here for two weeks, between us and Karen and Berit. We will get lots of potatoes this year. So, Erik, your grandfather is still living, how remarkable. . . . Greet him from me. Christian, our pensioner, will be 88 this October, and he still can take care of himself. Please greet your mother heartily, and your wife and brother. So you haven't got a little one yet? Live well all of you, and be commended to God. Your always devoted,

Barbro Ramseth

NOTES

1. Personal communication, Rolf H. Erickson. Additional information about the Ramseth family is found in the archives with the letters and in the privately printed family history by Ola Grandum, *The Family of Gammelutstumoen, Tynset, Norway,* trans. Rolf H. Erickson and Anette Norberg-Schulz (Evanston, Ill., and Kenosha, Wis., n.d.).

6

Politics and Gold Mining on the West Coast

Hans Hansen and Sivert Øien, 1890–1913

*A*lthough they came from rural backgrounds in Norway, the bachelors repre-
sented in this group of letters left the farming areas of the Midwest to go into
lumbering, fishing, construction, and business in the booming towns along the West
Coast. They also followed the lure of gold to Alaska and the Yukon Territory.

Most of the letters in this collection were written to Hans Pedersen Øien,
who was from Ørsta, Sunnmøre, Norway. He was born in 1864 and emigrated to
the Midwest in 1885, where he joined his uncle, Hans Hansen. After having lived
in both Minnesota and Washington, Hans Øien returned to Norway in 1895 and
took over the family farm. He died in 1945. Hansen was only five years older than
his nephew, and his letters all carry the salutation "Dear Friend."

Hans Hansen (also known as Hans Mathias and Hans H. or Hans M.
Oien) was born in Ørsta, Sunnmøre, in 1859. He emigrated to the United States
in 1881, going first to Minneapolis. He attended a business college there in 1885,
and was joined in the Midwest by his nephews Hans, Sivert ("Sam"), Mathias,
and Knut Pedersen Øien.[1] After about six years in the Midwest, he moved to Seattle. Hansen homesteaded in the Quillayute Valley of Washington, and after prov-
ing up on his claim, he worked on a large farm near New Westminster, British Columbia. He returned to Seattle after a few years and worked in a grocery store and
as manager of the Union Fish Company. He was active in the Populist movement,
and in 1896 was elected to the Washington State Legislature on the People's party
ticket, where he served one term (1897). He was noted in the legislature for "opposition to fish traps and earnest support of Hon. George Turner for United States
Senator."[2] Hansen wrote newspaper articles on political and reform topics and
planned several books. After serving in the legislature, he began traveling back and
forth between Alaska and Seattle, where he worked in various businesses and even

tried his hand at prospecting for gold. He died in Juneau, Alaska, in 1912 at the age of fifty-three.

Several letter excerpts included in this series were written by Hans Hansen's nephew Sivert (Sam) Øien. Sivert Pedersen Øien was born in 1869 and emigrated to Minnesota in 1887. After some time in the Midwest, he too moved to the West Coast. There he worked as a carpenter and tile layer and as a farmhand together with his uncle Hans. He also tried his hand at fishing, and spent several years prospecting for gold in the Klondike. After returning from the Yukon, he settled in Seattle, and worked in construction. Among other projects, he worked on the Parliament building in Victoria, British Columbia, in 1897. He married a Norwegian-American woman, and they had two children, James and Pearl. Sivert died in 1942.[3]

This section has been arranged in chronological order, with letters from Hans Hansen and Sivert Øien interleaved. The picture that emerges is one of a loosely knit community of men, mostly from the same area of Sunnmøre, who were close friends as well as relatives. Hans Hansen and Sam Øien often show differing perspectives on the same incidents, as well as relating totally different aspects of their lives. Hansen writes long, often philosophical letters containing much political commentary. Because his letters are so long, extensive editing has been necessary. He wrote many of his letters to Hans Øien in English to prevent others from reading them. His English spelling and punctuation are somewhat erratic, and judicious editing has been necessary for the sake of clarity.

Hans Hansen wrote to his father while his nephews Hans, Mathias, and Sivert were still with him in Seattle. Sedro is an area in Seattle.

Seattle, Washington
May 4, 1890

Dear Father,

I have received your dear letter of February, and thank you so much for it. I am very glad to hear that you are well, both spiritually and physically. I can likewise greet you with the news that I am also in good health. . . .

Quite some time has passed since I received your letter, so I ought to have answered it before, but . . . I have had little time to spare. . . . I came back from my land at the end of January, and since then have been working as a clerk for a Norwegian grocery store owner, E. O. Rindal. In addition to this, I have had much work with a youth association of the local Norwegian Lutheran church. The name of the association is "Fremad." We have meetings every Wednesday evening, so my free hours have been mostly taken up in preparing myself to take part in these meetings. We have had debates and discussions on topics that touch on both our religious and our civic duties. The association has made much progress and now has 67 members. We have published a magazine for youth, of which I am the editor. I really think highly

HANS HANSEN.

Hans Hansen. Photo from Thos. Ostenson Stine, Scandinavians on the Pacific, Puget Sound.

of this kind of association, where young people gather to talk about life and everything that entails. It gives one confidence . . . so I am now quite free of reserve . . . in speaking before an assembly. . . .

In two or three weeks I intend to go out to my land for a month's time. My land is of the best sort and in that I was very lucky, as it will be worth much more in the future than it is now.

Last fall I bought a city lot in a new place called "Sedro," which at today's prices would sell for three times the amount I paid. So I must say that luck has been with me these last years when it comes to the material life. And for that I am grateful. But it means much more to live for God. . . .

With regard to your question about my trip home, it is difficult to make any firm, final decision. However, I have certainly not forgotten that when I left, I promised I would come home again. It is just as much my in-tention now as ever before to come home to Norway, but I cannot fix the

time just now as something could possibly hinder me. Yet I live with the hope
that I once again will be seen in the first home of my life. With loving greetings from your son,

                                                            Hans Mathias

*Mathias, Hans Hansen's nephew and Sivert's brother, died of consumption in
1893. Hans gave a eulogy over Mathias, which he then printed and tried to sell. He
mentions having sent 150 copies of Mathias's eulogy home to Norway. In this letter
to Hans Øien, Sivert also mentions the eulogy, but from a different perspective.*

                                                    Seattle, Washington
                                                    January 22, 1894

Dear Brother,

I have just received your letter of the 17th of this month, in which
you send a great deal of scolding which I don't know if I shall take for myself
or if it is someone else who should have it. . . . You say that you want the
eulogy over Mathias. How do I know if you have gotten it or not? . . . As you
already know, I was out on my land when the eulogy was printed. I was there
over two months and Uncle came there the day I left, so I didn't get much
time to talk to him. He told me that the eulogy was printed and that he had
sent 150 copies home to Norway and likewise that he had sent to several
other places and so I thought that he had sent to you, too. When I asked him
if there were more left, he answered no, not unless I bought them. He has not
held back enough that I could get one unless I went and bought it from those
who have them for sale. He was here this summer trying to get money from
me to have it printed and I told him that I had no money to spare as times
were so bad . . . and then when I could get work I was sick for a month and
even so he got a little money from me to live on as he was here and had no
work all summer.

Now that Ole Mork has come back from Alaska, he [Hans] got the
twenty dollars that Ole owed Mathias and used that to get the eulogy printed.
According to what I have found out, he has sent it out to different people
who were going to sell it for ten cents apiece, and now they can't sell enough
to get the money back, so there you can see where Mathias' money is going,
and likewise how he is taking care of things, and I said that to him before, but
he is so obstinate that you can't do anything, and now it looks like I will have
the blame for that. Time will show I have done what I can. . . . I will send
you the eulogy soon, as soon as I find someone who has them for sale, and if
I get my money from Collins, then I will send you a photograph of the funeral, which was held in Seattle. Times are bad. I haven't earned a red cent

Hans Hansen with his three nephews, ca. 1888. Left to right, *Hans Hansen, Sivert Øien, Mathias Øien,* and *Hans Øien. Photo from Ragner Standal,* Mot nye heimland: Utvandringa frå Hjørundfjord, Vartdal og Ørsta.

since the 10th of September, so you can understand how I feel about the scolding, and with that I must stop for this time with a friendly greeting from,

S. P. Øien

Although Hans Hansen wrote this letter to Hans Øien in Norwegian, he used several English words and phrases such as memorial service, the speech of my life, *and* treated. *Hans Øien was in Gary, Minnesota, at the time he received this letter. Hansen mentions that he tried to get a post as "Chinese Inspector." This was apparently a political patronage job involving Chinese immigrants.*

Quillayute, Clallam Co.
Washington
March 14, 1894

Dear Friend,

I received your esteemed letter of February 12, and am very grateful for same. In the meantime, I will report that the night before I got your letter I dreamed of Mathias for the first time since I got out here on my claim. I saw us together and Mathias was so healthy and hearty and rosy-cheeked that I said to him that I had never seen him looking so well before. . . .

The memorial service held for Mathias was and is a witness to his character and life that speaks for itself. . . . The event was of a unique character. The eulogy was what I myself will always call *"the speech of my life."* There will never come another time in my life when my heart will be so touched. I gave his life story as far as possible in short and clear words, in keeping with his own manner of speaking. . . .

I haven't much news from here. I am struggling along as best I can, and this coming July I plan to prove up on my claim. My political friends in Port Angeles, . . . who I helped into well-paid offices, have treated me just the same way as these church brothers treated Mathias. Last summer I got the endorsement from the *state democracy* for Chinese Inspector (an office that pays $125.00 per month). But these folks in Angeles spoiled my endorsement, and that is just the repayment one gets when one has to do with false people, whether one meets them in church, in politics, or in a saloon, they treat you in the same way. Now that they have gotten what they are after, they don't want to know me anymore.

At the end of January I wrote a letter to Knut and one to Hans Brungot, but I haven't heard from them. You see, I asked them if they could help me with $10.00 each until I have proved up on my land. I must say that I am hard up, and if they couldn't help me then they could have said so . . . and I would have gone to another source. . . . As you understand very well, it embarrasses me to be in debt, but . . . I began to help and bear others' burdens before I had anything much for myself. I hope I will be helped in some way until I get through with my land. Then I will sell some . . . and that should pay what debts I have, and then I will sell more, for you can be sure I don't want anyone to lose a cent on me or be poor because of any of my actions. Yet I don't know anything better than to take things patiently, as all our fates lie in the hands of Divine Providence and mine, too.

I have no more to tell about this time. Let me hear from you right away. Many friendly greetings from me,

Hans Hansen

This next letter has the same date, and was no doubt a postscript to the previous one.

March 14, 1894

Good Friend,

Just as the mail came in, I got a letter from Sivert. You see, I had written to him to ask if he could help me with a few dollars, but that was not possible, he was having a hard enough time helping himself.

Therefore, I must ask you to see Hans Brungot and Knut and ask if they can or not.

I also received a letter from my former political friend, W. K. Clark. He thought that he and his friends had done me no harm, but yet in his remarks he admits that they had spoiled my endorsement for Chinese Inspector at Seattle.

Your friend,
Hans Hansen

Hansen uses many English words and phrases in this letter. He was an enthusiastic Populist, and ran on the People's party ticket.

Quillayute, Clallam Co,
Washington
April 28, 1894

Dear Friend,

As I have recently received two letters from you, I will take the opportunity to write to you, although I don't have much to tell about. . . .

It is now only a little over two months before I can prove up. I am longing for that day, so that I can clear up my affairs. . . .

I have now given up "all office-seeking" and joined "the People's party." We have a P.P. Club here, and in two weeks, I am going to deliver a long speech for the members of the club, and that will be published in *The People* of Port Angeles. I will send you a copy of the same.

I have no more news to tell you this time. With all best wishes and friendly greetings from me,

Hans Hansen

Sivert Øien tells how he and his uncle Hans are faring as they work on a large farm in British Columbia. The island they are on is in the Fraser River and is now part of greater Vancouver. Øie is the name of Sivert's home in Norway.

New Westminster, B.C.
November 18, 1894

Dear Parents,

Today I received your esteemed letter of the 14th of October, for which I am most grateful. I could have written much more often, but my negligence is too great, so you will just have to excuse me. First, I can report that both Uncle Hans and I are well and working for the same man on a large farm. The farm is 600 acres and is situated much like Øie, with a river on both sides. The island is called Lulu Island and is not in the United States but is in British Columbia, a part of Canada about 200 miles north of Seattle. We have been here since May and have worked every single day. I had intended to go up to Alaska this spring, but just as I was ready to go, I met the man I am now working for. I have worked for him before, he is from Sunnmøre. . . . There are now 23 men working here. I have been working as a carpenter almost the whole time since I came. I have built two large buildings and am now starting on one more . . . so I will have work for most of the winter. There is not enough snow here to matter, but mostly rain, more than in Washington. Times have been very bad in the United States the last two years, and they still are, so I had to leave for awhile, but when I finish here I will go back. . . .

You asked about your brother Hans, who you haven't heard from in a long time. He and I are sleeping in the same bed now and under the two quilts that you sent him from his father, so you can be sure that he has received them as well as the two silk handkerchiefs. I cannot tell you why he hasn't written, other than the same reason as mine, namely negligence. You must not believe that he holds anything against you for the settlement of your father's estate, for that is not the case . . . and by now you have probably received his last letter so you have gotten the message that he was sick some time ago, so he went to Seattle and saw the doctor and now he is pretty much well again. . . .

I must now stop my simple lines for this time with a friendly greeting from your son,

Sivert Øien

Hans Hansen probably wrote this letter fragment from New Westminster, B.C., in the fall of 1894, after his cabin in Quillayute burned down.

. . . All the letters and books that I lost, and all the letters that I had gotten from Mathias during his lifetime I had packed together carefully to preserve them, but those like everything else were ruined. . . . The fire was set on a dark rainy evening. . . .

I proved up my land in July, but I never moved back into my own house. Now I am on a big farm near New Westminster. Both Sivert and I are here. I came several days ago, but Sivert has been here for three months. We are working for C. Karlson. . . . He now has a contract from an Englishman to bring 570 acres of bottomland under cultivation. . . . [The rest is missing.]

Hans Øien was living in Minnesota, which is why his uncle Hans presumed he had had the pleasure of voting for Knute Nelson. Nelson and Boen were both Norwegian-American politicians in Minnesota.

New Westminster, B.C.
December 9, 1894

Dear Friend,

I have received both letters that you sent to me here. I must say that I am very glad to hear from you and to know that things are going well. I have been especially uneasy about you since the big forest fire in eastern Minnesota, but as I have seen the names of all the Scandinavians who were caught up in the disaster, I was assured that you were not in the danger that so many had to face. I do not like it at all that you are working in the woods, which I regard as one of the most dangerous occupations a man can have, next to fishing from Sunnmøre.

I haven't much to tell about from here. I am now in better health than I was when I wrote to you last. Dr. Day's . . . Remedies seem to have a good effect on me and by taking good care of myself and living as I should I hope to be even healthier than ever before. With the kind of misfortune I have had these last few years, and with my nature, which is to take everything to heart, there was nothing else to be expected than that my health would be broken. . . .

I am glad that I am free of my land. . . . As for my house, which burned down, it was not worth much, but I cannot forget that I have lost Mathias's letters. . . .

If I could get a position in a store in Seattle this spring, then I would go out there again, but not to run in politics. No! I am finished with all that insanity of running for office, I have had enough of it, and have experienced that it is as difficult for an honest man out here to get into office as for a camel to go through the eye of a needle. But I like to live where there are lots of people and where I can follow along with the times.

In September of last year I left the Methodist church and from that time until November when I went to Quillayute I taught Sunday school. . . . And if I stay in Seattle, then I will take a great interest in the Sunday school, but I will not join the church as a member. And I won't get mixed up in any of the many unnecessary organizations that they have.

I presume that you had the pleasure of voting for Knute Nelson for governor. It was too bad that Boen was beaten.

When you get this letter, let me hear from you. In friendship,

Hans Hansen

Sivert wrote to his brother Hans on the same day that his uncle did.

New Westminster, B.C.
December 9, 1894

Dear Brother,

As a long time has passed since you and I have heard anything from one another, I will break the silence by sending you some words. . . . I left Seattle early in May and since then have been up here working, except for a few days when I couldn't work because of a sore hand. There is very little news other than that everyone I know is healthy. Sam Stone is now down in San Francisco . . . working on board a government boat. Elias Larsen died last spring in Quillayute of nerve fever. Andrew Johnson, who worked on the sawmill out by Lake Washington, has gone crazy and is now in the asylum. Religious brooding was the cause. Louis Miller is married, and several weeks ago his wife had a boy, so he is also propagating the world. Gina Miller and Ole Sovig traveled to Norway some time ago. Sovig has been in Alaska a little over a year. Martin Olson is up in Alaska, he went up there last spring. Martha Morke went to Norway last spring, but will no doubt come back to America again. Her brother Andrew is in Tacoma, cleaning out saloons for a living.

I hear from Uncle that you have come back to the well-known city of Duluth. . . . I haven't had letters from Norway the whole summer until a few weeks ago. They were all well at home, but at the same time were very worried that they hadn't heard anything from you. They thought maybe you had been killed in the big forest fire that raged in Minnesota. But I wrote back and said that I would have heard about it, so they didn't need to worry. . . .

Knud Myklebust is in his old place, Andrew Rohde is in Seattle. This fall he bought himself a big salmon net and boat, so he has been foreman of a seine gang and done very well. For my part, I will no doubt take a short trip to Seattle at Christmas time to greet old friends and also buy some clothes, for up here everything is so expensive. After New Year I will be back at my old place, and I can stay here all winter and work a little. The pay is just enough to keep me in shoes and clothing, but it is better than going cold and hungry. I must stop for this time with friendly greetings from your brother,

Sivert P. Øien

Hans Hansen was still in Canada. He writes in Norwegian, but uses the English word damp.

New Westminster, B.C.
March 4, 1895

Dear Friend,

It is now a long time since I got a letter from you, so I don't know how you are doing. I don't have much to tell, only that C. Karlson wishes that you would come out here. He said that wages for you would be the same as Sivert and I get, $25.00 per month and board. Still, I don't recommend that you come back out here if you are having any thoughts about going back to Norway. Anyway, there is no certainty that Karlson will stay on this place either, though it does seem that he might stay here for the coming summer. He has the inside track with Alex Ewen, who owns the land, and next month seventy acres will be planted to potatoes, and Ewen also wants to help him get a contract to cultivate 1,000 acres of land that lie next to this place. If he gets the job, then there will be work for at least sixty men for a year's time.

I don't like the poor water here during the summer and it's too damp and rainy during the winter, so I am thinking of leaving in May in order to find a lighter, dryer climate. Maybe I can get work up in the mountains through the summer. My health is all right, and would have been first class if it weren't for the damp climate here.

You must write to me as soon as possible. I don't like to hear that you are working in the woods. Lumbering and cod fishing off Sunnmøre are two jobs I don't like at all, as they are so closely connected with danger. . . .

With these remarks you receive most friendly greetings from,

Hans M. Øien

Hansen sends some medical advice to his friends. Cannabis sativa *is also known as hemp, or marijuana. Across the top of the letter is written: Dr. W. A. Noyes, 820–822 Powers Block, Rochester, N.Y.*

New Westminster, B.C.
March 19, 1895

Dear Friend,

I have just received your esteemed letter and see that you are not well at present, and are using medicines for the first time. . . . I am enclosing in this letter a prescription for some medicine that is the best thing I know for stopping coughs, and so I am writing it out for you. The prescription is for *Cannabis sativa*, which is the only medicine that cures tuberculosis and all illnesses concerning the nerves and the lungs. . . . I have used the medicine for three weeks now and I must admit that it is already making me a new person. The medicine circulates through every single nerve in the whole system and takes away the poison that settles in the lungs and causes consumption. If your lungs are affected by strong cold or inflammation, then send for this medicine as soon as possible. Two boxes of the compound will last for six weeks and cost, sent from Rochester, only $5.00. The medicine aids digestion and the bowels in a remarkable way.

In friendship,
Hans M. Øien

Hansen writes about Fram, *a Populist newspaper in Seattle. For a time, Hansen was engaged to Birgitte Samonie Vinjevold from his home area of Norway. She was in Norway at the time this letter was written, but later lived in the United States.*

Seattle, Washington
July 6, 1896

Dear Friend,

I received your esteemed letter several days ago, and was very glad to hear that you are well. I have very little to report from here. I am in good health and am working as a subscription agent for *Fram*. . . . Sivert is out fishing in British Columbia and will be coming back again in six weeks and then will fish here.

Times are as bad as they have ever been in these last years. Politics is starting to heat up now, so that will be occupying everyone's minds from now until election day. Silver and gold are the topics of debate all over the country these days.

I have recently gotten a letter and a portrait of Samonie Vinjevold. That was unexpected, but I must say that she is the same beauty she was when I left Norway. I have never seen such a well-made portrait before. What will come of it I don't know, only time will tell. . . .

When I came back to Seattle just before Christmas, I took over the Bible class in Sunday school, and was the teacher until the 17th of May. In January at the election of officers for Fremad, I was elected president by a 4/5 majority, but there was the greatest excitement that I have seen at an election of this kind. There was such a fight for and against me that I couldn't do anything else than *laugh* at the craziness of those foolish people. Theodor Pederson, Andrew Nelson, and Knud Myklebust were my bitter opponents. They supported Gilbert Qvale, but they were not only beaten by an overwhelming majority, but branded themselves with villainy and shame by slanderous and indecent comments. As soon as I took the platform as president, the house became completely quiet. I brought in *The Reed Rules* at once and the meetings became as spiritual as a prayer meeting, and Fremad has never had such a fortunate period as the three months that I was president; good programs by the best speakers in the city, and full houses, but at the election in April I refused to accept the nomination unless I could be elected unanimously. I just wanted to show . . . that I was the man who knows how to keep them under control. . . .

With friendly greetings from,

Hans Hansen Øien

The Doctor Johnson mentioned here is Dr. Janson, son of the Norwegian author Kristofer Janson, who lived for a time in Minnesota. Two of his sons became physicians in Seattle. Hansen is still interested in Populist politics, and expresses disappointment at the defeat of William Jennings Bryan for president.

Seattle, Washington
November 12, 1896

Dear Friend,

As you can see, I wrote you a letter on the 6th of July, which has been lying in my album until now, the reason is that I didn't want to send the letter until after the election was over and the results known. I have the pleasure of informing you that I was elected representative from the 42nd district to the legislative assembly that meets in Olympia on January 9, 1897. You can certainly understand that I feel very happy over the outcome. My opponents fought against me with the bitterest possible means, with lies, falsehoods, and dishonor, but it was no use, I was elected by a large majority. My articles (three in all) in the *Seattle Times* regarding the monetary system, and the election speech that I delivered in Ballard, convinced the electorate clearly that I was the man for the office, so Rosleafe, Andrew Nelson, Hellestad, and Solberg couldn't do anything, even though they went from house to house and tried to get people to go against me. It is a good thing you were not here, or you might have sinned against that miserable Rosleafe, but the Swedes, except for him, voted for me almost to a man.

The other evening there was an election in Fremad for president. My friends wanted me reelected so I could go from here to Olympia as president. As soon as Andrew Nelson, Solberg and Co. understood that, they united themselves with the orthodox preacher element to defeat me (just like Herod and Pilate became friends when the Jews accused Jesus), but it was no use, they found out that my friends were too strong for them, and I was elected. It was the fourth time this year that I have bested that refractory element, so I am not the least bit surprised that they are sick and sore over their own humiliation. . . . The reason I was willing to accept the election as chairman was that those busybodies had gone around among the American church people and said that I had been kicked out of the Lutheran church for crooked work, and therefore I could, by my reelection, show people what blackmailers they are. Knud Myklebust both voted and worked for my election to the legislative assembly.

Sivert was sick this fall for a whole month, and lay in the North Seattle Hospital. It was some sort of constipation in his abdomen and he was as near death as one can be and still get well again. But Dr. Johnson (the son of Christoffer Johnson) cured him. Dr. Eames had him first, but he couldn't do anything for him. But as soon as Johnson had gotten his stomach in order, it didn't take more than eight or ten days before Sivert was as rosy and strapping as usual, although he was just skin and bone when Johnson took hold of him. Sivert is now in Victoria and together with Harstad has a contract for the tile work in the Parliament building. I was also sick during most of the election campaign, suffering from poor digestion, so I also went to Dr. Johnson and was well only one week before the election, so I delivered just one election speech, which was partially printed in the *Seattle Times*. I will send it to you later.

I don't have any other news, just that I am sorry Bryan was not elected president, the most honorable and greatest statesman in America. Never before has such a man appeared before the American people. Gifted, honest, and magnetic, without equal in this country.

If Birgitte Samonie Vinjevold is ever home, please invite her to come to you for a visit. . . . With these remarks I send you, with all relatives, friends, and acquaintances, most hearty greetings from,

Hans Hansen

Hansen writes on letterhead from the State of Washington House of Representatives. Most of the letter is in Norwegian, with some English words, such as apology. When he writes about his girlfriend, however, he switches to English.

Seattle, Washington
April 19, 1897

Dear Friend,

It is now a very long time since I received your letter, and I still haven't answered it. The reasons for this are many, lack of time is one, and the other and major reason is that I couldn't bring myself to write until I had arranged a settlement with the *Seattle Times*, whose apology I enclose with this letter so that you can see it. It was a hard job to get them to admit that they are blackmailers, but before I am through with them, the paper will find out that they are dealing with a person who understands how to hold them up to real justice. . . .

I presume that you have gotten the *Seattle Times* from January to April and from that you have seen the news both from the legislature as well as other doings from this side of the ocean. . . . But the *Seattle Times* by no means gave me a just report from the legislature, the paper tried as hard as possible to forget about me because they were so embittered that I wouldn't support Squire for Senator. But nothing in the world could persuade me to act against my own good conscience. Also, George Turner from Spokane was, in my opinion, the best man, so I worked hard for him, and got five other members to vote for him. But I could very well understand the bitterness of the Seattle politicians who were against me, since I was one of those who brought up the possibility of Turner being elected. . . . As you very well know, I don't run away when something debatable comes up.

I must admit that I am glad I have reached the position I wished for myself, but taking everything into account, what trouble and inconvenience there is in it and how little of what we call honesty is in the political life. Still, as far as I am concerned, I have a good conscience for every action I have taken part in, but even the honest person gets accused of dishonesty in politics, though as a reasonable person I don't worry much about newspaper talk. . . .

There is not much else in the way of news. Sivert is still working in Victoria on the Parliament building. . . . Our friends are beginning to disappear from Seattle. So many have gone to Alaska. . . . With the church (the Lutheran) it has gone from bad to worse since Mathias left here. They have no pastor now, and . . . the congregation is so split up that many have left, and those that remain are still fighting among themselves. . . . I for my part, as you know, am a little too liberal, straightforward, and openhearted to fit in with such company, but one thing I know is that I am at least more scrupulous than most of them. And I have so much good sense that I do not waste my time arguing with them on this and that in the doctrines and so on. . . .

I had a letter from Osborg the other day, he is in Astoria, and as usual is salmon fishing on the Columbia River. I was together with him here in town just before Christmas for three days, and had much discussion of both old and new. He is the same old boy as before. I asked him about Pernille Moe. Well, she has now married a widower . . . he said with his usual smile. Instantly he asked me about Samonie Vinjevold. I answered like this—She is all right. She isn't like your sweetheart, she isn't married, she is my sweetheart for ill and good.

Well, I will always remember the year 1896 as the most remarkable year I have lived as far as getting my way, and then there was also reconciliation between Birgitte Samonie Vinjevold and myself, that was the best of all. I was freed of much bother from my conscience. . . .

I presume that you will settle down at home now. I think that is the most sensible thing to do. And there are, of course, plenty of girls to choose between and . . . it seems to me you ought to go for Synneve Myklebust, that would be a sensible choice, I think.

What I will find to get in on this summer I don't know. I am thinking about going to Rossland, "east of mountain" as we say here in Seattle. Geo Turner has a rich gold mine there and I could get a job. I also have an aspiration to be Fish Commissioner, and if that should be, then I would have to resign as a member of the legislature. A few days ago I sent in my application to the governor, and the day after I got an answer from him that was complimentary in the highest degree. He viewed me as being an especially conscientious person and well suited for Fish Commissioner. It is seldom that an applicant gets any answer unless his show is good. But the office won't be vacant before next year. It is about the best office in the government, pays $2,000.00 per year, and the term is for four years. There is no money to be earned in the legislature, so you can understand that I would like to get the above-mentioned office, but as I have been so lucky in the past year, I cannot kick if I don't get it. I will be moderate and content myself with what providence has in store for me.

In regard to the youth organizations, things are quieter than before. Two weeks ago I gave a lecture for Fremad on "Sixty Days in Olympia." I got a crowded house. . . .

Evenson, a Norwegian, was elected auditor and my scheming more than anything else was what made it possible for him to be nominated. A number of Swedes, of course, were hurt that I had my own way too much. That was to be expected. Many of the club people were also envious that I arranged it so that Augusta Stromberg got a good position. They can't stand to see anyone else getting along well. Her mother was Norwegian and she herself is Norwegian through and through and that is why I was interested in helping them along as best I could.

A friendly greeting from,
Hans Hansen

Hansen writes this letter in English, for reasons that he explains in the text. From this date onward, all his letters to Hans Øien are written in English. Spellings have been standardized and punctuation has been added where necessary for clarity. Posten was a West Coast Norwegian-American newspaper.

Seattle, Washington
June 19, 1898

My Dear Friend,

More than a year has gone by since I received your last letter, and not yet answered. I am inclined to think that you are somewhat in doubt about my feeling of contentment in such a long time of silence. Well, I must admit that I have not been in the best kind of humor, neither have I been in a state of despair; but not all . . . in political life goes on roses. The sorrows, the falsehoods, the contempt that you have to go through is certainly more burdensome than the name and honor you receive.

Of course I paid no attention to that . . . howl . . . *Posten* made against me, nor to the charges of the *Times* as they had to take it all back, but I did get sorry because the governor virtually gave me his pledge to make me the Fish Commissioner and was simply false to the bosom of his heart. His word was no good, and so far as that is concerned it is just as well, because John R. Rogers is a has-been, a dead contemptible politician of the Grover Cleveland brand, and it is no honor to serve under his administration. Of course, it is $2,000.00 a year in the office, that is a good thing I admit.

But the war with Spain has taken away a great deal of the people's attention to politics—but that war is a mere money-making scheme now, as it could have been all over if the McKinley administration had used our army and navy for that purpose. But as it is they are working it backwards when they can to increase the national debt to pay political debt and to promote sons of dead politicians, . . . men who never shouldered a rifle in their lifetime. For an honest man who is sharp enough to see into all the cheating and plunder that goes on in the name of patriotism it is a pity to look at, and then to see the masses of people who are ignorant about official hypocrisy, and how they pay taxes and honor to the traitors to their own country and think they are heroes and patriots. It is enough to make a man disgusted and give up the battle for reforms altogether, as it looks very much as if honesty has no reward after all, but yet there is a time coming when truth will prevail that is sure.
. . .

I met Geo Turner here in Sept. last. He then said he would let me have all the money I needed to go into the retail grocery business this spring as he by that time would be in such financial condition that he could afford to do so. But then the war came and upset things, so he has done nothing of that kind, yet I had a letter from him in the spring. He said he did not have the money just then, but I could use his credit if I wanted to and that would be just as well, but I would not do that, as I wanted to deal in and by cash, as I then know just where I stand all along. He told me in reply that he will prove himself to be as true to me as I was to him in his fight to reach the U.S. Senate, the ambition of his life. And he knows that he could never have got there except for the remarkable fight I made in his behalf, that really surprised the people all over the state. No, he never would have got there except for my sharpness to save him from the plot the opposition had made to kill him forever.

On the morning of Jan. 28 (the day before he was elected), Tobiassen from Whatcom came to me and asked me to quit to vote for Turner. He then told me that Turner's men attempted to bribe him the evening before and at rollcall he was going to throw his story on the joint assembly, and as my name was ahead of Tobiassen I should join in with the gang, change and vote for Dick Winsor. I stood in a hard pinch as I and Tobiassen were the only two Norwegians in the Legislature, and when he should make such testimony before the joint assembly and I yet voting for Turner, I would go down in history as a contemptible bribe taker of the lowest kind. As the people would believe Tobiassen, and take him to be honest and I to be a rascal of a man. But I pleaded and reasoned with Tobiassen as I never have done with man yet, and admonished such forceful influence on him, that when twelve o'clock came and the ballot was taken he never said one word and afterward he said he was glad that I prevailed on him to not do so. In the meantime I had notified Turner about the danger, and he came at once and saw me and as everything went quiet in the evening Turner got the caucus nomination and the next day was duly elected. Tobiassen kept still as he knew that I was honest in my support to Turner and to save my name from blackmail he kept his mouth shut. Otherwise Turner never would . . . be U.S. Senator, and so I should think Turner is to depend upon.

Since New Year I have been working in a furniture store, but after the fourth for a time of six weeks I intend to go to Fraser River and fish salmon. . . . I can't expect anything from Turner before he returns from Congress by the end of next month. He should now be in a fix to help me out as he has sold the Le Roi gold mine, of which he is one of the largest owners, his share is at least worth $350,000.00.

. . . Sivert has gone to Alaska to the gold fields. He went in March. I have had four letters from him since he left. He is in . . . a splendid company, with a good outfit, men strong and healthy, and knows how to go ahead so I am hopeful they will do well.

I am now living in Mathias's shanty and writing this letter on the old table as you have written letters yourself.

All these matters . . . are not the cause why I have not written to you, but it is a cause that I shall describe from now on, which has really troubled my mind to a great extent and is also the reason why I write this letter in English, as I then know that no one but yourself will ever be able to read it, and as I trust you to be a real man you will not give away more than you see to be well for the other folks to know.

I suppose you know all about my engagement to Birgitte Samonie Vinjevold, but for the last nine months everything has not been well between us. Remarkably enough, she seems to have got it into her mind that I am not true to her. It was a great surprise to me, and has caused both me and her a great deal of sorrow. The matter of fact is that I have been and shall be true to her, that I shall stand by her if even mountains fall. . . . No matter what happens she can sleep sound on my sincerity to her so long as life lasts. No earthly power can induce me to be false to a woman. Never! Never!

I do not really know how it happens, but it must come in this way that I wrote to her, just as I did to you, about my kindness to the Stromberg folks, and she must have thought that I am intimate with Augusta R. Stromberg, and on that acct. become jealous. But there has been nothing of that kind. I and them folks are great friends and with Augusta in particular, but not so that in any way or manner interferes with my true love to Birgitte what-so-ever.

If I had not been engaged to Birgitte, as I am, it might have been different, but you know that I am a true man, and deceive no one, particularly no woman, and as I think more of Birgitte Samonie Vinjevold than any one woman I ever met, why should I not stand by her, I never will go back on her.

But that Augusta Stromberg is a great girl, and I suppose no one on earth thinks more of me than she does. She was taught by Mathias in Sunday school, and in two weeks she will send you her picture in honor of Mathias, and in the letter and with that picture will also be a hair of Mathias which I found in his old dictionary. I am sure that it is his, as the hair is so light it could not be either mine or yours and no others than we three have ever used that book. I found that hair when I came back from Olympia. I lost it once on the table but found it again.

And now as I am to close I must go back to politics, it is in my nature and I can't help it, my religion and politics is the same. I . . . will not run for the legislature this year, so many of the Populists have gone to Alaska, and I do not believe that my district will return Populists this year. Although I will be stronger than any other man that can be put up. But I have concluded not to run. But during the evenings since New Year I have studied and written six articles to be published during the coming campaign. Article 1: The Danger Why Liberty May be Lost. Article 2: Direct Legislation. Article 3: Judicial Reform. Article 4: Financial Reform. 5. Government Ownership of Railways, Telegraph and Telephone. 6. Taxes and Ownership of Land. Each article will cover four columns in the *Times*, and I hope to get them published, one each Saturday, and also in the weekly, if not in the *Times* in some other papers. I shall send you copies, and it will open the eyes to good many half blind men when they are read, and those who scorn and despise me will have to admit that Hansen knows a thing and two.

I got into politics, and as I am strong and healthy everybody says I am a younger looking man than I was when you left here. I shall, if life and God prosper me, aspire to be governor of this state in the future to come. . . .

Hoping you forgive me for my long silence. I subscribe myself to be, truly your friend.

Hans Hansen

Seattle, Washington
July 4, 1898

My Dear Friend,

Augusta Stomberg sends you her picture and also . . . a letter out of respect to the memory of Mathias. You must answer her, do it in Norwegian, she can read it, but not write it very good. I also send you that hair of Mathias in an envelope. You must be careful and not lose it. I have marked where it was placed. I have had a letter from Geo Turner lately. He is my true friend and as soon as possible he will do what he has promised me, but it may be fall or winter before he has his Le Roi affair so adjusted that he can do it.

I have just had a letter from Birgitte Samonie Vinjevold. . . . I have sent her the Indian Consumption Cures. . . . If she does not know how to use the medicine you can read the receipts for her.

I shall go to Fraser River, New Westminster, to fish salmon tomorrow and will be back before the end of August. . . .

Sincerely yours,
Hans Hansen

Sivert Øien went to the gold fields in March 1898, and wrote this letter to his parents from Dawson City. The end of the letter is missing.

Dawson City [Yukon Territory]
July 24, 1899

Dear Parents,

Since it is a long time since you last heard from me and an even longer time since I heard from you, I will be the first to break the silence. I can report that I am in good health and have been the whole time since I came in here. As far as money is concerned it has gone rather badly until now, but I can't complain. There are many here who have done worse than I have. This summer I am busy prospecting my mining claim, which I took up last fall. Right now I am sinking two holes, the one is forty feet deep in the earth and the other just fifteen feet. I hope to find something soon, though it is uncertain. It could be that I will have all this hard work for nothing as so many others in here. . . . However, whether this works out or not, I will stay here next winter and it could be that next summer I will go out to Seattle and stay there awhile and look after my affairs.

The winters here are rather cold, last winter it was 67 degrees below zero at the coldest and then there were many who froze their hands and feet. I, for my part, stood the cold remarkably well. Last fall I built myself a good warm log house to live in. I worked in the mines every day all winter and I like it quite well. It is the first time in my life that I have worked underground. Everything goes quite smoothly here except that we have to cook and bake and fix our own food as well as wash and mend our own clothes. That is more than I am used to, so I am really sick of that kind of work, but I have to stand it as long as I am in here. It is very expensive to live here. It costs 500 dollars a year just for food, and in addition comes clothing, shoes, and tools. Last winter we had to pay $2.50 for a pound of butter, a dollar for a can of milk, and a dollar for a pound of sugar and so on. But I think it will be a little better next winter as there are several hundred men here and more food on the market. . . . [The end is missing.]

Hans Hansen writes from Minneapolis, where he has gone to see his fiancée, Birgitte Samonie Vinjevold.

Minneapolis, Minnesota
January 20, 1900

My Dear Friend,

Once more in life I am in Minneapolis, Minn. I got a free pass on the N.P.R.R. and have been here now for two weeks and in a few days I shall return to Seattle.

My chief reason for coming here was to meet Birgitte Vinjevold. . . . Truly we have agreed to disagree. We are not by any means fitted to be one, and we are both the best of friends just the same. After all I believe there is nothing lost on either side and so I shall feel pleased. It may look queer to you folks at home, but to me it do not and further I shall always prove myself to be truly her friend so long as life lasts.

Minneapolis has got some splendid buildings since I left here twelve years ago. Well! I would sooner live here than in Seattle, and if it was not for my connection with Senator Turner I would remain right here as I would have a good show politically in this state.

Yours sincerely,
Hans Hansen

This letter fragment from Hans Hansen is written in English on letterhead from Buchanan's Fish Co. in Seattle.

. . . Sam Stone stays with me in the old cabin. He will go to Alaska next spring. He is very much surprised to see me so cheerful and displaying such good temper in the midst of the time when my engagement is broken up, but the truth is simply this, that I am ripe in matters of common sense, and am hardly a crank on anything in life, and so as to women, let me say, "There are just as good fish in the waters as ever was caught."

I am enjoying excellent good health and am strong physically, morally, and mentally. I am not wearying myself with political matters, but I am not yet through with politics. If I live I shall be heard from yet. I shall send you in a couple weeks an article that I have written on the coming campaign. Hoping you will enjoy life at home, I am,

Yours sincerely,
Hans Hansen

Sivert writes to his parents from Seattle, as he is preparing to return to the Yukon.

Seattle, Washington
August 20, 1900

Dear Parents,

As I am almost ready to leave again for the promised land of gold, I will take this opportunity to send you a few lines. I can report that I am still well, though I was somewhat poorly a while ago, but now that is all over. I will leave Seattle the 25th of this month for Dawson City and there I will stay next winter if my health remains good, and next summer I intend to come back to Seattle again. My uncle has also taken a trip to Alaska now. He left this month and will return in the middle of next month. . . .

I can tell you that this is a lively time in this town, great changes have taken place since I was here last, a lot of fine buildings have gone up, so this city will be a great one in time. Its population is now 75,000. I am enclosing a little picture from the Klondike where I was last winter. You can see me standing on top of a pile of earth with my dog beside me. My dog's name is Rover and he is the best comrade that I have in there. He is now here in the city with me, too. A friendly greeting from your son,

S. P. Øien

Hansen tells Hans Øien how the Norwegian-Americans in Seattle celebrate Norwegian Constitution Day, the seventeenth of May.

Seattle, Washington
May 25, 1901

My Dear Friend,

It is a long time since I wrote to you and also a long time since I heard from you. I have hardly anything new to tell you. Not a thing of any particular interest has taken place since I wrote to you in those days when I was to get married.

I was to Alaska last summer and took up five fishing stations. I may likely go up this summer again. I enclose my article on the 17th of May published in the *Times*. Strange things happen in this world, now I and the *Times* are on good terms. . . . The common and church people celebrated the 17th of May this year and entirely outclassed the Norse Club. We had 3,500 people at Salmon Bay Park and over 1,000 in Germania Hall. Governor John R. Rogers as orator and a splendid program. I must send Rector Steen a copy of our celebration proceedings that he may know that the Norwegians on the Pacific Coast remember the 17th of May 9,000 miles from Norway.

My mind is still on the political atmosphere as usual, and it will be no surprise to those who know me that if I live and God prospers me I will some day be a candidate for governor and Congress. It is what I aim for, but I must try to improve myself financially first, and my adventures in Alaska are of a doubtful character, but shall you ever make anything you must take your chances on it. Sivert is in the Yukon yet. I had a letter from him three weeks ago. He is alright.

Last winter I was sick of La Grippe for two months and I was lucky I got over it, but now I am strong and as usual in splendid good health.

Yours most sincerely,

Hans Hansen

Sivert Øien tells more about life in the gold fields.

Bear Creek via Dawson City
August 2, 1901

Dear Brother Hans,

After nearly four years of silence I have now finally heard from you. . . . I see to my joy that you are all well there at home and I can report the same about myself. I almost thought for awhile that you had forgotten me, though that is not to be wondered at as I have gone so far away and never let myself be seen again. However, you are excused as I see from your letter that you have sent me three letters in this period of time, so I ask your forgiveness for the hard letter I sent you last summer. . . .

I see you are married now and have a little daughter, which I am very glad for, and I see that you have settled on our birthplace. . . . I was very surprised to find out that I am now an uncle. For a while it looked like that was something I would never be! One thing I will say is that both you and brother Peter have done the right thing in getting married. Now you can have a pleasant home, and I who live up here in the cold north and have to cook and clean and wash and do all my own housework before and after my daily work, I understand what that means. Of course I have only myself to take care of, but for all that I am beginning to get tired of it, so next summer I plan to leave here for good. If I hadn't speculated so much I would be 3,000 dollars better off today and then I would have gone out this summer, but nothing ventured, nothing gained, according to the old saying and that's the way it is with me. Be that as it may it was my own money that I have used and I will suffer the loss myself. Even so I am in good spirits as though I should have thousands. . . . It is hard to send money out from here. I have much more money in my pockets here than I would if I only had an opportunity to send it out.

I have no news that would interest you, especially as you are unfamiliar with conditions here. . . . This summer we have had rather warm weather, a good deal warmer than Seattle is in the summer. Now we are having a drought and the water is so low that we can't do anything, but I hope we will soon get rain. My old partner, Harsted, who you must remember from Seattle, is in here now, we worked together last winter on 33 Eldorado. He is there this summer, too. I will send you a little picture of me and my comrades from last spring when we were sluicing. You can see me standing and grinning. Harsted is standing a little ways behind me with a spade in his hand and the one next to me is the foreman. I am under him, the straw boss.

You must greet Father and Mother from me. Maybe I will come home and visit you in a year or two for a short time. You must tell them not to worry about me because I can take care of myself and I am in excellent health. A loving greeting from your far distant brother,

Sam P. Øien

Hans Hansen tells of his trip to Alaska.

Seattle, Washington
January 22, 1902

Dear Friend,

When I returned from Alaska I received your letter. . . . Sivert is in Alaska and him and Godø as you remember well has a claim together. I hope they do well. . . . Guttorm Osborg and Sam Stone, your old friend, are also here for the winter and likely to go to Alaska during the spring. I expect to do the same myself. I was there last summer, but next spring if I live and things go well for me I will also turn my attention to the gold fields. I am not going to Dawson but only 1,200 miles from here on the coast to a place called Yakutat Bay and the Alsek River. I hope to strike it well at said place both with gold and in the line of salmon fishing as salmon and cod-fish are very plentiful at those places.

I have nothing new to speak about from here, the church on 4th and Pine is still there and Fremad exists as usual. I also go there now as in former years. But the old congregation is split. . . .

Seattle is now a big city just as large as Minneapolis was when you left, and I predict that Seattle will be a bigger city than San Francisco in ten years. Alaska is a wonderful country and will be well settled in time with Norwegian people.

Yours very sincerely,

Hans Hansen

Sivert writes from his claim in the Yukon.

Hillside no. 16 below Bonanza,
Yukon Territory
April 6, 1902

Dear Brother Hans,

I received your last letter of Dec. 26, 1901, a few weeks ago, and I thank you so much for it. It is really nice to hear a little now and again from my childhood home. It brings back memories of my childhood. . . . You said in your last letter that you had sent me a photograph of Mother and Father, but I have not received it. The reason that I don't get your letters is that there is another person by the same name and he takes my letters and doesn't bring them back to the post office when he sees that they are not for him. If I could catch the fellow, I would really make things hot for him.

As far as myself goes, I am healthy and strong, going out and working a little every day. Right now we are getting ready for the sluicing and then it depends on how much gold dust we get. You must greet Father and Mother and say that I am well and lacking for nothing. Next time I leave here it will be for good. Maybe I will go outside and go into some kind of business. This is all I know to write about for this time.

You and your family are greeted from your far distant brother,

Sam P. Øien

Hans Hansen is ever the optimist with big plans for the future in this, the last full letter from him in this collection.

Juneau, Alaska
June 1, 1903

Dear Friend,

I am again on my journey to Yakutat where I expect to be during the summer. . . . Sivert is yet in Alaska and when he intends to come down I have not the least idea. Provided I do well this and next summer I will go to the Old Country myself and look over the old ground once more. . . . But if I do it will be with the object in view to travel over all of Norway and lecture over Alaska as the New Norway on the Pacific Coast, and then on my return to this country to write a book to be named *Six Months in Norway* with pictures of Norway's grandest sceneries, and a book of that kind would sell well in America because it would guide tourists and further the book would contain sketches of industrial, social, moral, religious, and political life in its real and true stages of advancement. Of course this is simply a plan and only God and time can tell what may happen. . . .

With my best regard and good wishes to you all I am

Sincerely yours,

Hans Hansen

In this letter Sivert tells of the death of his uncle, Hans Hansen. Sivert indicates that he hasn't communicated with his family since 1904, when his brother Knut died. Some pages may be missing from the letter.

Seattle, Washington
January 31, 1913

Dear Old Father,

Years have gone by since I sent you my last letter, and now it is my lot to send you similar news as the last time. . . .

I must inform you with sorrow that your dear brother and my uncle Hans died on the 18th of December, 1912, in Juneau, Alaska of . . . kidney disease, from which he had suffered for several years. Two years ago he spent a whole winter in a hospital in San Francisco, California, and since that time he has been poorly. He stayed here with me when he was in Seattle. He stayed with me last spring for six weeks and I could see then that he would not live long. I told him that he could stay with me as long as he liked but he wanted to go back to Alaska again, and I am sending you the same information about his death that I got.

When he lay in the hospital in San Francisco I helped him with money, as did Guttorm Osborg, and as you can imagine, he was not able to pay us back, but we can manage for all that. As far as what he left behind, you folks in Norway can send to Bolstad in Juneau after it, for I don't want to have anything to do with it. I have had enough of dealing with such things and the consequences of being called a thief and cheater. Uncle has nothing here in Seattle that I know of. The reason that I have not written to you before about his death is that I didn't know the cause of it, which I just got from Alaska three days ago. The telegram said nothing about that.

This is all I have to say for this time, other than that I and my family are well. We have just one child, James, and he is doing well.

In case you wish to answer my letter, I will enclose a stamp. Greetings from your son and family,

Sam P. Øien

The friends who cared for Hans Hansen in his last days wrote this letter to Sam Øien. He must have sent the letter to his family in Norway.

Juneau, Alaska
January 3, 1913

Dear Sir,

I have received your letter of December 24, in which I see that you desire information about your uncle. We have been waiting for a letter from you so that we could let you know the situation. He had stayed with me since he came to Juneau and that did not cost him anything. He got sicker all the time, but I couldn't convince him to go to the hospital. The day before he died we had to take him up there anyway, but he didn't think he was going to die because he said he was getting better every day. I and J. N. Wahl took him up there. He didn't say anything to us about anything. He told us that he had $24 in one place and $90 in another place. We two and the nurse at the hospital looked in all his clothes and found nothing and when we came home we found $25.65 in his bed in a little purse. He had a cord around his waist and a red handkerchief tied to it which the undertaker found and in that he had $40 so altogether it was $65.65 but that wasn't enough for the funeral and the doctor so we took up a collection and gave him a fine funeral for he was entitled to that and we had enough money left to buy a little stone and set on his grave and fix the grave up.

The reason Vallantine sent the telegram was that in the first place, he was a friend of his and in the second, he is a business man here so the telegram would come to us right away and he helped us open the mail for he had lots of mail at the Circle City Hotel so we had someone with us to witness everything and we directed his funeral. He was buried December 21. He died quietly and peacefully, he just wanted to sleep. We asked him if he had any pain, he said no. He died at two o'clock in the morning so we were not able to be with him at the last, but he talked to us before we left him. Concerning his effects we have no knowledge. He had two telescope satchels here at my place. We have not gone through them other than to take off the locks and see that they are full of books and papers and letters, and we can send them to you whenever we hear from you that you will pay for the sending for we have done the best we can.

I suppose that you have an idea of what his illness was, so I don't need to tell you about that. We wonder if you know the date he was born and the year, so that we can put it on his gravestone. That is all I have to tell you.

Sincerely,

P. Bolstad

J. N. Wahl

NOTES

1. Ragnar Standal, *Mot nye heimland: Utvandringa frå Hjørundfjord, Vartdal og Ørsta* (Volda, Norway, 1985), 328–29, 369–70, 612–13.

2. Thos. Ostenson Stine, *Scandinavians on the Pacific, Puget Sound* (Seattle, 1900), 83–84.

3. Standal, *Mot nye heimland*, 613.

7

A Chicago Mother

Bergljot Anker Nilssen, 1923–1929

*L*ike Gunnar Høst, Bergljot Anker Nilssen came from an urban professional mi-
lieu. She was born Bergljot Karla Kjæregaard in the Norwegian town of
Fredrikshald (later called Halden) in 1891. Her father was a schoolteacher and
principal, her sisters and brothers became dentists and engineers. Bergljot helped her
father care for the family after her mother died in 1911, and then she worked in
several white-collar jobs before attending teacher's college. She and Karl Nilssen
were friends before he went to America in 1910. After several years, he returned to
Norway and they were married in 1915. They then emigrated to Superior, Wisconsin, but returned to Norway again in 1917. Karl worked for a time in Hamar,
where their son, Jens Trygve—often referred to as "Lillegutt" (Little Boy) in her
letters—was born. The Nilssens decided to return to the United States, and Karl left
in 1922 for Chicago, where he found a job as an engineer. Bergljot and their small
son followed in 1923.[1]

The letters reveal Bergljot Anker Nilssen's delight in her home and children,
her interest in their activities, and her concern for her family, both in the United
States and in Norway. She wrote faithfully and cheerfully to her in-laws, giving
them warm and intimate glimpses of family life. Her letters show a middle-class,
educated, urban family on the rise, moving from one apartment to another, to ever
better neighborhoods, and finally to a single-family home, a new brick bungalow.
She tells of buying a lot on a lake, the children's education, piano lessons, symphony
concerts, and visiting with other middle-class Norwegians as well as with American
friends.

In comparisons with Norway, Chicago and America generally come out
ahead, and she hints broadly to her brother-in-law, Eigil, that "there is plenty of
work for architects here in Chicago." The hints succeeded, for Eigil and his wife
eventually joined them in Chicago. Bergljot makes several cryptic references to some

157

unhappy experience in Hamar, which apparently was one of their motivations for moving back to the United States.

In 1929 Bergljot was operated on for cancer, but the doctors at the Norwegian-American hospital in Chicago informed her husband that she probably had only a year to live, and they recommended that she visit her father in Norway. She brought the two children, Jens and Evelyn, with her to Norway in 1929. Jens was then about ten and Evelyn three and a half. Bergljot died there in February of 1930.

The very first letter in this collection was written while Bergljot and "Lillegutt" were still aboard ship on their way to join Karl in Chicago. Her voyage was very different from that described by earlier immigrants, such as Berta Serina Kingestad.

S.S. *Stavangerfjord*
June 4, 1923

Dear Parents-in-law,

This evening we will arrive in New York, but we won't go ashore until early tomorrow. We have had a wonderful trip. It was stormy several days, but by then Lillegutt and I were so used to the sea that we didn't get sick. It is fun to be on the ocean when you don't get sick. . . . There are many pleasant people on board, and several times they have shown movies and had entertainment with singing, and yesterday was the Captain's dinner. It was very festive. Lillegutt is doing just fine, he has gotten better on the trip, but one day he was so unlucky as to fall down and hurt himself a little bit, but he got a cold compress, and is now all right again. I have been watching him all the time, but he moves quickly. It will be good to get him on land again.

On account of the new immigration laws, 400 people were held back in Kristiania, so there is lots of space on board. Lillegutt and I live and eat in first class. . . .

I am a bit nervous about tomorrow . . . even though I can manage the language. It is much worse for those who can't talk. The trip could easily have lasted for eight more days, it has been so lovely. We have been lying on deck sunning ourselves all day long, and have really had a nice time. Hearty greetings to all of you.

Yours,
Bergljot

Bergljot Anker Nilssen and Lillegutt (Jens Trygve). Probably taken at Long Lake, Illinois, ca. 1926. Photo courtesy Jens T. Anker.

3306 Fullerton Ave
Chicago, Illinois
June 18, 1923

Dear All of you,

Hope you are all well when you get this letter. Now the heat has come, and I am glad our house is more or less in order. Karl had rented the apartment and bought some furniture before we came. Karl and Lillegutt didn't recognize each other. Karl has a good position now, and he likes the new place very much. He has been there about three weeks. He leaves here about 7:30 in the morning and gets back at about 6:00, and of course they get an hour for lunch. I am glad Karl likes it so much. Yesterday we visited Thora Korsmo (she is a Nilssen) in Elgin. We took the electric train, which takes about two hours. The Korsmos have a car, and we drove around and then had a picnic together with some others. . . .

Our apartment unfortunately is located on a busy street with streetcars and many automobiles, so Lillegutt can never go out the door alone. Lots of Jews live around here. The apartment is beautiful and easy to care for, but it isn't so nice for Lillegutt. This morning we have been to a playground for children. It is in a large park where everything is arranged for children, with all kinds of toys for them. Lillegutt liked it very much, so we will go there often. The last place Karl lived was with an architect named Peterson. He and his wife are both Americans and they don't understand Norwegian. We are together with them a lot. They have a boy who is five years old. Lillegutt speaks Norwegian and Bernhard English and they play wonderfully together. . . .

Today it is terribly hot, so the letter will reflect that. I will write more, and more clearly, when it gets cooler. Lillegutt speaks of you often, but he doesn't want to go back to Norway, he says. He knows a number of words, and understands everything, so I hope it goes quickly for him. Then we will speak only English here at home. Write soon. Hearty greetings.

Yours,

Bergljot and Lillegutt

Chicago, Illinois
September 9, 1923

Dear Mother- and Father-in-law and Adda,

Many thanks for your letter, Mother-in-law. You ask if we got a house close to the office where Karl works, but Karl works down in the center of the city in a twenty-story building. There is terrible traffic down there and only stores and offices, so no one lives there. Karl takes the elevated train to the office and back. It takes about half an hour, exactly 35 minutes. We like it

Evelyn Grace and Jens Trygve Anker Nilssen. Chicago, Illinois, ca. 1925. Photo courtesy Jens T. Anker.

very much in Chicago. I am glad we came to America and we don't envy you who have to move to Kristiania. It is so unpleasant there, but I hope you won't be disappointed. . . .

We have gotten into a pleasant group of Norwegians. The Norwegians here are better educated than in Superior [Wisconsin]. We get together with a number of engineers. Two weeks ago on Sunday Thora Korsmo . . . and Ester . . . were here from Elgin. They were so enthused about our apartment and how we had fixed it up. Saturday we went to my cousin outside of Morris. It was the first time we have been on a farm in America. They met us with the car in Morris. The farm is a little ways outside of town. There was a big old-fashioned house with big old trees around it. It was a beautiful place, I would never have believed it could be so pretty. They raise mostly maize (sweet corn) and hogs. My cousin was very sweet and pretty. They have five children. Her husband is of Swedish descent, and spoke excellent Swedish and was very attentive and entertaining. Sunday we drove to Morris in the afternoon and drove around in the area. . . . [The rest is missing.]

Chicago, Illinois
October 21, 1923

Dear Parents-in-law and Adda,

Many thanks for the letters. . . . It is cold here now, but we have had a lovely fall. The fall is almost the best time here in America. Lillegutt is very well, and he eats well too. We hope he is getting used to the climate. He does not go to kindergarten anymore. He went for two weeks, but apparently the children laughed at his Norwegian clothing, so now he is very particular about what he puts on. His language has deteriorated. He mixes Norwegian and English, and has a wonderful American accent.

. . . We are fine. The days go so quickly. Karl leaves here at 7:30 in the mornings and isn't home before around 6:00 in the evening. I always have enough work to do. Monday, washing, Tuesday, ironing, and every day enough to do. Three lodgers make a lot of work even if they only get breakfast. But they are nice, kind young men, and they seem to like it here. . . .

Lillegutt says such funny things. The other day he said to Karl that it was nicer to be in Fredrikshald than in America, but you know we have to be here. He talks about you all the time, and remembers all kinds of things you have said and done. It's a long time since we heard from you, but we expect letters more often, now that you have . . . fewer to write to. Karl is always worn out, so there will be no letter writing for him, so you'll have to make do with my letters. Hearty greetings.

Yours,
Bergljot

Bergljot's brother Skjalg has joined them in Chicago.

Chicago, Illinois
December 4, 1923

Dear All,

Thanks for your letter, Mother-in-law, which I just received. According to the newspaper, this letter should reach you by Christmas if it is sent from here today. Karl wrote a letter several days ago. We have had a wonderful, mild fall, though there have been several cold days. I have hung the wash out every single Monday, and gotten it dry, but yesterday it didn't work, unfortunately. Fall is the nicest season in Chicago.

Lillegutt uses his Norwegian stockings without saying anything, and I am glad that I have several pairs for him, but he is very fussy about all his other clothes. Everything has to be bought in America. He has gotten a new winter coat and hat. He doesn't want to use his old coat when he is out playing in the yard, and even less when he is on the street. He keeps a sharp lookout that he has clothes like the others. Thanks for being willing to knit stockings for him. He has black boots, so black is best. . . .

Helga is so kind, and we are together with them a lot. Karl likes her husband. They have interests in common and are in the engineering society together. You ask in your letter if we like it here in Chicago, or if we are only saying it to comfort you. Well, we like it very much—in spite of the fact that it is a dirty city and very noisy. In the long run, one might get worn out here, and one wastes a lot of time on the elevated train and the streetcars. And if you want to go somewhere, you can't walk like at home, because the distances are too great. The people are nice here, and fortunately there is no snobbery like at home. I get quite sick at the thought of all those unpleasant people. When Norwegians get together here, they always say our country is "all right" but that it is good for people to get over here a little. If we hadn't been at Hamar, we might not have seen it that way perhaps. Most people have it easy at home, here we have to struggle for our existence a little bit.
. . .

The other day I was on Milwaukee Avenue together with Mrs. Jørgensen (Lillegutt wasn't along, so don't worry). We jumped when five revolver shots were fired not many steps from us. It was full of pedestrians, cars, streetcars, so we couldn't see anything, but the traffic simply continued on its way, no one cared about what had happened.

This evening Skjalg is coming here. I am so glad that he got into the country. Supposedly they are stricter now at letting people into the United States. It looks like we are getting bad times here, but many believe it will get better by spring. Lillegutt is well and has grown. He says so many strange things. One evening after he had gone to bed, he started to cry and say, "You mustn't die, Mommy, before I grow up. Eat lots of salt herring, so you will live a long time." He had heard Mrs. Jørgensen say a long time ago that it was good for you to eat salt herring. He has stopped saying "Papa" and "Mama." Now it is "Daddy" and "Mommy."

This will be a pleasant Christmas for you. . . . We haven't sent you any Christmas presents this year, as much as I wanted to. But I will wish you all a very merry Christmas and a happy New Year—with thanks for the old year! Karl is well, though he is working hard, but he likes his post. Hearty greetings from Lillegutt and me.

Bergljot

In Norway, December 23 is known as "Little Christmas Eve."

Chicago, Illinois
January 15, 1924

Dear Parents-in-law and Adda,

Many thanks for your letter written on December 18. It just came now, and I am writing immediately for it sounds as though you are worried about us, and that you think we are not well. But that is completely unnecessary, for we lack for nothing and are all fortunately healthy. Before and during Christmas things were in a bad way here, we all had colds, one after the other. . . . On Little Christmas Eve Karl stayed in bed . . . and Lillegutt stayed in bed a few days, too. Luckily I managed to stay up. Now we are all fine again—you have to expect to get a few colds during the winter.

Skjalg is living here, he has been sleeping in the dining room, but today I gave notice to one of our roomers, as I didn't like him, and so Skjalg will get his room. It was too much with so many. Next winter I hope we don't have any roomers, for it is a lot of work, even if they only get breakfast, but what won't the German do for money, as the saying goes.

Lillegutt has started kindergarten every afternoon. I have promised him a tricycle this summer if he will go there, so now he never misses a day. I have to take him there and fetch him. It is so pleasant down there—two teachers play with the children, and they learn to bow and behave themselves. Lillegutt knows a little Norwegian girl there, so now he likes kindergarten. He has gotten good in English. Today he said, "Jeg har en sweetheart og det er Aunt Adda in Norway." He speaks English and Norwegian on top of each other. You would laugh if you heard him. He has gotten so tall, he is one of the tallest in the kindergarten.

Karl likes it very much in America, so he never regrets leaving Norway. You have to work more here, but then you feel better, you don't get tramped on, like we were in Hamar. I am so glad that time is over! I have gotten an American friend, Mrs. Vanderworth. She has a little boy, Kane. It is so much fun to be with Americans, for you learn so much. . . . The apartment here is cold, so I don't think we will stay here next winter. But it has been cold this winter, colder than for twenty years, they say. Now we are having summer weather again, so it goes up and down.

Many thanks for the money you sent to Lillegutt. We bought a sled for him. . . . Americans are generous with Christmas presents, so Lillegutt got gifts from all his friends. He got a desk and chair, which he uses every day. I don't think you should try to knit stockings for him this year. But if you want to knit some at some later time, there won't be so much duty to pay if you write the value on the package as low as possible when you send them. . . .

One of my roomers is engaged to a woman in Norway, and I got a beautiful embroidered and crocheted tablecloth sent from her for Christmas. I got a card from his father, so I was quite touched by all the attention.

Hope you are all well. Hearty greetings.

Yours,

Bergljot

Chicago, Illinois
February 27, 1924

Dear Parents-in-law,

It's awhile now since I heard from you, but I hope that you are well. Fortunately we have recovered from our colds, but this winter Lillegutt and I have had colds continuously. The doctor says it is because of the change in climate. . . . It was the same for Karl last winter. Lillegutt had a terrible earache one night. Poor little thing, it hurt so much, but now he is just fine. He goes to kindergarten every day. I wish you could hear him tell about school. His language is so strange, he mixes the languages, but at school or when he is with Americans, he speaks only English. He has gotten a new winter suit, so now he is dressed in American clothes. Only his cap is Norwegian, but his teacher praised his cap, so it is "all right" for him.

We have had terribly cold weather this winter, but now it is beautiful, and the sun is shining into the livingroom. We have a nice apartment, and have made it really pleasant. But I don't want to stay here another winter. We don't have a basement, as there is a store on the first floor, and they use the basement for storage. So I have to wash clothes in the kitchen, and also have to dry them there, and that is very unhealthy. The washing machine (electric) is excellent, and when I wash every Monday, it isn't such hard work.

Skjalg is living here, and we have rented out the third bedroom to two boys from Stavanger, so there is enough to do in the house. But my brother will soon go East or South, as there is not much textile industry in Chicago, though he has had work since the second day he came. Karl is rather nervous, but is otherwise healthy. We haven't been to Elgin since November. . . . I hope we can make it this summer. It would be good for Karl to get out of Chicago a bit.

Hearty greetings to both of you and Adda. Greet everyone!

Yours,

Bergljot

Chicago, Illinois
April 16, 1924

Dear Parents-in-law

Many thanks for the letter. It is so good to hear that you are all well, and that you like it in Kristiania. But I think I would long for the garden in Fredrikshald. Father-in-law especially must miss the garden he worked in every spring. Maundy Thursday and Good Friday are this week, but we keep on working. We only get Easter Sunday off, so there is no rest during Easter. . . . Lillegutt got a tricycle today, so he is practicing this evening in the kitchen.

April 24. This letter didn't get sent, so I will finish it now. On Saturday evening before Easter we were with some Norwegians. . . . We are together with many pleasant people, but we seldom go away, and never have anyone here during the week. We cultivate our social life on Saturday evening and Sunday. On weekdays only the ladies visit each other.

My brother is now working in South Chicago, so unfortunately he doesn't live here anymore. He is earning well, and that is wonderful. I have four renters in all now—so there is lots to do and in this country they change sheets and pillow cases every week, and they are supposed to get two terry cloth towels every week, so I have a rather big wash on Mondays. Karl has just found out that he gets eight days of vacation this summer, and he is happy about that. But he is quite worn out, so he needs it. . . .

Saturday we are going to Elgin and staying until Sunday. It is always so pleasant at Thora's, you can't imagine a finer person. . . . Helga Hansen is together with lots of people from Fredrikshald—I never knew that Fredrikshald people were such terrible gossips! So if you want to know about silver smuggling or other smuggling in Norway, it isn't difficult to find out about it here. . . .

Karl never writes letters, but leaves it to me to take care of. A person gets quite restless here in the big city, and so it seems that I never get time to sit down and write. Lillegutt really likes it here now. Everyone says he has changed so much since last year. He is the tallest in kindergarten, and has gotten quite plump now. He hasn't had hives here in Chicago, so the climate seems to be excellent for him. Hearty greetings to all of you from all of us.

Yours,

Bergljot

Chicago, Illinois
May 20, 1924

Dear Parents-in-law and Adda,

Many thanks for the letter! I hope your arthritis gets better when the weather gets warmer, Mother-in-law. We have had a cold spring. Today, the 20th of May, we have a fire in the stove and are using winter clothes. We have had a few warm days, but then it got unbearably cold. . . .

Yesterday Karl went to Evanston and Highland Park on company business—it was absolutely beautiful, he said. Only rich people live out there. So now he has decided to buy a lot and build a summer house in Long Lake. . . . The lots are going up in price everywhere around Chicago, so it doesn't pay to wait. . . .

Helga Hansen has joined the Free Church here in Chicago. And there are some pretty strange things happening there. One of the people who is big in the Free Church was after me several times, but I had to say to him that I would never join. We have been visited by several Norwegian pastors, but we will see where we end up living before we join. I like an English Lutheran church better than many of the Norwegian ones.

May 24. The letter wasn't sent. Thanks for the letter you sent for my birthday. I don't understand how you can remember all the birthdays, Mother-in-law. That is my weak point. Skjalg came here this morning at 9:00 but went to Kensington at noon. He is living in Kensington and working at Ford's factory in "Ford City"—about two hours' journey from here. He had night work, and so came up here without sleeping and then back again to work. He makes good money, but works terribly hard, poor boy. . . . I have always read that working conditions at Ford were supposed to be so ideal, but things must have changed since he got to be a rich man.

Tomorrow, Sunday, between 6:30 and 7:00, we will drive with the Brynildsens to Long Lake to find the lot. We will also look at a house that is for sale there. The Brynildsens are from Fredrikshald, fine, pleasant people. They have lots of money, a house in Chicago—near Long Lake, and two cars.

. . . Karl likes it at the office and he is looked up to and admired, and that is just what he needs after the experience at Hamar. Karl even came home and said that the boss of the factory came with some work for him, and said that it was difficult and so he didn't think the others could do it, so Mr.

Nilssen had to take it. Karl gets all the difficult assignments at the office, and he has to supervise the two others. Karl won't like it that I am writing this, but after what happened at Hamar, it will be fun for you to hear it.

Lillegutt now has a whole bunch of little girls to play with. He speaks English with a vengeance. I will try to write more often. Karl never writes letters, so you will have to be satisfied with hearing from me. Hearty greetings to all of you.

Yours,

Bergljot

Chicago, Illinois
June 17, 1924

Dear Parents-in-Law and Adda,

It is such a long time now since we heard from you, so I hope you are all well. We haven't had any summer yet. One day it can be terribly hot, and the next day can be winter weather again, but sometime it will have to get warm this year, too. On Friday Lillegutt will be finished with school. Thursday the kindergarten will have a big party. Everyone will bring ten cents, and the teacher will buy ice cream and cake for the children. Yes, in this country they have fun in school. The big children put on a comedy and danced. They learn to behave and to perform from an early age, and the children aren't any more difficult than Norwegian children. In February Lillegutt will start first grade, so in the fall he will continue with kindergarten. He plays outside all day now. His playmates are all Jewish. A little girl, Luzille, comes and wakes him every morning. I am happy that the boy is thriving, and he looks well. Last year he couldn't talk to the children, so he was lonely, and then I felt sorry for him.

No doubt you have read in the papers about the bad times we are having here now. Lots of people are unemployed. It is not like in Norway, where you get three months' notice. Here you have to leave the same day. Karl is secure where he is. He is the next one after the head engineer, so the others would have to go before he would.

In the next letter I will tell you more about our summer plans. We still haven't decided for sure, but for now we are planning to buy a lot on Long Lake. Hearty greetings to you all.

Yours,

Bergljot

Chicago, Illinois
September 14, 1924

Dear Parents-in-Law,

It is a very long time now since we heard from you, but I hope that everything is fine. We are having a cold fall and have already had a fire in the stove. Usually the fall here is warm and pleasant — the best time of year — but this year it won't be. We are trying to get another apartment, as this one is very cold during the winter. It is terribly hard work to try to get an apartment here in Chicago, where the distances are so great. First you have to look at apartments that are advertised, and then there are many that are not advertised, but only put a sign in the window. So now Lillegutt and I have traipsed up and down the streets for over a week. We would like to live around Logan Square close to Humboldt Park. We also have to rent out a couple of rooms this winter, and around here that isn't hard to do. The apartments are terribly expensive. I hope that next winter we can move to another neighborhood. More and more Jews are moving in here.

As you know, we are having bad times here, but things are beginning to get better. Karl has been very busy this summer, but now he is in the engineering division again. My brother Skjalg was called back to Ford again after having worked rather hard on a farm this summer. He is earning well now, but working hard. No, here in this county you just have to hang in there and work hard, there is no use in striking and loafing.

Lillegutt has gotten so tall, and he never speaks Norwegian any more. If we ask him to speak Norwegian, he can't do it. We haven't sent him to kindergarten as we are going to move, and he may have to go to a different school. He will start first grade in February and then he will be six years old. We are thinking about sending him to an English church for Sunday school, as it can be hard enough for him to manage in one language. . . .

Why does Adda never write? I hope that you are all well, and that you are comfortable in Kristiania. . . . Hearty greetings from us.

Yours,

Bergljot

Chicago, Illinois
October 10, 1924

Dear Parents-in-law,

We haven't heard from you since the last time I wrote, hope you are all well. Poor Eigil, who is out of work, I surely hope he has gotten something now. Karl started in a new position on Monday. He really likes it there. They get dinner at the office every day, so that is really nice. Lillegutt and I go apartment hunting every day, but we still haven't found one we like. . . .

Saturday and Sunday we are going to Long Lake. We call our house there Sunny Hill. You can see a bit of how it looks in the pictures. It is painted yellow — almost creamy yellow with brown trim. The colors are beautiful. We are now going to plant trees and dig up the garden. Karl has almost finished making shutters and storm doors for the winter. . . . Karl loves the house in Long Lake, and wants to go there every week while the weather is still somewhat good. . . .

We can learn to make all kinds of things in night school. Mrs. Ingolfsrud and I have been going and learning millinery for a month now. I have sewn myself a very elegant black velvet hat. It is so pretty you could believe it was a model from Marshall Fields. When we have finished learning millinery, we can learn to make lamp shades and then dressmaking. It is so much fun to learn to help oneself.

Why does Adda never write? It would be fun to hear from her. Hearty greetings from us all,

Yours,

Bergljot

Chicago, Illinois
January 18, 1925

Dear Parents-in-law,

Many thanks for the letter, which we received yesterday. I see that you must not have gotten my long letter with the description of our new apartment, so I will tell a bit about it again. All the rooms are much larger than in the one we had before, except for the kitchen, which is small, but much cozier than the old one. The apartment is modern (six rooms) and really nice. We have no less than five large clothes closets, and three of them are like small rooms. Everything has been fixed up, but it is a lot to keep clean. The owner lives on the first floor; he has a delicatessen . . . and he takes care of the heat, so that is nice and simple. Now they are painting the hallway, and he is laying a rubber rug in the stairway and hall, so it will be easy to keep clean. Lillegutt has only three or four blocks to Mozart School. . . . It is much safer for him here. He will begin school in earnest in the first grade in February. Last Sunday was his first day at Sunday school. He started in the Norwegian church — Zion Church — just one block from here. The religious instruction is in English.

We have started teaching Lillegutt to speak Norwegian, but it is difficult for him. He mixes the languages terribly, and speaks Norwegian with an American accent, so it is quite funny to listen to him.

All the children at Helga Hansen's have the measles, and there are sick children in every other house in Chicago. I hope Lillegutt escapes the measles this year. My brother Skjalg was here for Christmas Eve and Christ-mas Day, and we had a really nice time. Yesterday he went to Buffalo to get into his own line of work. All winter he has been in South Bend—a town of about 90,000—three hours from Chicago.

January 28. My letter didn't get finished. Skjalg has now gotten a po-sition in his own line of work, and is in Worcester, Mass. Times are very bad in this country now, the newspapers promise great things for 1925. Toward spring, it will no doubt get better. Poor Eigil, who is out of work. For engi-neers and architects there is plenty of work in Chicago, but he can't get into this country, and to you, America means something terrible. . . . But for me, America is preferable to Norway. If you are out of work and having a hard time here, no one knows about it, while at home, it is a topic of discussion for everyone. Karl is now going to a night class to become an American citizen. Since the war many offices require you to be a citizen in order to work there.

. . . Lillegutt is completely wrapped up in school now. You should hear him tell about the presidents. He recites them one after the other, and we have to read about them to him. He says that he will write to you as soon as he learns to write. Fortunately, he has been well all winter. Now he has two little Norwe-gian boys to play with, so I hope he is finished with having Jewish friends. The Jewish children are sweet and pretty, but their homes are not clean.

On January 10 Karl was in bed with a cold. . . . He was in bed for three days, but now he is quite well again. People have been so sick with colds this winter, they have been sick for weeks. But Karl took it in stride. The Christmas magazine and the books for Lillegutt came just before Christmas—many thanks for all of it. Greetings from all of us.

Yours,

Bergljot

Bergljot has had a baby girl, named Evelyn.

Chicago, Illinois
October 25, 1925

Dear Mother-in-law,

Happy birthday! I hope you will have a healthy and happy year. Many thanks for your last letter. Karl said he would write, but nothing ever comes of his letter writing. Luckily all four of us are healthy. I have been rather tired, but if I take it easy I will soon get my strength back again. Baby is very good, and seems to be thriving. She hasn't disturbed us one single night yet. I thought that Lillegutt was good, but Baby is even better and calmer. She smiles and talks in her own way, and is really sweet. I talked with Lillegutt's teacher the other day, and she said he is one of the smartest boys in the class.

We study with him every evening, which I think is excellent. Karl is eager to study with him, and he is the one who does it mostly since "Sister" came. I really want him to do well in school. But he is certainly not musical. He sings "My Country 'Tis of Thee" and many other songs with a vengeance, but so terribly off key that it is awful to listen to.

. . . How is Eigil doing? Here in Chicago there is lots of work for architects. Hearty greetings to Father-in-law and Adda and yourself.

Yours,

Bergljot

With this letter, Bergljot begins referring to her son as Jens instead of Lillegutt.

Chicago, Illinois

February 7, 1926

Dear Parents-in-law,

Now we have all had colds, one after the other. Evelyn was quite sick last week. Doctor Dohrmann examined her, but she was all right, it was just a cold. She is a very strong baby, he said. Now she is well again. She is seven months old, and has gotten a high chair for the occasion and has been sitting in it for quite a little while. We are having dangerous weather this winter, first it is freezing cold, and then summery. There has been lots of sickness this year, the doctor said. Karl has gotten glasses. They are good for his eyes, he says. In any case, they suit him admirably. Jens has now moved up to second grade. In the schools here they move up in February. He has gym, and is learning writing and arithmetic. He will soon be able to write to you. He has managed to avoid getting colds this winter.

We are thinking about moving in a few months. It is tiring to have such a large apartment and renters, especially when I have to do everything myself. Every week I do a large washing and ironing. I would like to have less to do, and the children take up so much time, for in a big city they have to be watched closely. I am looking forward to getting a smaller apartment, three or four rooms and a kitchen. We are thinking of moving a little out of Chicago, but it isn't certain. . . .

We are wondering how things will go for Adele and Eigil. It must be terrible to be out of work. There are wonderful opportunities for architects here in Chicago now. I really hope they come over, then we will be a big family over here. Hope you are both well and that Mother-in-law's leg is better. Karl sends greetings.

Yours,

Bergljot

Chicago, Illinois
April 16, 1926

Dear Parents-in-law,

Every day we are waiting to hear from you, but nothing comes. We write to you more often than we hear from you. Hope you are all well. Next week we are going to move. Our new address will be 4343 Schubert Avenue. We will be living in the third house from Kelvyn Park—on Schubert Avenue. It will be one and a half blocks from Kelvyn Park School. It will be very nice out there for the children. We will live on the second floor—six rooms—that is, five rooms and kitchen—veranda outside the living room and veranda outside the kitchen. We had not intended to rent out any rooms, but Mr. Dahl who lives with us now asked if he could stay with us until he gets married in a year. Lillegutt will get his own room, and he is very excited about that. Evelyn is so chubby and nice, and an unusually good little child.

Has Eigil heard whether he will come over here? A young lady from Kristiania applied in January to come over, and was supposed to find out in April if she could come in August—so Eigil should also find out in April. We have been to a party with a Norwegian-American minister . . . who is a teacher at the Bible School in Oslo. Everything was bad in Norway, he said, and spoke so awfully about Norway, so he ought to be denied permission to enter the country.

Fortunately, we are all well, we have had a few colds this winter, but nothing else. Evelyn already has three teeth. She says Mama and Papa. She tries to stand in her bed. We have summer and winter weather one day after the other, everyone is hoping for more stable weather, one gets so tired of the long, cold winters in Chicago. Many greetings to all. . . .

Yours,

Bergljot

Chicago, Illinois
July 12, 1926

Dear Parents-in-law,

Many thanks for the letter that just arrived. It is too bad to hear that you are so bothered by arthritis, Mother-in-law, but the summer heat should help a bit. I surely hope that Eigil will hear by July 15 whether or not he will be admitted to the States, and that we will hear the results as soon as possible, as we are very eager. Has Adele applied to come over? She surely knows that the law is rather strict, so even if Eigil is over here, it won't help her to get into the country.

Karl has not been terribly well all spring and summer. He has just had X-rays of his teeth—two have been pulled that were infected in the roots. Two others were also infected, and he will get them pulled on Thursday. The dentist thought he would feel much better, as so much can come from bad teeth. . . .

It was unbearably hot on Evelyn's birthday. The newspapers said it was the hottest day in ten years. We had three mamas here with three babies. Evelyn didn't understand what was going on, and took a nap just as the guests arrived, but Lillegutt thought it was fun that she had her birthday during the heat so he could have ice cream. He is outside all day playing in the Kelvyn Park playground where they have all kinds of equipment. The park is beautiful, with many shade trees, and here in Chicago you can walk on the grass, not like at home in Norway where you can only walk on the paths. Karl was off on the 4th of July, of course, and we took a picnic lunch to the park and stayed all day.

Fortunately the traffic around the park has gotten better. When we first moved here, we were worried about the way the cars speeded around here. Everybody talked about it, but nobody did anything about it. Lillegutt came home one day and reported that a boy in his class had been run down right outside the school. Karl composed a letter to the Chicago police, and I wrote and signed it. They pay more attention to complaints from ladies in this country. I got a letter from the chief of police—two detectives came to investigate, and they promised to fine the speeders so that the speeding on Kostner Avenue would be stopped. One evening when Lillegutt and I were out walking, we saw two cops arresting one car after the other. Lillegutt was wild with excitement when he saw the cops were after the cars, and said (in English), "That's your fault, Mother, you're smart."

The Leveroos have invited us to Superior this summer. Karl doesn't get any vacation and Evelyn is quite troublesome right now, so it is better to stay put. She has seven teeth now, and is a good crawler, but doesn't walk. She is chubby and nice, but Lillegutt thinks she is too fat. One morning he was sitting and looking at her for a long time, and then he said, "Eve hasn't got any nice face, she is too fat." He says so many funny things. He was moved up to the highest group, and the teacher told me he was very smart. I am glad that the boy has a good, clear head. . . .

Hearty greetings to both of you and to Adda.

Yours,

Bergljot

Chicago, Illinois
November 4, 1926

Dear Mother-in-law,

Best wishes for a happy birthday. This letter will come late, but there is always something in the way. First I had blood poisoning in my right hand, and my whole system got poisoned, so I was very sick, and then Karl was quite run-down. Now he has started taking cod-liver oil and has been to see my clever Doctor Dohrmann. He is supposed to have quiet, and there has been little of that in our house lately. Evelyn is getting a new tooth soon, and she has been quite bothersome for several weeks. She cries Mama and pulls at my skirts. Jens has started playing the piano and that is so much fun. He is doing so well at school and is the best one in writing. He has lots of fun in the park up here, and has many friends he can discuss football and baseball with, so that it is a pleasure to listen to them. They are very interested in the World Series, and they all have their own opinions.

You asked in your letter if we had good help while I was sick. There is no help to be had here, but I was sickest on Saturday and Sunday, and then Karl was at home. Monday morning Helga was here, and otherwise I had to manage with my left hand. Karl can take care of himself without much fuss.
. . .

I have sent you the pictures we took of Evelyn in the park this summer, and since then we haven't taken any, but when I get more I will send them to Adda. Hope you are all well. Greetings to Father-in-law and Adda and yourself.

Yours,

Bergljot

Chicago, Illinois
December 5, 1926

Dear Parents-in-law and Adda,

We seldom hear from you, but I will send a few words anyway. This letter should reach you just in time for Christmas. . . . The last week I have had "grippe," so I stayed in and have not gotten to the stores. I am sending a little package from the children, but please excuse me if it doesn't arrive by Christmas Eve. Eigil and Jens are at the movies this afternoon. This morning I went to the Norwegian church, where they had a big choir that came marching in with long black robes and white collars. The English Lutheran churches all use robes like that, so almost all the Norwegian churches imitate them. Karl is very well now, luckily, but he still has to be careful with his eyes. He takes cod-liver oil regularly, and that has helped him a lot.

Jens went to birthday parties two days in a row last week, and now he is just waiting for his own birthday. He has already invited eight boys. "You don't care how many I invite," he said to me, so it looks like it will be a busy day. I am so happy for the children's sake that we live in Kelvyn Park, for there is a big difference in the children here and down on Fullerton. Evelyn is chubby and good and tries to talk all day long, so now it won't be too long before we can understand her.

I wish both of you and Adda a very merry Christmas from the children and us.

Yours,

Bergljot

Although this letter is dated January 1926, it must have been written in 1927, since Eigil is living with them.

Chicago, Illinois
January 16, 1926

Dear Parents-in-law and Adda,

Thanks so much for all the Christmas letters—the money, the sack, the bib, and the pictures. Everything arrived safely just before Christmas. Unfortunately . . . the children were sick the week before Christmas. Evelyn was really miserable, so we called the doctor. He thought she had eaten something that disagreed with her, but I am sure it was her teeth that made her sick. Four molars broke through, and she has been sick with every single tooth. Now she is completely well again. It is too bad you can't see her. I haven't taken any pictures of the children since this summer, but when we get better weather I will take pictures of them to send you. Then Karl got "grippe" just two days before Christmas, and it lasted a good week before he felt well again. When the children were sick, Eigil ate several meals out, and he no doubt got something that disagreed with him, for he was sick, too. So there weren't many takers for the ribs, just sick people all over the house. It is good when everyone is well and things go in their usual course.

We have bought an excellent radio, so we have beautiful music. I am enclosing a radio program for today (Sunday), so you can see that we have enough music. I think that Eigil is getting more comfortable with conditions over here, for he has been in good humor for quite some time now and everything is going well. He has his own room—off the living room. He begged to live with us when he came, and said he couldn't stand to live with strangers. We don't have any roomers now, and we have never had any boarders. I hope we are finished with having strangers in the house. I had thought of asking Eigil to eat out after New Year's, as it is a bit extra, and he comes home later than Karl, but since he was so unlucky as to get sick from eating out, I haven't had the heart to ask him to do it. I can manage until Adele comes. For three days we have had terrible cold, and lots of snow for Chicago. . . .

Lillegutt would like to write to you, but he still isn't good enough at writing. He reads fluently, but is just now learning to write and spell. The children here learn to read without learning the sounds—just to recognize the words—but, my goodness, how quickly they learn this way. Before Evelyn came, I used to go to the school a lot and observe. It was interesting to see the different methods of instruction between home and here. . . .

I hear that everyone in the family still has long hair, and I am glad of that. And you haven't fallen for the new fashion either, Adda. I hope you are all well. Hearty greetings.

Yours,

Bergljot

Chicago, Illinois
March 25, 1927

Dear Parents-in-law,

Thanks so much for the card from Mother-in-law. It is good to hear that she is beginning to get better. When summer comes and you can get out in the fresh air, then you will feel completely well again. Both children are coming to visit you today. Isn't our big boy fine? Evelyn was frightened and has a scared expression, but she is chubby and good. Basically, she is sweeter than in the picture, but the photographer set her on a table, and that frightened her. We have had many warm days, so she has gone walking in the park, and has been so happy to get out of sitting in her buggy that she laughed aloud for joy. . . .

I heard today that it is difficult to get work, and the employment offices downtown are full of Norwegian newcomers. The factories won't accept Norwegian immigrants because they are so lazy. Isn't it a shame that Norwegians should have gotten a reputation for being lazy? But when they have been in this country for two or three years, then they put on a little speed. Today in a bakery on Fullerton I met a girl who had been in the first year of teacher's college when I was in the second year. She was a teacher at home for five years, and then came over here with her father and brother three years ago, and now she is clerking in a bakery. Change is the spice of life!

Our address will now be 2650 Kildare Ave., probably from the 15th of April. I have written about this before. It's too bad about all the mail that gets lost. . . . Karl asks me to greet you. Hearty greetings to Adda and both of you.

Yours,

Bergljot

Chicago, Illinois
July 8, 1927

Dear Mother-in-law and Adda,

Many thanks for your letter, which came yesterday on Evelyn's birth-day. We hadn't heard from you since the letter we got on May 20. Both children have had chicken pox, but now they are well again. . . . We have been out almost every Sunday since the children got well. It's so good for Karl and the children to get out in the country a bit, so we won't be at home any Sundays this summer. Evelyn is good at traveling, so it is no bother. Karl is still working overtime on Tuesdays and Fridays, so those days he doesn't get home until 10:30 or sometimes 11:00 at night. We had a terribly hot week, and then he worked three nights. You have to work hard in this country if you want to get anywhere. . . .

Hearty greetings to Father-in-law and both of you from us.

Yours,

Bergljot

Chicago, Illinois
January 22, 1928

Dear Parents-in-law and Adda,

As Karl is so busy and it does not look like he will get around to writing letters, I had better take over. Thank you so much for the money you sent the children for Christmas—and many thanks for the Christmas letter. . . . This Christmas we had Jens in bed. Just before Christmas he went out skating in the park, and when he got tired he sat down on a rock and got a terrible cough. He stayed in bed for about ten days, but now he is completely well again. Evelyn is fine, she has just gotten two molars, and naturally coughed a lot just before they came through, just as she has done with every tooth she has gotten. She has an excellent appetite, and also gets cod-liver oil, so she looks like the picture of health.

Yesterday Jens and I went and saw the Norwegian film that the Norwegian America Line has been showing in many cities here in this country. We saw cities and towns all over Norway. Krogh sang—over here they say he is Norway's best singer, but I don't believe that can be true. His voice is nothing compared to the voices I have heard in the opera here. Neib from Tistedalen played the violin. The hall was filled, and it was interesting to hear people speaking Norwegian with English words mixed in. There were people there who had been in this country for thirty or forty years, and it was moving to hear their comments when pictures from their home areas were shown. Jens was enthusiastic about the sports at home, and he asked, "Why can't we go to Norway for a few years?" But you can't live off the beautiful country, so he wouldn't have what he has here. Three Norwegian children's homes and two Norwegian old folks' homes have been invited to the performances. There will be six showings in Chicago—and all will surely be to a full house.

We are having a mild winter this year, but have had several periods of cold. We have a pleasant, warm apartment now, as opposed to the cold one we had last year. I hope you are all well. Hearty greetings from the four of us.

Yours,

Bergljot

The Nilssen family has moved to a new brick bungalow. The end of this letter, which describes the new house, is unfortunately missing. "Blaamand" is a Norwegian children's song.

Chicago, Illinois
April 16, 1928

Dear Mother-in-law,

Thank you for your letter. It is good to hear that you are quite well and it sounds like you are enjoying yourself in Oslo, where you have so much family. We got a card today from Louise and her husband. They can take their next trip abroad to America and see a little of the New World. In a few years we will be having the World's Fair in Chicago—1934. We have heard from Norway that the laundry at Lillehammer went bankrupt, so now Father-in-law can stop regretting that Karl sold it.

The children are well. Jens has had a bad cold three times this winter, but not Evelyn. Jens is in fourth grade, and I play the piano with him every single day. He can already play little pieces, and is very good. Evelyn can sing "My Country" and "Blaamand" completely right. She has a powerful voice for such a little one.

In a week we will be moving to 2832 Natchez Ave. We have bought a five-room brick bungalow. The house is very pretty and brand-new. We can fix up the upstairs. . . . [The rest is missing.]

This time Karl, instead of Bergljot, writes to his parents.

Chicago, Illinois
August 12, 1928

Dear Mother,

It is now a while since we have written. Thanks for the presents to

Jens and Evelyn, and thank you for your letter. . . . The house we have bought is well within the city limits, but even so it is like out in the country. I walk to Grand Avenue (about a twelve-minute walk) and take the streetcar to my office in the "loop." It takes about an hour to get there. Going home I often take the train. It goes from Union Station at 5:21 and I get to Gale-wood Station about 5:50 and am at home by 6:05. I get home at about the same time if I take the streetcar, but it is a long ride. It takes about six minutes to get from Galewood Station to Grand Avenue. I start at my office at 9:00 in the morning—get one hour for dinner and am through at 5:00. Saturdays from 9:00 to 12:00. We have shorter work hours in the state government where I have worked since January. I have one week left before vacation—two weeks—and we are thinking of traveling out of Chicago. . . .

Well, time flies, it is now over eighteen years since I drove down to Fredrikshald Station . . . and left for America. I have been away from Norway ever since except for the six and a half years we were at home. . . .

Your devoted son,

Karl

Karl has added a note to this next letter.

Chicago, Illinois
October 31, 1928

Dear Mother-in-law,

Happy birthday! We hope you are well and have a nice day. The children often talk about Grandma, and I wish you could get to know them both. Jens has had fun today. It is Halloween, and children get to do whatever they want today. Jens put on Karl's old work clothes, put a wool scarf around his neck and an ugly old hat of Karl's, and then he had a mask in front of his eyes. I made him a beard with a burnt cork. He was dressed as a "ragman" and went around with his friends ringing doorbells and making a real racket. Evelyn thought it was too bad that she couldn't go along, so we found an old mask for her and Karl took her out for a bit. "Now we are going to have fun," she said. It doesn't take much to amuse them. Evelyn is growing so fast, and she is a very sturdy little girl.

Karl isn't completely well. He is going to make a glass porch on the house. He will get a carpenter to help him. Behind the kitchen we have a big open porch, and the kitchen will be much warmer when it gets finished. We have furnace heat—hot air. We have a big stove (furnace) in the basement with pipes going to all the rooms. It is colder out here than where we lived before, for this is the highest point in Chicago, and it is not so built up, so it is more open. It is healthy for the children here. . . . Both of them have gotten better since we came out here.

You ask in your letter about our garden. The lots in Chicago are small and the houses close together, so we won't have any big garden. This year we didn't get much done. An old Italian came with some tomato plants, and even planted them for us. We got about five bushels of tomatoes, so I have canned a lot, and made soup, and gave away many bushels. Over here they can lots of tomatoes. I also canned a bushel of peaches—crab apples—apricots and all kinds of things. Made jelly out of purple grapes and also juice. I also made some grape wine. So now we have some things in the cellar for the winter. It was a shame that our stay in the country had to be so short. When we had been in Williams Bay for a week, I got such terrible hay fever that I couldn't breathe, and had to sit up in a chair at night, so we had to come back to town. It was too bad for Karl and the children.

Thanks for your last letter. Hearty greetings to you and everyone.

Yours,

Bergljot

Dear Mother,

This letter will arrive after your birthday, but I hope that doesn't matter. Happy birthday. . . . B. has written about what you asked about—the garden and trees and so forth. The lot isn't so big and the place is new. But I am going to plant some trees this spring both in front of and behind the house. A house with a real garden and shade trees would cost too much. You can't get that within the borders of Chicago anyway—then you have to go out of town. I have now ordered windows and materials to build the porch on the back. The wind comes from that direction.

It is now only a few days before the presidential election. The outcome of the election will make a big difference in whether we have bad or good times. . . .

The children are well. B. has started playing the piano—takes lessons twice a month, so she practices a lot. Jens practices, too, and Evelyn also wants to climb up on the piano bench. Today I had to buy a mask for her. She called it an "ask." Greetings to everyone from your devoted son,

Karl

Karl has again added a note to Bergljot's letter.

Chicago, Illinois
December 16, 1928

Dear Mother-in-law,

The last letter we sent you was on your birthday, I hope you got it. We haven't heard from you for a long time. I sent a little Christmas package from the children. We are all well, fortunately, and I hope we escape the flu that is going around here now. You may have read in the newspapers that it began in the West and has now spread eastward. They were talking about closing the schools here, but haven't done that yet. We have had mild, rainy weather for a week. Today it snowed a little and the children had so much fun in the back yard. Evelyn gets so excited when her big brother lets her join in with his friends, and in her enthusiasm she said, "Jens is a good boy today." Jens is going to be in a play at school, and he is very proud of himself.

Karl has had lots to do with the house. You may know that he has made a glassed-in porch—ten French windows on the back porch. He always finds something to work on, and he likes to have things to putter with. Maybe I told you that my brother Skjalg is going to Germany in January. He has gotten a position there for an American company, and will be paid in dollars. He will come to America every time a new machine comes out, probably every other year. He has been really lucky, but he deserves it, because he has been so energetic and not afraid to work hard.

I want to wish you all a very happy new year. Hearty greetings.

Yours,

Bergljot

Merry Christmas and a Happy New Year to all of you. We sent a little package, hope it gets to you. We have enclosed the back porch, did all the work myself. It is good protection against wind and weather.

Evelyn is now talking well. . . . She is big for her age, and in good health. Jens has now gotten so far with the piano that he and Bergljot can play duets. We are having some cold days just now, . . . but today it has been milder again.

I have the day off on Monday, so that will be three and a half days of vacation. At the same time as the presidential election we had an election for governor in the state of Illinois. Emerson was elected, so Small will be gone in January—there may be a new "Director" or "Supervisor" at the Illinois Waterworks where I work, but otherwise we don't think there will be any big changes. However, if Floyd Thomson the Democrat had been elected, then there would have been all new people at the office.

I had better stop with these lines. Hope you are all well.

Greetings,

Karl

Chicago, Illinois
January 22, 1929

Dear Parents-in-law,

Thanks for the letter and the money you sent for Christmas. It was too much. We were all well during Christmas, usually one or another is sick, so we had a really pleasant Christmas. The children got many presents. Evelyn was so excited about the Christmas tree. Jens has started school again after vacation. In February he will move up to the fifth grade. Time goes so fast, and now Evelyn wants to be a school girl, too. She plays with Jens's school bag, and pretends to go to school. Her little Swedish friend, Hazel, visits her often, and they play school and all the dolls are pupils. We have had quite a lot of snow and have had to shovel a lot around the house. Evelyn has her little broom and snowshovel, so she is always busy. . . . Karl and the children are doing calisthenics now—Evelyn is mostly a spectator, but you should hear her laugh.

We heard the Chicago symphony orchestra in Orchestra Hall just after Christmas. There are 100 men, and they play beautifully. Of course we can hear them on the radio, but still that is not the same as being there. Hope you are all well. Hearty greetings to you and Adda from all of us.

Yours,

Bergljot

Many thanks for the Christmas present. We had a small Christmas tree as we do every year. Evelyn was excited about the presents and the tree. Jens is so big now that he doesn't believe in Santa Claus any more. It has been rather cold in January, but as we have a good house we have been warm enough inside. B. is now taking a trip to town and Jens is out skating. Evelyn and I are going to go for a walk. . . . Hope you are all fine. Greet Adda and the others.

Greetings,

Karl

Bergljot Anker Nilssen was operated on for cancer in 1929. The letters Bergljot wrote between September and December of 1929 from Halden, Norway, where she was staying with her father, are not reproduced here. In them, she wrote about the children and their activities, worried about Karl, who was still in Chicago, and remained cheerful and optimistic in spite of her steadily worsening condition. In her first letter, just after arriving, she wrote, "I hope to get stronger in awhile." In the next letter she wrote, "People have been extremely kind to us while I have been sick, and you can't imagine how helpful the Norwegians in Chicago are." She reported that the children were becoming quite good at speaking Norwegian, and that Jens was studying to keep up with his class in Chicago, where he was to enter the sixth grade in February. She reported on going to Oslo for X-ray or radium treatments, and apologized for not having enough money to send her mother-in-law a nice present for her eightieth birthday. By November, she reported that she was much better, and had been up for half an hour that day. The pain had eased some, she wrote. In December, she apologized for writing her Christmas letter in pencil, but as she was in bed, it couldn't be helped. She was in so much pain by this time that she had to take morphine drops, but she expressed the hope that the pain would stay away. She hoped to learn in January whether there had been any improvement since the radium treatments, which had left her very weak. Her last letter was written right after Christmas. Again, she wrote charmingly of the children, and reported on the doings of their friends in Chicago. She mentioned having felt a little better the last few days, but otherwise, she noted, "I have not been well at all." Bergljot Anker Nilssen died on February 2, 1930, at the age of thirty-nine.

NOTE

1. Personal communication, Jens T. Anker, son of Bergljot Anker Nilssen.

8

A Brooklyn Builder

Christ Gundersen, 1908–1945

*L*ike Bergljot Anker Nilssen, Kristen (Christ) Gundersen lived his life in America *in a big city. Unlike her, however, his origins in Norway were rural. Gundersen was born on May 20, 1875, in Øvrebø Parish, Vest-Agder. He came to Brooklyn in 1900, was trained as a mason, and worked in construction for forty-six years. In 1906 he married Thora M. Berentsen, who died in 1937. The Gundersens had four sons, George (who died in childhood), Edwin, Chester, and George, and two daughters, Lilly and Gudny. Gundersen established his own construction business, which he ran through the prosperous years of the 1920s and through the hard times of the 1930s. In his letters he talks about his children, first in school and then as they go out into the world of work; he describes the ups and downs of his business and comments on American political and economic conditions.*

The Gundersen children were all well educated, and the oldest son, Edwin, became a Lutheran minister. Lilly Gundersen married Dr. Bernhard Christensen, who later became president of Augsburg College in Minneapolis. Christ Gundersen died on March 13, 1949, in Woodville, Wisconsin, at the home of his son Edwin. [1]

Gundersen's letters were nearly all written from Brooklyn, New York, between 1908 and 1945. Most of them are addressed to his brother, Karl Skogstad. The letters are intermittent, with long periods of silence in between. Of course Gundersen may have written other letters that were not preserved in this collection. Communication between the brothers was cut off by outside forces during the German occupation of Norway in World War II.

Gundersen writes choppy and often incomplete sentences, with erratic spelling and punctuation. His handwriting is also quite difficult to read, and names are particularly hard to interpret. He frequently leaves letters unsigned, or signs them simply "Brother." His letters give us a tantalizingly brief glimpse of what life was like for a Norwegian-American in Brooklyn during the first half of this century.

All of Christ Gundersen's letters are written on letterhead from his construction business, which in 1908 was located at 355-61st Street.

Brooklyn, N.Y.
March 1, 1908

Dear Brother Karl,

Many thanks for your letter and card, which we have received. We are very happy to see that you are all well. We are also all well, hale and hearty all of us. George is a little crabby, he has a toothache, otherwise big and strong. Will soon send a photo of him and Thora. Thanks for everything you wrote about the folks at home, it is always so much fun to hear from old Norway. I see from your letter that you would like to get out in the world, but you have time enough—I was 25 years old when I left. You mustn't think of leaving Father, for you are now his best support. I often regret that I left Father and Mother, whom I could have helped, so therefore stay home and be of help to them.

You ask in your letter if you can use the bicycle. You may have it and I hope you have many pleasant trips on it. Have you heard whether anyone found my umbrella while I was home? I lost it the evening I left, and you must have it if it is there. Write to me if the rings are bad on the bicycle and I will send you a couple of new ones. They are cheap here, and Thora's sister is going home this spring, so we can send them with her. The last time I wrote, I had such a long distance to get to work, but now I am lucky to have only four blocks. I have a big contract and need lots of people. If only I can be fortunate and earn something. I have a smaller job that I have to start this week so I have enough work to do. This will be a busy summer.

Yes, now it would be wonderful to be in Norway, the beautiful bird songs and the fragrant spring air make me homesick, here it will soon be springtime, and then there will be only a week or two before the hot weather suddenly comes.

. . . I will send you some newspapers. Wouldn't you like to learn English? I will gladly send you some books and you can learn a lot from them. . . . I hope that you will continue to be good at writing, and you won't have to wait long for an answer from me. Greet Father, Mother, and Sister. Thanks for Mother's letter. Greet all friends. But most of all greetings to you, dear Brother.

Kristen and Thora

Christ and Thora Gundersen on their wedding day. Brooklyn, New York, 1906. Photo courtesy Mrs. Bernhard M. Christensen.

Brooklyn, N.Y.
May 14, 1911

Dear Father and Mother, Brothers and Sisters,

Many thanks for your letters, which we received two weeks ago. I see that everything is well at home, which we are very glad to hear and we can say the same. The boys are well and everything is going as usual. I am working every day, and Thora has her hands full. Edwin is a wild little scamp, always on the move, and is just starting to walk. We sent a photo of both boys with Aunt, . . . maybe you have gotten it. The large photo of Father and Mother is finally ready and we will send it at the first opportunity. It is a long time since I wrote, but it is strange, the more seldom one writes, the less one has to tell about.

Anna Stølen was here last Sunday and said farewell. Was leaving for Norway. She will probably come and say hello to you. We should have sent a little with her and I promised to come down before she left, but something always came up, so nothing came of it. We are having a very cold spring. Today it is a little warm for the first time this year. . . .

Write back right away and tell just as much as the last time, it is so much fun to hear from old friends. Many many greetings from us to Father, Mother, Karl, Anna Kristine and everyone we know.

Thora, K, and the boys

Mushom is the name of the farm in Øvrebø, Vest-Agder, where Gundersen's family lived. At the time he wrote this letter, he was on a trip, probably to Gloucester, Massachusetts.

Gloucester
September 29, 1918

Dear Brother Karl,

It's already several weeks since I wrote to you, would like to know how things are at Mushom today. It is an unusually nice day here in Gloucester. It is one o'clock and I just came from church. There are several churches here, but few who visit them today. Was in the Methodist church. The minister preached about the Bible and how it had grown strong because it wasn't written by sinful men but by God. It is so good to hear a learned man who can clearly state his case, and tell why we should believe and especially in the American language, which is so powerful.

Yes, brother, I have so much I would like to tell you but the letters have to be short and many are lost. I seldom hear from Norway, but it is best

The Builder. Christ Gundersen in Brooklyn, ca. 1940. Photo courtesy Mrs. Bernhard M. Christensen.

to keep writing often. We are all well here, have a well-laden table every day and can buy what we need. A large number of our young men are in France now and more are ready to go. The first draft took those between 23 and 33 years, and then the second round those between 19 and 45, which I am in. But those from 20 to 35 will go first, and I have six months before I will be called, and you know I won't have to go since I have such a big family. We were 13,000,000 men in the last draft. Uncle Sam has people, money, and everything that is needed.

Since I came up here I have seen what an immensely rich land the U.S. is. Here there are fields as large as the eye can see and grass that is two or three feet tall, but no one cuts it because it isn't needed. They can't use so much hay. Here you can get permission to cut the thickest meadow completely free if you need hay. I looked at a big farm that I thought a little bit about buying. It was the most beautiful piece of land I have ever seen, and big enough to feed four horses and eighty cows. Fields, farm machinery, tools, two horses, 300 chickens, eight pigs, sixteen cows, an eight-room house, barn, stall, chicken house and more buildings for $11,000. He was ready to trade even Steven for the two buildings we own in Brooklyn, but then I thought about Father and Mother. It is easy to get rid of a house, but a farm is much harder. We want to come home and see you all as soon as there is peace again. Greet everyone.

Your devoted brother,
Kristen

Gundersen has been home on a visit, and is on his way back to the United States.

London
April 20, 1920

Dear Brother and family,

Thanks for the visit. Yes, now it is already several weeks since we saw each other and I still have not gotten home. Have been very unlucky. It began the same evening that I left Kristiansand. We went out, but there was fog, so we went in to the dock again and couldn't continue until one o'clock, then we came to Rekefjord, stayed there one night, then I got a boat to Flekkefjord, by train to Stavanger, by boat to Bergen, and then — my passport wasn't right, which the fool of an agent in Kristiansand didn't tell me. So I had to get a new passport from the American consul in Bergen, and that took a week. I went back to [unclear] and was there for four days, and then got a telegram that my passport had arrived and then to London, but here we have to wait for four more days for the first boat to the U.S. I am well and doing

Christ Gundersen nearly always wrote on letterhead from his construction company.

fine, but I don't recommend that anyone travel this way, it is terrible. I have seen most of London, but it does not appeal to me in the least. Hope you are all fine. Many greetings to you and yours.

Your Brother

According to his letterhead, Gundersen's construction company has moved to 1056-73rd Street and 451-45th Street.

Brooklyn, N.Y.
March 11, 1923

Dear Brother and family,

It's a long time since we heard from each other. Hope you are all well, we are all in good health, and have no reason to complain. This has been a hard winter, especially for me, we haven't had much work, just two or three days a week, and then we earned accordingly. But now it is spring and we have lots of work that is well paid. We pay masons $13.00 per day, and helpers $7.00. A week's income for us, which we pay our workers out of, is from $600 up to $2,000. But if only you can get lots of money to pay out, then you can manage to earn it, too. We have one contract for $2,100, one for $2,300 and one for $9,000. The one for $9,000 is a Norwegian Free Church that will soon be finished.

I had a visit from a Gundersen . . . and he said that Father was so badly cared for, he wasn't getting enough food, and he was really in poor shape in all ways, and then he had a message to me . . . that you had agreed to declare him incompetent. There is not a person on earth who we, you and I and all our brothers and sisters, owe as much to as Father, so therefore let us pay a little bit of that debt to him. Send me a long letter and tell how much he needs to make life a bit more comfortable and I will try to send what is necessary. Can't it be done in such a way that Kristen S. and Guri can stay at home and take care of the farm for Father? Doesn't Father have a horse? Write about that. Buy one if that will be helpful to him and you. I will help you to pay. I wrote to E. Vehus, who wrote to me about coming home, that I would try to take a trip to Norway this fall. Now we must try to do the best we can, and I am sure that it will come out right. Tell me, do you want the farm? I will never live at Mushom.

Write soon. Greetings from

your only brother

Brooklyn, N.Y.
July 4, 1923

Dear Brother Karl,

Many thanks for the letter, which I received long ago. Thank you for all you wrote, it was good to hear how Father is, and we are more at ease now. . . . We will never live there, so I will do all I can so that you can get it if you want it. I have been in the U.S. too long and will never move away from here. We have everything just fine here all of us . . . and God gives us what is best for us in this life. But our time is certainly taken up, we have lots of work, and lots of workers . . . so we have enough to do this summer. . . .

October 21, 1923

My letter has been lying here for a long time. And now summer is over. It has been a busy summer for me. For two months we have had five or six jobs going at the same time and the weekly wages went up to $2,000–3,000, but now it is a bit better, so I can get time to breathe at least. I have greetings from the son of K. Hegeland, he worked here awhile for us, and several other boys from Øvrebø. It would really be fun to see Norway one more time, but that will no doubt never be. This spring we were about to send Lilly and Edwin to Norway, but as you see, nothing came of it. We bought a car and have traveled lots this summer, up to 250 miles on a Sunday, and we have seen more of the U.S. this year than in all the years since we came here. I have sold the old car and gotten a brand new one, it is up-to-date in every way and . . . cost $2,680.00. A terrible price for an ordinary contractor to pay for a machine, but it is worth it.

I am busy all the time. . . . We have now bought a truck, and I drive around in that all day. . . .

Edwin and Lilly will be confirmed this winter. Lilly . . . will graduate from grade school this spring. That is well done, she is only twelve years old. Edwin is fourteen and will go until . . . 1924. He has a good record, has never missed a day . . . and has the best grades in the class. He has played the violin for two years, so you can just imagine the good music we have. This evening he and Lilly are playing at church.

Now they are coming home, and it's about time to settle down. . . . Hearty greetings to you and your family from us all.

Brother Gundersen

Brooklyn, N.Y.
February 8, 1925

Dear Brother Karl,

Thanks for the last letter, which we received two weeks ago. Thought you had forgotten us completely. Glad to see that you are well. We are all fine, and everything is going as usual. See from your letter that B. Jylebæk is dead. Well, there are probably many I would miss among those I knew. . . . It is strange how time flies, especially over here where everyone is always so busy that you can't get to your grave fast enough unless you drive a car.

It has been quiet for me for awhile but now it's getting busy again. We have a large building that will be finished in a few weeks. We had lots of work last year, but I think there will be more this year. We were unfortunate enough to lose $10,000.00 on a job last summer. So now we are barely out of the hole this spring. We have paid our debt and cleared our name without taking any of our private property and so we'll have to do better this summer. Times are still good, and we are beginning to be known and so we get better prices. Last year we built a Norwegian (Lutheran) church that came to $51,000.00 and a Free church that cost $48,000.00. It is good to build churches, the money is assured, but we had to wait a whole year, so I was in bad shape.

I see from your letter that you haven't heard from us. I have sent you two letters that I haven't had answers to. I wrote to you about the farm, that you could be prepared to have my place, for I will never return to Norway. If it should happen that we would see Norway again, it would only be for a short visit. I also wrote and said that if I could help you with anything, you should let me know. We also sent a big package with many dollars worth of clothing. My wife thought that you wouldn't like getting used clothes, but what we sent was almost new. Try the post office in Kristiansand and maybe you can get it. We sent two packages to Guri, but she has apparently just gotten one. . . .

I see from your letter that Father is feeble and stubborn. We laughed hard when we heard that you didn't have permission to repair the roof for him. I had greetings from him from Tomas Hægland, who asked me to go to Norway. I wrote the same as to you, to talk to Father and tell him that you had my place, but that letter must have gone the same way as your clothes. And then I wrote a really long letter to Kristine and told her about the schools and the schoolwork and the children's grades in school. We now have two out of elementary school and into high school. Now I will try to be really diligent in writing to Norway.

We thought you had FORGOTTEN us over here. Over here people always say, when Mother is gone, then Norway is forgotten. Let's not let it be that way with us, Karl. You write about coming to the U.S., but that wouldn't be a good thing for you now that you have a family, and you can surely find enough to do where you are. Norway will soon wake up, don't you think? Norwegian postage has gone up in price. . . .

Hearty greetings to everyone from all of us.

Your Brother

Brooklyn, N.Y.
October 8, 1928

Dear Brother Karl,

Many long days since I wrote to Norway. Not so long ago, I received a money order from you for $263, but no letter, so I don't know why. Had a letter from Sister . . . and from that see that you are all well, and now and then I meet people who give me a little news. . . .

We are all healthy so we have much to thank God for, but there have been hard times and it is still difficult for me. I have been so unlucky as to lose $6,000, and that is hard for one like me, who has no capital. Just about everything I had in the business is in the hands of the lawyers. We will hope for the best. All the children go to school, you know, so I have a costly household. Lilly has now started university, which takes four years and $$. Edwin will graduate in January 1929. He will then be an engineer and if he wants to continue, he can borrow money. He has been with me this summer. He and I had no free time. He is a good driver, and drove the truck for us. Chester goes to high school, he wants to be a lawyer. It is strange, when one writes so seldom, one has little to write about. Yes, in 1930 a trip to Norway, but if it goes like this summer nothing will come of it. It would be fun once more to see Norway and old friends, but if we can't use the car and drive a little, then we don't go anywhere.

Here it is so pretty and lively and the best place on earth. So it is strange that so many take trips to Norway. We now have many fine roads, very wide, up to 200 feet, and cement or asphalt, so it is really a joy to drive. This summer I got a fine for driving too fast. $10.00. I drove the car 43 miles an hour and the police caught me (but I have driven 65 and I didn't think it was so dangerous).

I have sent many letters to you but I never get an answer. My letters must be STOLEN in Kristiansand. Try to catch the thief. Send me a little letter soon, Karl. Greet Father and everyone I know. But heartiest greetings to you from

Your Brother

Brooklyn, N.Y.
New Year's, January 1, 1932

Dear Brother and family,

Happy New Year, and thanks for the old! Well, now Christmas is over, it is 1:30 on New Year's Day, so it's best to send you a few words. Thanks for the letter, which I received a long time ago. Strangely enough, I have been busy this winter, working every day, so there has been little time for writing to Norway. We are all fine, Mother is not in such good health. She had such a bad cold at Christmas time that she stayed inside. Christmas has been quiet, I have slept a good deal. On Christmas Day, Thora's brother and wife together with Kristensen were here, that was all. We have fine weather, not cold or snowy. But today it is raining. Yesterday there was a celebration as the old year went out, and then there was a big fire a ways from here. A Catholic church burned up.

Everyone seems to be glad that 1931 is over, but I scarcely think that this year will be any better. It is true that the war years are over, and many find it difficult to manage and cannot live in luxury like before, and then they just cry out that the times are so bad, and believe it is the government's fault. You try to tell them to cut out a little expense, such as house rent for $70-85. One can get a house for $30-35 . . . cars and much else that we couldn't afford twenty years ago. The living standard has gone down thirty percent, but now try to get day wages down. Many would rather suffer a little. . . . I met a man yesterday evening who was drunk and hungry. He had 60 cents but he wanted to have enough for a proper dinner, and my answer was, you have more money than I, you can ask for 25 cents. . . .

Thanks for the card and the Christmas magazine you sent us. . . . See from your letter that you are expecting to get paid. . . . Thanks for everything that you have done for us, and don't send the money. Though I have had a hard time, I can stand that much, but now I have a few jobs . . . in January, so we hope it will be better. I can bid on quite a little work, but I also feel that the war years are over.

Saw from your letter that you have planted trees. . . . That was well done, but write what it cost and the appraisal. It's fun to hear a little, the boys have fun with it and want you to be paid. Edwin came home during Christmas week and has been working with me, but now he has to go back. He has a hard way to go, but is in good spirits and has a very fine reputation from school. (Just six years left). . . .

Greetings from all of us to all of you, but especially to you from

Your Brother

January 11, 1932

Brother Karl,

That's the way it goes, your letter has laid quietly for eleven days, so it will be old before you get it. We are as usual. I am still working, but if I don't get something new soon, it will be over. There are many looking for work here, but I think people complain too much. It is about like it was before the war, but I think it will be worse next year. Now we are having a presidential election, and then there is always little to do. It's been that way as long as I have been here.

Have you thought about coming to the U.S. this spring? I will help you as best I can, and we can find something for you to do, so it is up to you. Do as you think best, if you can get away from home, but earning big money here is over. I am satisfied if I can keep things going, and now it is a consolation to me that some of the children will soon be through with school, and then they can be of some help. But then they move out to their own homes and have enough to make it themselves. George seems to have the best mind, he beats everyone. The school principal wanted to move him up to the high school. There were six boys here in Brooklyn who were moved up, but George is so young, and for him to get into a group of boys who are twelve or fourteen years old didn't seem like a good idea to us, so we let him stay two more years in junior high. Well, now my letter is so long that you will get tired of it.

Thank you for what you sent George for Christmas. It arrived, and he wondered how many miles the ball had traveled. He wants to go to the Brooklyn Technical School, and then to flying school, and then take a trip to Norway in his own plane. He is busy writing laws, he has gotten a group of boys to form a club, and there will be rules — no smoking, no swearing, and so on. He is the president and gets more respect than you would believe. It costs five cents to be a member of the club.

Greet all your dear ones from all of us.

Your Brother

"Glade jul, hellige jul" is "Silent Night" in Norwegian. When Gundersen writes "T. Haal" and "T. H." he is probably referring to Tammany Hall, the corrupt Democratic political machine in New York City, whose influence declined due to the reforms of Mayor La Guardia (1934–45).

Brooklyn, N.Y.
February 1, 1934

Dear Brother and family,

Thank you for your letter, which I received yesterday, and for the money. $300 and $260. The first amount was enough, so we can manage for awhile. *Do not send more.* See from your letter that you and others there have been sick. Yes, health is the best thing in life. Thora is better today. She has been in bed for a week. She was so poorly that the doctor wouldn't let us see her. She has a bad heart, and will go fast, but today she wants to get up.

I haven't worked this week, but it looks a little better, it isn't nearly as bad as the newspapers say. People were used to having enough money to buy anything they wanted, and that can't be done now. I didn't work much last summer, and besides, it was impossible to collect any money. I had $1,200 outstanding, now there is $800 left. I think I will get that, too, but it takes time, people don't have money. Edwin is working hard to get on his way, he has a big exam coming up. His face lit up when he saw your letter. . . . George is through with junior high and has started high school. . . . He won a medal for the best grades, 98 and ½ average. Lilly is working, Chester is working—so I can take it easy soon.

I see that Bernt . . . moved from Mushom, that was too bad. I remember when father guaranteed for him so that he could get the farm. Now he is old and worn out and he has to leave. It was so hard to say good-bye to him when we were home. Little chance of seeing him again.

February 4, 1934

As you see, your letter has had a rest, I was called out to look at a fire. . . . Maybe I'll get it, it will be three or four weeks' work. Thora is still well and takes care of the house. We have cold weather, and a little snow, so many have jobs clearing the snow away. I have applied for a position as a permanent mason for the city, but haven't heard anything yet. We have a new city council, so it should be better. It is terrible the way *T. Haal* has treated us. In 1933 there was $20,000,000 of tax money in *graft*. Here there were some on [unclear] and were paid each month . . . in spite of the fact that the man was dead for eight years. Others were so lucky they had a position, but didn't know in which office, just where they should pick up their wages. It costs more to run N.Y. and Brooklyn than the whole country of Norway. But now it is over, we won this fall. It is said that T. H. bought 100,000 stones . . . for $5–10 apiece. This has gone on as long as I have been here, but where will he get his money from, now that he has lost his position?

I was so happy when I heard that Torkel and Kristine visited you at Christmas with the radio. We often sit by the radio, and at Christmas we heard "Glade jul, hellige jul" all the way from Norway, and then a speech from Copenhagen. I hear that the Jews are going to build such a strong station in Jerusalem that the whole world can hear them.

It has already begun. It is strange how the prophecies in the Bible come so naturally to fulfillment. They have now invented an electric light here that can be seen for seven miles. You would only need two to light up your whole way to town. The time is near that heat can be saved for a cold winter day. The Bible tells us it is our duty to subordinate the earth, and that is happening a little at a time . . . but humanity is rebellious toward God and all His goodness and we are punished and put back—another war and perhaps many hundreds of years back. . . . The time will come when virtue will reign and no more war. . . . [The end is missing.]

Brooklyn, N.Y.
February 24, 1935

Dear Brother and family,

I am ashamed of myself today for my negligence in not answering your last letter. You wrote that you wanted me to look around for a car. You can get a car for $150–300, used. I saw a new Ford eight-cylinder, four-door, six-passenger for $600. If you write and let me know what you have thought of buying, then I can help you. But you must find out how much duty you have to pay. I have heard that you are not allowed to import used cars. Here you can buy cars cheap.

We are all well. Thora is in reasonably good health this winter, but very weak. Chester works in N.Y. in an office, Lilly is at a seminary in Nuhemsted, 250 miles from here. She was home for Christmas, she will be through in May. A long school session. Edwin works for me every day, and then he goes to school from seven to ten o'clock every evening, so his time is taken up. But he wants to get ahead. Today he is in Philadelphia at a big meeting and I am glad that he got that trip together with his comrades. He is always thinking and talking about you folks in Norway, so you will surely see him some fine day. Gudny works in an office in N.Y. She has gotten herself a Danish boy who she says she loves, but I don't like it. . . . Hope she will forget him, we are all against him, except Thora. . . . George is in high school, third year, . . . and the cleverest of all.

Times are bad here in the U.S. Worse than they have ever been before, everything is so expensive now, it is about double what it cost to live in 1930. Butter is now 46 cents and it was down to 17 cents. Now we have a sales tax on everything, two percent (food is not included). The taxes have gone up and up. Water rates have doubled, and I think that if Roosevelt gets to stay in office for another term, then it's all over for the good old U.S. Now the state is putting out $2,000,000,000,000 [sic] for the destitute who don't have work. We now have 11,000,000 men without work in the U.S. In 1930 wages were from $10 to $16 per day, now after N.A.E., the New Deal, they are fixed at $15 per week. Who can live on that? That is all Chester gets, $15 per week, and Gudny has the same. Edwin and I always work on contract and sometimes we can be lucky and earn a little bit. I am well known in Brooklyn, so we have kept things going with repair work. We have had five small repairs since New Year's, and we have three that we will start on, so we can't complain. I don't hire much, we two manage it alone. We have had many strange contracts. Last summer we were without work and I didn't think we could take time off. So I knew a Jew who needed a garage built. He was a tailor and I went and talked to him and said that I wanted to have clothes instead of money. He got a garage and we got winter clothes. A dentist got his house repaired and E.C.G.L. and I got our teeth repaired. Yes, that's the way it goes in the U.S. nowadays.

We have had good weather this winter, one snowfall with seventeen inches of snow, and now we are waiting for spring. Greet everyone heartily. Most of all greetings to you from,

Brother

Thora Gundersen died in 1937. At the time he wrote this letter, Gundersen was living with his son Chester and his family.

Brooklyn, N.Y.
January 19, 1940

Dear Brother and family,

Thanks for your letter, which I received a week ago. It takes a long time for a letter to reach us now. It's good that you are all well and everything is as usual. We are all well, all three of us are healthy and have enough to do. Chester works with me. So it is easier for me now. I live with him. Telma is still working, so we take care of things as well as we can, but she is very kind and everything is going well. I have never had it better.

I took a trip west to Edwin and Ester at Christmas time. Edwin was married this fall to Ester Larsen from Minnesota. Her father has a farm. She is a gifted woman, and has gone through college and is educated as a nurse. I didn't have time to go west for the wedding, but Chester and Telma were there, and then Edwin and Ester came to Brooklyn and stayed with me for a week, and then went west again to his new home and church. His first church was in . . . a city of 30,000, a large church, yes, the second largest, but he had someone over him and then he had to speak Norwegian over the radio once a month. Then they were offered another call out in the country, with three churches to serve and he took that. Here he gets a free house. A really nice house with eight rooms and a yard. He starts his new call on January 1, 1940. I traveled west on December 23, 1939, and got there at ten o'clock on Sunday, so I got to hear his last Norwegian sermon in the big, fine church . . . and it was full. Then we went home, where Ester had a wonderful dinner.

At four o'clock we traveled to Ester's home, which is 25 miles out in the country, but the roads are good and Edwin has a new Ford, so it goes fast. At Larsens they had a real Christmas with lots of genuine Norwegian food. Edwin had devotions and then Ester played and sang, which she is a master at. She has a sister who is married in Canada. So now Larsen and wife are alone, have three servants, but they had gone home for Christmas. Mrs. Larsen is very pleasant and it was hard to say good-bye and I hope I can get time to stay there again sometime. At eight o'clock we left again, it was cold but clear skies and a little snow. The church bells were ringing in Christmas, "Peace on Earth." What strange feelings one gets when one thinks of all the things that sin has spoiled for mankind.

Our next stop was in Minneapolis, with Lilly, Bernhard, and George. I had promised to be there at four o'clock, but Ester sent Lilly a telegram — so they were ready for us. We came at nine o'clock and there were many guests, the table was set and waiting. . . . There was a little creature who wished

Grandpa, Aunt, and Uncle welcome and Merry Christmas. That was little Nadia, who was three years old in June and whom everyone admired for beauty and good behavior. . . . She was busy handing out packages, which there were a lot of. Her father has explained to her that it is . . . not Santa Claus who gives us presents for Christmas. She got six fine new dresses, two of real silk all the way from China, so she has clothes enough for the year, and then a whole lot of toys. She thinks everyone is good and kind, and she has a little sister whose name is Naomi. . . .

Yes, Lilly has a pleasant and beautiful home and a fine husband, but he . . . has too much to take care of. She has a servant, but is going constantly from the telephone to the front door, two children, and visitors upon visitors. When the girl sets the table she must always leave room for two or three more. Yes, one evening we were nine to begin with, but before we quit, we were twenty-two at the table. There is plenty of company at the home of Dr. B. M. Christensen. This summer he is coming to Brooklyn on a trip, so I hope he can get rested up.

I stayed with Lilly until January 4, 1940, and then Edwin came and I went with him and helped him move. Had to buy more furniture, it takes so much to fill eight rooms, but now he is set. I think he has found the right place, the people are so fine. He lives in a little place about like Mosby, there is a little church there . . . and then he has another church four miles out and then a third, which is the largest, seven miles out. So he will have enough to do, but he is acquainted with conditions out there and that is a good help for him.

Well, you asked if I thought you should sell the forest. . . . It should be however *you* think best. Do as you want. . . . Yes, if only I could be a little more diligent about writing, it doesn't take so long for me to scrape together a letter, but it takes a great EFFORT and then I have four children who have to hear a little from me, too. George writes every week. I am very proud of him, he has been a great joy to me. I was so afraid that he would go the wrong way, but now he is more settled and wants to continue with school, which is my wish. He asked me so nicely about quitting and starting with me, but I told him no, if you quit school, then you have to take care of yourself. It wasn't easy for me, but it went well, and he is a *good* boy. I didn't see much of George at Christmas time, he worked in a flower shop during Christmas vacation and earned $60. He has a business sense like few others. This year, too, B., L. and children, George and I were invited to the Bishop's here in Minneapolis. Dr. B. and Bernhard are such good friends and I go along as a hanger-on, but George couldn't come, so we talked about him, and B. asked what George was going to be, now that he has only two years left until he is through with college and just nineteen years old. Well, now we will see when the time comes, I said, and the one word better than the other was said about George — If only God gets him completely under His will, but I certainly believe that will happen. He has such clarity and truthfulness, keeps away from all sinful amusements, for he understands already now that sinful amusements have bad consequences and are empty pleasures. He loves life and healthy sports and is polite and helpful and slow to make new acquaintances.

If you can read this, then you are better at figuring out my handwriting than I am. So to end with hearty greetings to all, but especially to you, dear brother.

Your Brother

The new letterhead tells us that the Gundersens have moved their business to 619-73rd Street in Brooklyn.

Brooklyn, N.Y.
June 8, 1945

Dear brother and family,

It is good to sit down and write to you with the thought that this letter will reach you. Thank you for your letter, which I got on the sixth of this month. It is so good to know that everyone is living and not starving too much. I have gotten one letter from you. So sister Targjer is dead. I have written twice to you, but no answer. We have heard more about the misery on the radio than from you. Thank God it is over!

In Brooklyn we have no shortages, can get just about anything we want. Edwin is an army chaplain in Germany, he has been doing that for two years. He is really good at writing and sending packages to me. He has the rank of captain in the U.S. Army. He has done much good and seen many horrible things. His wife and two girls are at home with her father, who has a farm in Wisconsin. Lilly has four girls, no boys. She is well, her husband is now a professor, and well liked by everyone. Chester works with me and I live with him, his wife is nice to me, but I have no use for her family. They have a boy who is four years old, called Bobby. Gudny is in California, I saw her two years ago. She has two boys. . . . Yes, I have nine grandchildren, a large family. George is in the Coast Guard—he worked first in a shipyard, but then he is at the age where as soon as Uncle Sam is out of people, then it is time to go—and he and I agreed that that must not happen. God hears our prayers, for the last day he was free, he got a job with Standard Oil, in a boat that went from N.Y. to Boston, and he was in that two and a half years. Then he got free schooling and now he is an engineer on a large boat that goes from the West Coast, with a salary of $250 per month and free room and board. He sends me $100 a month, which I put in the B. . . . He is not married, doesn't go out much and is quiet and kind. As long as he was on this coast I could see him now and then, but now it will be Christmas before I see him again. But he is good at writing to me.

Since Mother died I have lived with Telma and Chester and four years ago I took him as a partner. He is a good businessman and it has gone well. We have more work than we can manage. We have ten men working for us, but should have had twenty. It is hard to get workers, and we have had much to do for the U.S. and therefore Chester wasn't taken into the army, because I am too old to work, but since I got to be seventy years old, this is the first Sunday I haven't worked. So I am in good health. In 1944 I broke my right foot. I fell 22 feet, and it took a long time, but now I am well again. As you can see, I have moved farther down 73rd Street, and remodeled 1056 for three families. Where we live is a one-family with a large yard, a seven-room house. We have several houses, seven altogether, so there is enough for us to take care of.

You write about many who have passed away. . . . As soon as things have settled down in Norway, I will take a little trip across the ocean. . . . It will be good to meet those who are still alive. . . . Now it is over. And who is to judge—God alone. You asked if I had heard from Inga's boys. I have talked to [unclear] and he said they were well, he has been here in Brooklyn two times—but I have not heard from them . . . and now I have lost their address. I am sending you a photo of Edwin from Germany. He is carrying a parachute.

Yes, I am coming to Norway to stay for one year. And it could be that I will take little Nadia, Lilly's oldest girl. She is so good at writing to Grandpa, so we are really good friends. She is seven years old and so clever, and it is always "Come to us, live with us." Well, I know that I am welcome there by all of them—but I am too young to settle down yet.

Now I will quit for this time. . . . Yes, God has been good and has spared all of my dear ones from this terrible punishment, which has gone over the whole earth. If there is anything I can do for you, Brother, please let me know, and I will be happy.

Write. Write. You are my only brother. Hearty greetings to all of you and God bless you,

Your Brother

NOTE

1. Obituary found in the Norwegian American Historical Association clipping file, and personal communication, Mrs. Bernhard M. Christensen.

Maps

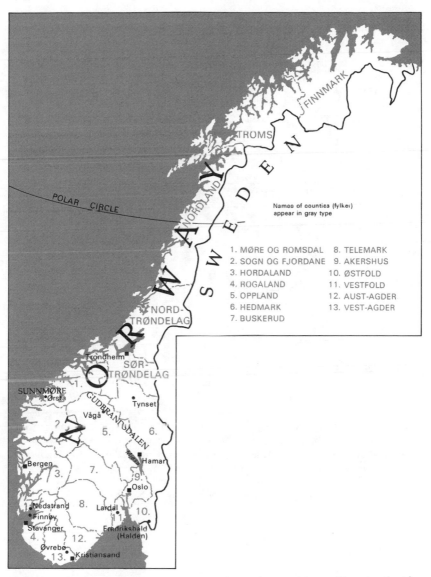

The writers of these letters came from eastern, southern, and western Norway. Map adapted, with permission, from The Promise of America: A History of the Norwegian-American People, *by Odd S. Lovoll, University of Minnesota Press, 1984.*

Andreas Hjerpeland lived in Iowa and southeastern Minnesota before homesteading in Barnes County, North Dakota. His post office changed from Dailey to Kathryn. Gunnar Høst lived in several small towns in the Red River Valley, as well as in the city of Grand Forks. He started his own business in Leeds, North Dakota, around 1901, and lived there the rest of his life. Map adapted, with permission, from The Promise of America: A History of the Norwegian-American People, *by Odd S. Lovoll, University of Minnesota Press, 1984.*

Berta Serina worked on farms near several small towns in Illinois. She moved to Rowe (near Pontiac) when she married Knud Tuttle. The Ramseth family came first to Bristow, in Vernon County, and then settled on a farm in Shawano County. Although they stayed in the same place, their address changed from Frazer to Lessor and then to Rose Lawn. Map adapted, with permission, from The Promise of America: A History of the Norwegian-American People, *by Odd S. Lovoll, University of Minnesota Press, 1984.*

Hans Øverland worked on the railroad in western Montana.

Urban workers and adventurers Hans Hansen and Sam Øien lived both in cities, like Seattle, and wilderness areas in Clallam County, Washington, and Alaska. Sam Øien even joined the Klondike gold rush, and had a claim near Dawson in the Yukon Territory.

Selected Bibliography

Selected Bibliography

NORWEGIAN-AMERICAN HISTORY

Andersen, Arlow W. *The Norwegian-Americans*. Boston: Twayne, 1975.

Bjork, Kenneth O. *West of the Great Divide: Norwegian Migration to the Pacific Coast, 1847–1893*. Northfield, Minn.: Norwegian American Historical Association (NAHA), 1958.

Blegen, Theodore C. *Norwegian Migration to America, 1825–1860*. Northfield, Minn.: NAHA, 1931.

Blegen, Theodore C. *Norwegian Migration to America: The American Transition*. Northfield, Minn.: NAHA, 1940.

Flom, George T. *A History of Norwegian Immigration to the United States: From the Earliest Beginning Down to the Year 1848*. Iowa City, Iowa: privately printed, 1909.

Lovoll, Odd S. *A Century of Urban Life: The Norwegians in Chicago before 1930*. Northfield, Minn.: NAHA, 1988.

Lovoll, Odd S. *The Promise of America: A History of the Norwegian-American People*. Oslo: Universitetsforlaget, 1984.

Norman, Hans, and Harald Runblom. *Transatlantic Connections: Nordic Migration to the New World after 1800*. Oslo: Norwegian University Press, [1988].

Qualey, Carlton C. *Norwegian Settlement in the United States*. Northfield, Minn.: NAHA, 1938.

Semmingsen, Ingrid. *Norway to America: A History of the Migration*. Trans. Einar Haugen. Minneapolis: University of Minnesota Press, 1978.

Strand, A. E., ed. *A History of the Norwegians of Illinois*. Chicago: John Anderson, 1905.

OTHER COLLECTIONS OF SCANDINAVIAN-AMERICAN LETTERS

Barton, H. Arnold, ed. *Letters from the Promised Land: Swedes in America, 1840–1914*. Minneapolis: University of Minnesota Press, 1975.

Blegen, Theodore C., ed. *Frontier Parsonage: The Letters of Olaus Fredrik Duus. Norwegian Pastor in Wisconsin, 1855–1858*. Northfield, Minn.: NAHA, 1947.

Blegen, Theodore C., ed. *Land of Their Choice: The Immigrants Write Home*. Minneapolis: University of Minnesota Press, 1955.

Farseth, Pauline, and Theodore C. Blegen, trans. and ed. *Frontier Mother: The Letters of Gro Svendsen*. Northfield, Minn.: NAHA, 1950.

Hale, Frederick, ed. *Danes in North America*. Seattle: University of Washington Press, 1984.

Hale, Frederick, ed. *Their Own Saga: Letters from the Norwegian Global Migration*. Minneapolis: Minnesota Press, 1986.

Haugen, Eva Lund, and Einar Haugen, trans. and ed. *Land of the Free: Bjørnstjerne Bjørnson's America Letters, 1880–1881*. Northfield, Minn.: NAHA, 1978.

Jevne, Per, ed. *Brevet hjem: En samling brev fra norske utvandrere*. Trondheim: Adresseavisen, 1975.

Malmin, Gunnar J., ed. *America in the Forties: The Letters of Ole Munch Ræder*. Northfield, Minn.: NAHA, 1929.

Munch, Helene, and Peter A. Munch. *The Strange American Way: Letters of Caja Munch from Wiota, Wisconsin, 1855–1859*. Carbondale: Southern Illinois University Press, 1970.

UNDERSTANDING THE EPISTOLARY FORM

Altman, Janet Gurkin. *Epistolarity: Approaches to a Form*. Columbus: Ohio State University Press, 1982.

Eddy, Beverly D. "Peter Nansen's Epistolary Fiction." *Scandinavian Studies* 58 (1986): 10–24.

Hampsten, Elizabeth. "Editing a Woman's Diary: A Case Study." *Women's Personal Narratives: Essays in Criticism and Pedagogy*. Ed. Leonore Hoffmann and Margo Culley. New York: MLA, 1985. 227–36.

Hampsten, Elizabeth. *Read This Only to Yourself: The Private Writings of Midwestern Women, 1880–1910*. Bloomington: Indiana University Press, 1982.

Hoffmann, Leonore, and Margo Culley, eds. *Women's Personal Narratives: Essays in Criticism and Pedagogy*. New York: MLA, 1985.

Hustvedt, Lloyd. "Immigrant Letters and Diaries." *The Prairie Frontier*. Ed. Sandra Looney, Arthur R. Huseboe, and Geoffrey Hunt. Sioux Falls, S. D.: Nordland Heritage Foundation, 1984. 38–53.

Kissel, Susan S. "Writer Anxiety versus the Need for Community in the Botts Family Letters." *Women's Personal Narratives: Essays in Criticism and Pedagogy*. Ed. Leonore Hoffmann and Margo Culley. New York: MLA, 1985. 48–57.

Perry, Ruth. *Women, Letters, and the Novel*. New York: AMS Press, 1980.

Schlissel, Lillian. *Women's Diaries of the Westward Journey*. New York: Schocken, 1982.

OTHER WORKS CONSULTED

Brinchmann, Chr., Anders Daae, and K. V. Hammer. *Hvem er hvem?* Kristiania: Aschehoug, 1912.

Commager, Henry Steele, ed. *Immigration and American History: Essays in Honor of Theodore C. Blegen*. Minneapolis: University of Minnesota Press, 1961.

Derry, T. K. *A History of Modern Norway, 1814–1972*. London: Oxford University Press, 1973.

Fox Valley Norwegian-American Sesquicentennial, 1825–1975: The Prairie Land of the Sloopers. [Ottawa, Ill.]: Fox Valley Norwegian-American Sesquicentennial Association, 1975.

Fuglum, Per. *Norge i støpeskjeen, 1884–1920*. Oslo: Cappelen, 1978. Vol. 12 of *Norges historie*. Ed. Knut Mykland. 15 vols. 1976–80.

Grandum, Ola. *The Family of Gammelutstumoen, Tynset, Norway*. Trans. Rolf H. Erickson and Anette Norberg-Schulz. Ed. David Paul Dowse. Evanston, Ill., and Kenosha, Wis., n.d.

Haugen, Einar. *The Norwegian Language in America: A Study in Bilingual Behavior.* Vol. 1. Philadelphia: University of Pennsylvania Press, 1953. 2 vols.

Jervell, Hans. *Nordmænd og norske hjem i Amerika, samt kirker, skoler, hospitaler, alderdomshjem og lignende institutioner reist væsentlig av nordmænd.* Fargo, N. D.: Hans Jervell, 1916.

Kleiven, Ivar. *I heimegrendi: Minne fraa seksti-aarom.* Kristiania: Aschehoug, 1908.

Knutsen, A. *Utvandrere fra Rogaland: Utarbeidet ved A. K.* Haugesund, Norway: Haugesunds Dagblad, 1942.

Molland, Einar. *Norges kirkehistorie i det 19. århundre.* 2 vols. Oslo: Gyldendal, 1979.

Nedstrand herad i hundrad år, 1837–1937. Stavanger: n.p., 1937.

Our Heritage, Leeds-York, 1886–1986. Leeds, N.D.: Leeds History Book Committee, 1986.

Rogaland Fylke gjenom 100 år. Rogaland fylkesting: Stavanger, 1937.

Seventy-five Years, Leeds-York, 1886–1961. Leeds and York, N. D.: Board of Directors, Leeds Interprises, Inc., and Diamond Jubilee, York Committee, 1961.

Skårdal, Dorothy. *The Divided Heart: Scandinavian Immigrant Experience through Literary Sources.* Oslo: Universitetsforlaget, 1974.

Sørensen, Jon. *Fridtjof Nansen: En bok for norsk ungdom.* [Oslo]: Jacob Dybwads Forlag, 1942.

Standal, Ragnar. *Mot nye heimland: Utvandringa frå Hjørundfjord, Vartdal og Ørsta.* Volda, Norway, 1985.

Steenstrup, H. J. *Hvem er hvem?* Oslo: Aschehoug, 1930.

Stine, Thos. Ostenson. *Scandinavians on the Pacific, Puget Sound.* Seattle: n.p., 1900.

Ulvestad, Martin. *Nordmændene i Amerika: deres historie og rekord.* 2 vols. Minneapolis: History Book Company, 1907 and 1913.

Wist, Johannes B., ed. *Norsk-Amerikanernes festskrift 1914.* Decorah, Iowa: Symra, 1914.

With, Nanna. *Illustrert biografisk leksikon over kjendte norske mænd og kvinder.* Kristiania: n.p., 1920.

Index

Index

Compiled by Mary Hove

Solveig Zempel is an associate professor of Norwegian at St. Olaf College, where she has taught Norwegian language and literature since 1976. She graduated from St. Olaf College in 1969 and received her Ph.D. in Scandinavian languages and literature from the University of Minnesota in 1980. Zempel has previously published translations of two works by O. E. Rölvaag, a novel entitled *The Third Life of Per Smevik* (co-translated with Ella Valborg Tweet), and a collection of short stories entitled *When the Wind Is in the South and Other Stories*.